THE FUTURE OF MONEY

THE FUTURE OF MONEY

ROBERT A. HENDRICKSON

PRENTICE-HALL, INC.
Englewood Cliffs, New Jersey

THE FUTURE OF MONEY by Robert A. Hendrickson
© 1970 by Robert A. Hendrickson
All rights reserved. No part of this book may be
reproduced in any form or by any means, except for
the inclusion of brief quotations in a review, without
permission in writing from the publisher.
Library of Congress Catalog Card Number: 70-101523
Printed in the United States of America · T
ISBN 0-13-345876-8
Prentice-Hall International, Inc., London
Prentice-Hall of Australia, Pty. Ltd., Sydney
Prentice-Hall of Canada, Ltd., Toronto
Prentice-Hall of India Private Ltd., New Delhi
Prentice-Hall of Japan, Inc., Tokyo

To
REILY,
ALEX
and
ROB

Acknowledgments

I wish to express my appreciation to Mr. R. G. Davis-Poynter for his understanding of the need for a book of this kind and for his review of the manuscript and his many valuable comments and suggestions.

I wish to thank Mr. Thomas H. Lipscomb for his dedicated, efficient, and skillful editorial work in preparing the manuscript for publication.

I am grateful for valuable insights into various aspects of the subject matter to The Honorable Harold Macmillan; to Mr. Louis Stone, Economist of Hayden, Stone, Inc.; and to Mr. Stewart B. Clifford of First National City Bank, New York.

And I am deeply grateful to my faithful secretary, Mrs. Jean A. Alden, who typed and retyped with exemplary care and patience.

Grateful acknowledgment is hereby made for permission to quote material from the following sources:

Galbraith, John Kenneth. *The Affluent Society,* reprinted by permission of Houghton Mifflin Company.

Harrod, Roy. *Reforming the World's Money,* reprinted by permission of St. Martin's Press, Inc., Macmillan & Co., Ltd. (London), and Macmillan Company of Canada Limited.

Jewkes, John. For material appearing in *The Wall Street Journal,* and reprinted by permission of that publication.

Macmillan, Harold. *Winds of Change 1914–1939,* reprinted by permission of Macmillan & Co., Ltd. and Harper & Row Publishers, Inc.

Myers, C. V. For material appearing in the June 1968 edition of *Myers' Finance Review,* Calgary, Canada.

For several charts from "New England Letter" published by The First National Bank of Boston.

CONTENTS

PROLIFERATION OF WEALTH • THE MORE INTRINSICALLY WORTHLESS
MAN'S MEDIUM OF EXCHANGE, THE RICHER HE IS—AS LONG AS
FAITH ABIDES • A ROSE IS A ROSE, AND PAPER MONEY
IS ACCEPTED BECAUSE IT IS ACCEPTED, BECAUSE IT IS
ACCEPTED • NEITHER ISIS NOR OSIRIS: THE LOST SECRET OF
ANCIENT EGYPT • THE ETERNAL FASCINATION OF GOLD • "TO A
SHOWER OF GOLD, MOST THINGS ARE PENETRABLE" • YOU CAN
PUT IT IN YOUR TEETH BUT YOU CAN'T EAT IT • ECONOMIC MAN,
THE WOODEN IDOL OF THE MIDASES • THE FORGOTTEN MAN—
REMEMBERED • PURSIDES VERSUS MIDASES—THE HUNDRED YEARS'
WAR BETWEEN GOLD AND PAPER • MONEY, PEOPLE, AND GOVERN-
MENTS IN THE FRAMEWORK OF THE INTERNATIONAL ECONOMY

STANDARD: AND HOW IT CAME AND WENT • AN AUTOMATIC INTER-
NATIONAL MEDIUM OF EXCHANGE INDEPENDENT OF GOVERNMENTAL
ACTION • "YOU SHALL NOT CRUCIFY MANKIND UPON A CROSS OF
GOLD" • THE "AUTOMATIC GOLD STANDARD" AND THE "INVISIBLE
HAND" OF THE FREE MARKET • THE GOLD-EXCHANGE STANDARD:
GIVES CENTRAL BANKERS A FOOT IN THE DOOR OF THE MONEY
MANAGEMENT VAULT • THE CRASH AND THE DEPRESSION, AND THE
DEMAND FOR A VISIBLE HAND • BRITAIN USHERS IN THE REIGN OF
KEYNES • "ARE WE TO ACCEPT ECONOMIC DETERMINISM, OR HAVE
WE FREE WILL?" • LEVEL OF EMPLOYMENT AS THE MEASURING ROD
OF CURRENCY MANAGEMENT • HAMMERING OUT KEYNESIAN ECONOM-
ICS ON THE PARLIAMENTARY ANVIL • "UNEMPLOYMENT IS NOT IN
ITSELF A HARMFUL THING—THE REAL PROBLEM IS NOT HAVING
ENOUGH MONEY" • THE NEW DEAL HELPS BREAK THE CHAIN OF
ECONOMIC FATALISM • DON'T TALK ABOUT KEYNES IN THE U.S.—
JUST QUIETLY DO WHAT HE SAYS SO THE SOUTHERN BLOC WON'T
NOTICE • IT IS EASIER TO PRODUCE VOTES WITH CURRENCY THAN
WITH PRODUCTIVITY • DEVALUATION STRIPS AWAY A COUPLE OF
GOLD TIERS, BUT A TIER ALWAYS REMAINS • PURSIDES MAKE THE
U.S. THE HAVEN FOR THREE-FIFTHS OF THE WORLD'S GOLD, NOT-
WITHSTANDING JOHN MAYNARD KEYNES

INTERNATIONAL CLEARING UNION • A NATIONAL OVERDRAFT, OR
RUBBER CHECKS THAT DON'T BOUNCE • DON'T PILE UP TOO MUCH
MONEY IN YOUR IMF ACCOUNT OR YOUR CREDIT WON'T BE ANY
GOOD • A RELAXED VIEW OF EXCHANGE RATES • WHERE TECHNICIANS
WOULD MEET IN SECRET, AWAY FROM THE NATIONALISTIC WHISPER-
ING GALLERIES OF WASHINGTON • JUST A LITTLE OLD INTERNA-
TIONAL "STABILIZATION" FUND—THE WHITE PLAN • BRITAIN'S
POSTWAR BLOCKED STERLING BALANCES AND TODAY'S U.S. GOLD
RESERVE DEFICIT TO FOREIGN PAPER DOLLARS • GOLD AS THE BASIC
MEDIUM OF EXCHANGE IN BOTH THE KEYNES AND WHITE PLANS •
THE WHITE PLAN AS THE BASIC CHARTER OF THE FUND • WHITE'S
UPTIGHT EXCHANGE RATES AS THE FINICAL HANGUP OF A FIDDLE-
END FUND • SCARCE-CURRENCY PROVISIONS—RESPONSIBILITY FOR
MAINTAINING TRADE AND INVESTMENT AT A HIGH LEVEL SHOULD
BE SHARED BY ALL • CONGRESS DEFINES THE DOLLAR'S VALUE IN
TERMS OF GOLD, AND MORTISES A GOLD HINGE INTO MONEY MOVE-
MENTS • THE RECREANT INVISIBILITY OF THE FUND

OMY • AN ECONOMIC FAMILY OF MAN • MAKING A PROCRUSTEAN
BED • A NATIONAL SOVEREIGN IS A PRISONER IN ITS OWN HOUSE •
"NOTHING HAS ALTERED MORE SINCE MY YOUTH THAN THE RELA-
TIVE STRENGTH OF THE BRITISH ECONOMY" • BRITAIN SURRENDERS
THE ROLE OF MONETARY ATLAS TO THE UNITED STATES • A RUN ON
THE STERLING AREA BANK • THE SIXPENCE CONTINUES ON THE
WRONG SIDE OF THE LEDGER • "TOUCHES ON THE TILLER" OR
"HAMMER BLOWS ON THE ECONOMIC THERMOSTATS" • THE DIREC-
TIVES ARE HANDWRITTEN ON THE WALL BY THE VISIBLE HAND OF
THE INTERNATIONAL ECONOMY • AN ECONOMIC UNION WITH THE
COMMON MARKET, OR THE UNITED STATES, TO LOOSEN THE PRO-
CRUSTEAN BED • FRANCE IS NOT RESPONSIBLE FOR THE SQUALLS
THAT BROUGHT DOWN THE POUND AND THREATEN THE DOLLAR
(ACCORDING TO DE GAULLE)—BUT NOT IMMUNE FROM THEM,
EITHER • AN UNEASY ARMISTICE BETWEEN THE FRENCH FRANC AND
THE WEST GERMAN DEUTSCHEMARK • "GOLD IS THE SUN AND THE
DOLLAR IS THE EARTH. THE EARTH REVOLVES AROUND THE SUN
AND THE RELATIONSHIP DOESN'T CHANGE" • THE GREAT SOUTH
AFRICAN POKER GAME IN GOLD • "WE LIVE IN TIMES WHEN SILENCE
IS GOLDEN"—AT LEAST IN SOUTH AFRICA • "BRING MORE BUYERS TO
THE MARKET, AND INCREASE THE DEMAND, AND THE PRICE WILL
FALL": U.S. TREASURY ECONOMIC DOCTRINE, GOLD DIVISION • HAPPY
ENDING: AS THE TREASURY FAILED TO JAWBONE DOWN GOLD, AND
THE UNITED STATES TRADE POSITION DETERIORATED, AND BY ALL
ECONOMIC STANDARDS DISASTER LOOMED, EVERYTHING ACTUALLY
GOT BETTER

---

9 • THE UNITED STATES ECONOMY ONCE WAS AN ISLAND, ENTIRE OF ITSELF—NOW IT IS STUCK WITH THE ENTIRE WORLD, AND VICE VERSA • 143

GOLD RUSHES BACK TO WHERE IT RUSHED FROM, WITH A PUSH
FROM HITLER • HALCYON DAYS IN INNOCENCE OF INTERNATIONAL
PAYMENTS PROBLEMS • A WORLD OF NATIONAL GOVERNMENTS IN
ECONOMIC SHACKLES • ADJUDGED BANKRUPT BY THE GOLD-EX-
CHANGE STANDARD WE IMPOSED UPON OURSELVES • RETURNING THE

DOLLAR TO SOUNDNESS IN THE WORLD ECONOMY • "AN OUTSIDE ELE-
MENT, ARTIFICIAL AND UNILATERAL, WEIGHING ON OUR NATIONAL
PATRIMONY" • THE DECLINE OF THE UNITED STATES IN FOREIGN
TRADE • JAPANESE SNAPSHOTS OF AN AFFLUENT SOCIETY • OVER-
VALUED U.S. DOLLARS GOOD ONLY FOR OVERPRICED U.S. GOODS •
AMERICAN MULTINATIONAL CORPORATIONS AS SALVATION AND CATAS-
TROPHE • THE WORLDWIDE PENETRATION OF MULTINATIONAL COR-
PORATIONS • U.S. ENTERPRISE ABROAD AS THE THIRD BIGGEST
ECONOMY IN THE WORLD • DO MULTINATIONAL CORPORATIONS HURT
THE U.S. BALANCE OF PAYMENTS? • WHO NEEDS A TRADE SURPLUS
ANYWAY? NOT THE WORLD'S BANKER • CROSSING NARROW POLITICAL
BOUNDARIES OF NATION-STATES • ARM'S-LENGTH TRANSACTIONS
ACROSS NATIONAL BORDERS? • THE THRUST OF AMERICAN ECONOMIC
HEGEMONY—AT HOME NO LESS THAN ABROAD • MULTINATIONAL
CONTROLS FOR MULTINATIONAL CORPORATIONS • FACING UP TO THE
MULTINATIONAL CORPORATION—"THE AMERICAN CHALLENGE" AS
THE CHALLENGE TO THE WORLD, AND TO AMERICA AS WELL

---

10 • EVERYBODY HATES INFLATION UNLESS THEY LOVE IT: GERMANY, FRANCE, URUGUAY, AND THE UNITED STATES, AND SOME CURIOUS CURES • 159

A BIGGER RAISE THAN WALTER REUTHER WON • "ENHANCEMENT" AS
DEBASEMENT—AND INFLATION AS NATURAL PHENOMENON • WHAT
HAPPENS WHEN THERE ARE NO LINKS BETWEEN PAPER MONEY AND
INTRINSIC VALUE? • GOVERNMENTAL RESPONSIBILITY FOR INTEGRITY
OF MONEY • PRINTING PRESS MONEY—FROM HARD LUCK TO HARD
CURRENCY • FRANCE CAPITALIZES THE ASSIGNAT BY CAPITAL PUN-
ISHMENT • URUGUAY—MODEL OF A MODERN WELFARE STATE • FULL
PAY AFTER RETIREMENT AT FIFTY-FIVE • CREEPING INFLATION TURNS
INTO A TROT, AND A TROT BECOMES A GALLOP • DEBASEMENT OF
PUBLIC MORALS AND PRIVATE SOULS: INFLATIONARY VIVOISM •
VIVOISM, DECAY, EMIGRATION, OR DESPAIR • ROBBING FROM THE RICH
AND GIVING TO THE POOR TO REVERSE THE EFFECTS OF INFLATION •
COASTING ALONG WITH CHRONIC INFLATION • CHRONIC INFLATION
IN EUROPE, AT A CREEP INSTEAD OF A GALLOP • INVESTING FOR IN-

CHILLING GLOOM • THE PAPER BLOC VERSUS GOLD • GLOOM AND
DOOM FROM MIDASES TOO • A BANKER DOESN'T KICK A DEPOSITOR
IN THE TEETH • WHAT COULD HAPPEN TO THE DOLLAR? • IF THE
WHOLE INTERNATIONAL MONETARY SYSTEM COLLAPSED, WOULD
ANYBODY HERE NOTICE THE CATASTROPHE?

GOLD IN THE MONETARY SYSTEM IN THE VERY LONG RUN • THE STRONG PREFERENCE IN MOST COUNTRIES FOR GOLD OVER OTHER RESERVE ASSETS • THE U.S. AND BRITAIN CAN ACHIEVE BALANCE-OF-PAYMENT SURPLUSES ONLY BY DRIVING OTHER COUNTRIES INTO DEFICITS—UNLESS THE MONEY VALUE OF NEW GOLD MONETARY RESERVES RISES • REFORM OF THE SYSTEM IS A PRECONDITION FOR CURING THE U.S. DEFICIT, NOT THE REVERSE • HOW A RISE IN THE VALUE OF THE ANNUAL GOLD OUTPUT WOULD SOLVE THE DEFICIT • ARGUMENTS AGAINST INCREASING THE GOLD PRICE, WITH SOME BUILT-IN REBUTTALS • ALLOWING U.S. PRIVATE CITIZENS TO OWN GOLD "IN THE NATIONAL INTEREST" • IF SDR'S REPLACE GOLD AS THE PRIMARY INTERNATIONAL MEDIUM OF EXCHANGE, WHO CARES ABOUT THE GOLD PRICE? • THE GAGGLE OF GOVERNESSES MUSCLING IN ON MARX, OR HIM ON THEM • DOUBLING THE VALUE OF EXISTING GOLD RESERVES WOULD BE MORE BELIEVABLE THAN MORE SDR'S AND A WHOLE LOT BETTER LOOKING • THE GOLD-EXCHANGE SYSTEM CAUGHT IN THE CROSS FIRE • THE UNANNOUNCED AND UNMOURNED DEATH OF THE GOLD-EXCHANGE SYSTEM • AS THE ONE UNIVERSAL GOD OF MONEY, GOLD IS DEAD • THE GOLD BOOM AND THE CRASH • AN END TO EXPECTATIONS OF INFLATION? • SURVIVING BY MONETARY MANAGEMENT IN A POVERTY-WRACKED, DANGEROUS, AND ENVIOUS WORLD • WE SHALL ALL BE SUBJECT, IN FINE, TO A GAGGLE OF GOVERNESSES

THE REGULATION OF EURODOLLAR DEPOSITS • INTERNATIONAL RE-
SERVE SYSTEM REGULATION OF EURODOLLAR AND OTHER INTERNA-
TIONAL CURRENCY DEPOSITS • ADJUSTING NATIONAL CENTRAL BANKS'
RESERVE REQUIREMENTS FOR INTERNATIONAL DEPOSITS • EACH
COUNTRY'S NET POSITION WITH THE FUND WILL BE DETERMINED IN
INTERNATIONAL DOLLARS • THE INTERNATIONAL RESERVE SYSTEM
AND THE WORLDOLLAR IN FULL-SCALE OPERATION • SPECIAL DRAW-
ING RIGHTS WOULD BE ACTIVATED SOLELY IN DENOMINATIONS OF
WORLDOLLARS • USING "OLD GOLD" AS THE WORLDOLLAR MONETARY
BASE, AND "NEW GOLD" FOR ADDITIONS TO WORLD LIQUIDITY • THE
INTERNATIONAL RESERVE SYSTEM ASSUMES ALL U.S. LIABILITIES TO
FOREIGN HOLDERS OF DOLLARS • WITH ONE WORLDOLLAR CURRENCY
THE NEED FOR ENFORCING FIXED EXCHANGE RATES DISAPPEARS • A
SIGH FOR THE LOSS OF ONE ILLUSORY SOVEREIGNTY FOR ANOTHER

---

20 • ONE NEW WORLD OF MONEY • *322*

THE MONETARY ATLAS SHIFTS THE WORLD OF MONEY TO THE IN-
TERNATIONAL RESERVE SYSTEM, AND ALL HIS GOLDEN APPLES AS
WELL

INTRODUCTION

In March 1968, homeward-bound American tourists who walked up to the currency exchange windows at Paris' Orly Airport, handed over United States dollar travelers' cheques and asked for French francs to buy Otard cognac, Caleche perfume, and Hermes scarves for the family back home received the shock of their lives: The cashiers refused to accept American paper dollars for French francs. At London's Heathrow that same weekend, travelers got an even bigger jolt: Their good old Yankee dollars could not even be exchanged for British pounds—the new ones, which had been freshly devalued only four months earlier.

But a few months later, in November 1968, Frenchmen at Orly were paying almost any number of French francs for those same American paper dollars, and in Frankfurt no one would exchange a German mark for any number of francs. Nobody had any idea what a franc was worth, if anything, so the authorities simply closed the currency exchange windows and refused to take in any more, or give out any dollars or marks in exchange for them.

The finance ministers of all the leading Western countries hustled over to Bonn for yet another crisis meeting. When it was over they announced in their generous, gentlemanly way that they had agreed to give France a $2 billion standby credit. At the same time, they said, France would officially devalue her franc by about 10 percent. They snapped shut their attaché cases, issued the usual cheery communique on the successful resolution of all current currency problems, and left for home. The next day, seeing them safely gone, President de Gaulle stunned them and the world by announcing, in his elegant, ungentlemanly way, that all their talk of devaluing the franc was an "absurdity." Absurdity or not, a week later the franc was trading in the free currency exchange markets at a 15 percent discount from its official rate of about five to the dollar. It was never the same afterwards. Five months later France repudiated President de Gaulle's financial policies and out he went.

Germany had refused to revalue her mark upward, and this in turn

1

had forced the franc down in all free markets. This also had the side effect of forcing Britain to raise her already high purchase taxes on alcohol, tobacco, gasoline, and clothing by 10 percent to "save" the pound from devaluation once again.

In August 1969, the new French government acknowledged the inevitable and officially devalued the franc by 12.5 percent. The following October Germany "set free" her deutschemark (entirely contrary to the fixed exchange rate rules of the International Monetary Fund, but with the tacit consent of its managers) and allowed the deutschemark to rise against the dollar and all other world currencies to a rate 9.3 percent above its old level. This time they didn't flatly refuse to accept your dollar for deutschemarks at the exchange windows at Orly or Heathrow or Frankfurt; they took it, but instead of receiving back four deutschemarks for it, you got back only about 3.65. The practical effect of the "revaluation" of the mark was devaluation of the dollar. Having lost two world wars and suffered the most devastating period of inflation the world had ever known, Germany had finally emerged as the world's big economic winner. The military loser had forced the victors to say economic "uncle."

Jet-set society, whose fortunes ordinarily keep them pretty well insulated from the economic storms that buffet the rest of us, began to learn in January 1968 how the world money crisis affects all of our lives. President Johnson proposed a graduated tax on American travelers' expenditures above $7 a day outside the Western Hemisphere. Beyond the $7-a-day limit, the traveler who did not plan to sleep in the heather in Scotland or a gritty youth hostel in Venice, and steal apples and chickens for provender, would be taxed at 15 percent for the first $8 above the $7 exemption, and 30 percent for all spending above $15. The President announced that these stern measures were absolutely essential for saving what was left of our gold. All of a sudden one of the most precious of all freedoms, the freedom to travel abroad, was to be curtailed by a travel tax intended to save a hoard of a monetary metal that no individual citizen is allowed to own.

Jet-set society reacted with electrifying acuity. The *Wall Street Journal* reported that Mrs. Oates Leiter of Washington felt staying home would be mighty tough:

"What's going to happen to the art collector? What will we do if some simply marvelous picture comes on the market at Christie's in London? Will we go over and get it or not?"

Mrs. Leiter, who had been spending about four months a year on

2

"spur-of-the-moment trips to Europe and the Far East," said she "will try to stay home more now," but added that, "it might kill me."

The 30 percent spending tax on one day's impulse purchase of a $500,000 Cézanne at Christie's would be $150,000, no laughing matter even in high society.

Huntington Hartford, heir to the Great Atlantic and Pacific Tea Company fortune, opined, "I don't think the average jet-setter will be much influenced. There is a slight smell of dictatorship to all this."

The consensus view, or the conventional wisdom of the "average jet-setter," was summed up best by Charlotte Ford Niarchos, Henry Ford's daughter who had been briefly married to Stavros Niarchos: "I haven't given it much thought."

We are All Usurers Now

In 1965 you could get a mortgage for as little as 5½ percent, and plenty of mortgage money was available. At times in 1966 and 1968 you would have had to pay 7 percent or more, and in 1969 you would have paid 9 percent or more. Mortgage money was often impossible to find, although it often seemed easier when "tight money" was 9 percent than when it was 7. To close the loan you also had to pay "points" or discounts, or service charges, and maintain balances with the lender, which made your effective rate of interest still higher.

Usury is the exaction of an unconscionable rate of interest, and in school we all learned that great moral opprobrium falls upon people such as Shylock who exact it. Most states and countries have laws that forbid it. So heinous is the offense that the penalty is sometimes forfeiture not only of all the illegal interest, but of the principal loaned as well. In New York the maximum legal rate had been 6 percent for more than 100 years. But in 1969 New York City could not even sell its own tax-exempt bonds except at rates above 6 percent, so New York had to raise its 100-year-old 6 percent usury ceiling. Something more than just a transitory change, something completely beyond the control of even the strongest of local governments, had breached all historic money standards ever known in the United States.

The "Great Credit Crunch," and One Still Greater

During August and September 1966, the period that later became known as the "Great Credit Crunch," three-month United States

3

Treasury bills yielded around 5.60 percent, one-year tax-exempt notes 4.25 percent, and top-grade bonds of telephone companies were priced to yield about 5.95 percent. In 1966, 4.25 percent government bonds due in 1992 traded at 88⅜ and yielded 5.05 percent. Credit markets were chaotic. For a few days banks could find no buyers at any price for the highest grade long-term tax-exempt bonds they were desperately trying to sell to raise lendable cash. The banks were all but "throwing them away." But little did we know in 1966 that this was only the beginning.

Three years later, at times in 1969, one-year Treasury bills yielded over 8 percent, Federal Home Loan Bank one-year notes 8.35 percent, high-quality tax-exempt one-year notes around 6 percent. A-rated utility bonds were priced to yield around 10 percent, and AAA-rated Bell System Company bonds were yielding around 9 percent. That same 4.25 United States Government bond that was yielding a seemingly astronomical 5.05 percent three years earlier was yielding more than 6.75 percent. And when a new issue of United States Treasury 8 percent notes maturing in May 1971 declined to the point where they were yielding 8.09 percent the Federal Reserve system finally relaxed its prevailing "tight money" policy enough to step in and buy the bonds in the open market, to stave off complete chaos in the credit markets.

INFLATION VORACIOUSLY FEEDING ON ANTI-INFLATIONARY MEDICINE

When President Johnson took the anti-inflationary medicine that professional economists unanimously recommended at the time, including a reduction in Federal spending and suspension of the income-tax credit for new corporate investment, the great credit crunch of 1966 relaxed its grip. The President proclaimed that all was now going to be well with the economy, and the professional economists as with one voice chimed in with a grand amen.

But as it turned out, the supposedly anti-inflationary medicine of 1966 brought on an ever-quickening rate of inflation for the next three years, and produced the "Greater Credit Crunch" of 1969.

All through 1967, 1968, and 1969, professional economists administered still stronger doses of anti-inflationary medicine—higher interest rates and a 10 percent income tax surcharge—and confidently predicted a business slowdown by the end of the year. Some

4

went further and warned against economic "overkill." None forecast what actually happened: an increasing rate of business activity, more wage and price increases, and accelerating inflation all through 1969.

Revered principles of neo-Keynesian economics had been applied to the United States economy and had completely failed to work. They had, in fact, worked in reverse. Economists tiptoeing their way to seminars given by archheretic Milton Friedman on "quantity of money" economics surreptitiously slipped their old texts into the first trash basket they passed and looked the other way.

WHEN THE OLD NEST EGG HATCHES OUT PEA-SIZED

If you had put $100 in cash in your safe deposit box in 1939 to have handy as a "nest egg" or "just in case" and took it out to spend on food, shelter, and clothing in 1969, it would have bought you only $38 worth in 1939 terms. One hundred dollars put away during the comparatively stable 1957–1959 period would buy you only about $78 worth of the essentials of life now. If you are a married man with two children you had to take in $14,440 in 1969 to buy what a $5000 income bought a man in the same position as yours in 1939. You must earn 188.8 percent more today just to keep even with your counterpart of thirty years ago. You must earn $6332 a year to buy what $5000 bought just ten years ago. This is what the relentless rise in the cost of living and Federal income and Social Security taxes does to the typical non–jet-setter.

An American who starts to work at 18 and who must live with a 5.5 percent per annum inflation will see prices double before he is 31. And he will see prices doubled for the third time in his adult life before his 57th birthday. If a healthy constitution and modern medicine keep him going he will see prices doubled for the fourth time before he is 70. When he reaches 70 he will have to pay 16 times as much for whatever he buys as he did when he started out. His dollar will have shrunk to $.06-1/4, or by 93.75 percent. If he lives in a city like New York, prices will have doubled four times before his retirement age of 65 and five times as he reaches his 76th birthday. At 76 he will have to pay 32 times as much in dollars and cents as he did when he took his first job, and his dollar will be worth a mere $.03-1/8. He would have to pay $1.60 for a pack of chewing gum and $4.80 for a cup of coffee. The penny, nickel, dime, half-dollar, and single hav-

5

ing altogether disappeared, a small $2 piece of base alloy would be left as the lowest denomination in the currency which he used.

At the 4 to 5 percent annual rate of inflation that began after the escalation of the Vietnam war in 1965, prices double in fourteen to seventeen years; at the 7 percent annual rate of the early part of 1969, prices double in ten years.

PRICES OF EVERYTHING DOUBLING EVERY DECADE?

A 30 percent spending tax on foreign travel to stop the "gold drain"? Five or six or seven international currency crises in a couple of years, and two or three "money crunches"? The highest interest rates in the history of the United States, along with the lowest bond prices and the highest taxes? Prices of everything doubling every decade? Governmental authority dutifully administering to the economy all the prescriptions you learned in your freshman economics course and producing results opposite to the confident predictions of the professional economic doctors?

These things do not usually make big black newspaper headlines, or punchy visual TV news items. But they are reason enough for every layman to inform himself about the future of money, in self-defense if for no other reason.

Will a loaf of white bread cost 50 cents in five years or $3? Will a standard Volkswagen cost $2000 in five years or $5000; and $10,000 in thirty years? Will a secretary with the same skills as one who now starts out at $160 a week start at $300 a week in five years? Will the three-bedroom split-level house that now is advertised for $30,000 be $60,000 in five years? $150,000 in thirty?

Will the Dow Jones Industrial Average stand at 400 or at 2500 five years from now? Will the U.S. rate of unemployment be 4 percent or 3 percent or 6 percent or 10 percent? Will the U.S. gross national product increase from the 1969 annual rate of about $920 billion to $1200 billion or to $1500 billion, or fall to $500 billion? Will the "prime" interest rate be 4 percent or $8\frac{3}{4}$ percent or 10 percent or 20 percent? What will individual income tax rates be? Will an ounce of gold be $35 or $70 or $150 or $10?

Professional economists are not much help with the answers to these practical questions. The logical extension of one or another of various theories put forward by prominent economists in recent years

6

can provide a plausible basis for any one of the figures hypothesized by these questions.

WHY SHOULD ONLY THE MYOPIC AND DENTURIC BE EXPECTED TO CORRECT THE NATION'S BALANCE OF PAYMENTS?

We in the United States are not the only ones caught in the grip of the onrushing world money crisis. When a money crisis fastens on an advanced country, its options for all policy decisions grow fewer and narrower. Most arresting is the example of Great Britain, clamped in the world money vise and squeezed until the world begins to think of her, and she of herself, as Little England.

Before the Labour government took office in 1964, there was a National Health Service charge for medical prescriptions of about 25 cents. When the Labour Party dropped the prescription charge, free prescriptions became one of its proudest achievements. But in January 1968 British pledges to Swiss central bankers forced Prime Minister Wilson's government to suggest reimposition of the prescription charge. Jennie Lee Bevan, one of the party's leading personages, threatened to quit the government. Mrs. Shirley Summerskill, a doctor, cried in Parliament: "Charges would mean the end of the service. A gesture to foreign bankers is no justification for betraying the National Health Service."

In 1969, when 25 percent increases were proposed for dentures (which had ranged from $5.40 for a single denture with up to three teeth to $12 for a full set) and spectacles (which had ranged from $1.50 for each single-vision lens to $2.40 a lens for bifocals), Mrs. Summerskill leaped into the breach once more, with the cry, "Why should only the myopic and denturic be expected to correct the nation's balance of payments?"

People are not the only form of life on our planet involved in the future of money. The crisis crops up in curious contexts, and Britain's balance-of-payments problems brought at least one small gain for the world's ecology. Her long-range strategic plan to withdraw from bases east of Suez for budgetary reasons was balanced against a proposal to build an airbase on the tiny Indian Ocean atoll of Aldabra, an isolated sanctuary of flightless rails, web-footed boobies, and other remarkable and ancient species of wildlife. Later, however, still more exigent budgetary reasons knocked out even this budget-balancing base. When Harold Wilson announced the further cutbacks to Parliament, saying, "We have decided not to proceed with the Aldabra project," David Stoddard, a biologist who had once led a scientific expedition to the atoll, was somewhat relieved but far from satisfied: "It is a little sad," he said, "that it was a sterling crisis and not scientific opinion that made the government change its mind."

In any event, thanks to the money crisis no splay-footed Tommies will be dislodging any web-footed boobies or flightless rails on far-away Aldabra after all.

A NATION OF MENDICANTS LIVING ON INTERNATIONAL HANDOUTS

Way back in June 1965 Peregrine Worsthorne saw how the vise of the international money crisis was closing on Great Britain when he described, in the *Sunday Telegraph*, the pageantry of a ceremony celebrating the 750th anniversary of Simon de Montfort's Parliament. His caption was "Pathetic Pomp at Westminster," and his conclusion was stinging:

> There is nothing inspiring in having to recognize that we are a nation of mendicants living on international handouts. Those Tory M.P.'s who complained about the farce of last week's ceremony in Westminster Hall were a forbidding portent. Their unprecedented failure to respond to the customary sounds and symbols of patriotic emotion demonstrates with startling clarity just how weak these traditional forces have come to be. A serious recession could well find them pitifully unavailing.

Are international monetary matters natural phenomena like inclement weather or tidal waves, which we must suffer and endure but can do nothing about? Or is there some way we can begin to understand what is going on and not just sit idly by looking on helplessly as our wherewithal washes out to sea, or, more accurately, shrinks in our pockets or our bank, no matter how securely we may try to preserve it?

The main purpose of this book is to suggest how you can begin to understand what is going on in the world money system, foresee what is going to happen next before it does, and act to protect yourself and your money accordingly. Another purpose is to tell the story of the world money system, one of the greatest inventions of mankind. A third is to show you that the world of money is truly an international world, one world, that every day grips each separate country, and each of us, for better or for worse more tightly in its vise.

THE FUTURE OF MONEY IS THE HEREAFTER OF YOUR WHEREWITHAL

It is axiomatic that money is not everything, but in this day and age it is not so easy to say what else is, if anything is. Every part of our lives, and the lives of all nations and of the world, is bound up with money, the surfeit of it or the lack. The future of money includes what you can do with those copper-edged quarters and freshly printed Federal Reserve notes in your pocket, what you work for and why, what pleasures you can afford and cannot; your bank credit, your stocks, bonds and insurance policies, your taxes, your rent and your mortgage, your new house, your old apartment and your pension. It is the bite that Social Security withholding takes out of your paycheck, and the bliss of cashing in those blue payment checks completely tax free. It is your children's education, your family's security, your will and your descendants, or, as your lawyer usually puts it expensively in a will, your issue *per stirpes,* down to the last generation.

Some might add that the future of money is your fate, your demon, or your god. You know it means a lot to your church, if you still have one. T. S. Eliot described us as "the decent Godless people, their only monument the asphalt road and a thousand lost golf balls." So it also involves asphalt roads and golf balls. The future of money is the hereafter of your wherewithal.

TO DISPEL THE SPECTRE OF CATASTROPHE—A WORLD ECONOMIC SYSTEM AS THE CENTRAL FRAMEWORK OF A WORLD COMMUNITY

A still broader claim may be made for money: The world economic system may be the best hope left for the ultimate salvation of the world and its people from irreversible disaster. Professor Richard A. Falk, the Milbank Professor of International Law at Princeton University and research director of a worldwide inquiry sponsored by the World Law Fund concerning world order in the 1990's, recently issued this warning:

9

Man may be skeptical about following the flight of the dodo into extinction, but the evidence points increasingly to just such a pursuit. The planet and mankind are in grave danger of irreversible catastrophe if the political structure that now prevails is not drastically changed during the next few decades. We live in a high-risk environment, and the trends that create the present level of risk continue to increase the danger and to reduce the possibilities of creatively controlling it.

The steely tone, the exhaustive research implicit in his air of having marshaled all relevant first-hand evidence, the judicious balancing of levels of risk, all invest Professor Falk's views with a chilling credibility that is more terrifying to our cool modern temperaments than any fervid jeremiad could ever be.

The only way Professor Falk suggests for changing the trend toward "irreversible catastrophe" is a drastic change in the "political structure that now prevails." In the world's present "political structure," the only entity that seems to offer any hope for bringing about such drastic change is, of course, the United Nations. Yet it seems powerless to act in the meaningful way that Professor Falk demands. Moreover, that suave and seemingly imperturbable Burmese gentleman, U Thant, Secretary General of the United Nations and by virtue of his office diplomat at large to the world, dashed even the faint hope left to us by Professor Falk when he told a meeting of leaders from thirty-five countries who gathered in 1969 to discuss strategy for the Second United Nations Development Decade of the Seventies that we only have ten years left:

> I do not wish to seem overdramatic, but I can only conclude from the information that is available to me as Secretary General that the members of the United Nations have perhaps ten years left in which to subordinate their ancient quarrels and launch a global partnership to curb the arms race, to improve the human environment, to defuse the population explosion, and to supply the required momentum to world development efforts.

All of us can agree with Professor Falk and Secretary General U Thant that the four main threats to life on our planet are wars of mass destruction, overpopulation, pollution, and the depletion of resources. None would deny that money could do as much as anything else to relieve them. They overlap and they have a cumulative effect. A problem in one such area intensifies the problems in the others: A war increases pollution and depletion of natural resources, and if the past is any guide, overpopulation will not be relieved by the slaughter, because birth rates will rise above the number of corpses. Ultimately, all four problems are caused by the discretion vested in national governments, and individual choice. As John Maynard Keynes once pointed out, the "paradox of aggregation" is that the definition of rational self-interest is different for the individual than for the community of individuals. If your car's exhaust is polluting the air we are all breathing, your contribution to the general pollution is so infinitesimal that there is no rational incentive for you to forbear from driving your car, or to spend money for an expensive antipollution filter. The same logic applies to a private corporation's behavior in pursuit of profits, and also to each separate government and nation in its pursuit of wealth, power, prestige, and national security.

Would an appeal to your individual conscience make you stop driving your car? Would an appeal to the conscience of a nation, Red China for example, make it destroy its stockpile of hydrogen bombs? Is the United Nations, which has disappointed so many bright hopes, the central framework of political and moral control that can translate the interests of the world community into actions that will impose controls on the nations on a global basis? U Thant's comments are far from reassuring.

Politically and morally the world and all its separate peoples and nations are chaotically divided. This is what the United Nations faithfully reflects, and what renders it so impotent. Professor Falk's hope for a drastic change in the political structure that now prevails seems a vain hope that leaves his prospect of tragedy unrelieved. Is there nothing else to provide the necessary central framework of control? What about the world economic system itself?

Such strength as the world economic system has in its present primitive form arises as much as anything else from the absence of national politics in its operations. When national politics intrudes on international economics the system suffers its most serious strains. Germany's refusal to revalue the deutschemark upward until after her 1969 Fall elections kept the world currency markets in a state of constant jitters, reinforced by occasional currency crises, for well over a year. But if the world economic system could somehow be made to grow and prosper without being crushed by the increasing political burdens that would automatically fall upon it as it did, the universal respect for and belief in money might ultimately become the foundation of an apolitical central structure of world organization whose frame of reference would be the essential long-term interests of the world community and all of its separate peoples and nations considered as one group of fellow passengers riding on the only planet they have. The powers of money would serve as traces drawing them together in the interests of all in a way that no political system ever could.

THE CRISIS-GRIPPED CAPITALIST MONETARY SYSTEM AND THE BARBAROUS RELIC

There are really two separate, but tenuously interrelated world economic systems, the free world economic system and that of the Soviet Union and its satellites and dependencies, and also a number of peoples and nations somewhere between the two who belong to neither.

Far from being ready to become the pivot of the future economic government of the world, the free-world's system is quivering under ever more frequently recurring signs of crisis all the time. Not only do these hurt us and all the other peoples and countries within it, but they also provide the Soviet Union with confirmatory evidence that the entire capitalist world is finally staggering into the oft-postponed final collapse the Marxists have predicted for it decade after decade.

Tass, the Soviet news agency, gleefully ridiculed one of the gold crisis meetings that the finance ministers of the ten richest free-world countries held in Bonn to sort out one of the recurring franc-mark messes: "These half measures will hardly stabilize the crisis-gripped monetary system of the capitalist world, or safeguard it from new crises in the near future." Recurring free-world currency crises, the intensifying pace of inflation, the historically high levels of interest rates, the wide swings in the market price of gold have not been mirrored by corresponding signs of distress in the more primitive Soviet and satellite economic system. So there is no reason to laugh off these dire prophecies from Tass as quickly as we did its claims for the communist invention of baseball.

12

Unconcern, Incredulity, and Contempt for the Role of Gold

In March 1968, when the international rush to exchange paper dollars for gold had brought on a gold and dollar crisis, *Time* magazine quoted a Los Angeles drug salesman named Peter Davis, age twenty-eight, as saying, "I have the same feeling about gold that I get when I read the society pages. What goes on in high society has no effect on my life—and that's the way it is with gold."

Much of "high society," broadly defined to include professional economists, goes along with Peter Davis' views. Ever since John Maynard Keynes called gold "a barbarous relic," most United States Secretaries of the Treasury and most of the best known professional economists—Paul Samuelson, Harry Johnson, Richard Cooper, and many others—have also looked upon the role of gold in the world monetary system with a mixture of incredulity and contempt.

But the American traveler who scurried nervously through the homeward-bound flight gates at Orly during the March 1968 gold crisis, his pockets bulging with uncashable paper dollars and travelers' cheques, would refuse to agree with Mr. Davis, or the professional economists, that what happened to gold had no effect on his life.

Rashes of Speculation and Other Symptoms of Gold Fever

Dollar troubles for Americans at Orly and Heathrow were not the only symptoms of the 1968 gold crisis. Back home in New York, Benjamin Stack, senior partner of Stack's, the oldest and largest coin dealer in the United States, reported that before the November 1967 devaluation of the British pound, United States $20 gold pieces had sold for $50. After devaluation the price jumped to $60 and then began to increase gradually to $70 and finally to $80 and more during the week of March 17, 1968. One of Mr. Stack's competitors even reported a bid of $98 for a $20 gold piece. Mr. Stack said:

> We found speculators and gold hoarders coming out of the woodwork trying to buy gold in any shape, manner, or form. People began to come in to buy coins who had obviously just been to their savings banks to draw out whatever they had. These were people we never saw before, and the bills that they had with them to buy coins were still crisp from the bank. The prices of-

fered were so insane that we stopped selling gold coins Thursday afternoon. We had over 2000 telephone calls from people who wanted to buy gold coins, and yesterday we had several thousand more all before one o'clock in the afternoon.

Along the cobblestoned Sharia al-Haghan—the street of the goldsmiths in the Moussky, Cairo's vast bazaar—reports of the world gold crisis caused only a modest flurry. There had been a 7 percent rise in the price of gold jewelry and gold coins, but the really big news was a shortage of the ornamental nose clips with which some Nubians and Bedouins still adorn their wives.

The Egyptian man in the street is forbidden by law to buy gold bullion, so he stocks up on gold jewelry and coins for hoarding, and because he mistrusts all banks. Massive and roughly made jewelry in which fine workmanship represents the least possible element of value is the most popular. But the 7 percent rise in the price of gold itself did not bring very much excitement. One dealer, a member of the seventh generation of a Moslem family of gold dealers whose first had sold mementos to Napoleon's soldiers, conceded, "There is some excitement—but people are always excited here."

THE DOLLAR IS DEFINED BY GOLD AND NOTHING ELSE—
AND SO IS THE RUSSIAN RUBLE

The dollar is defined in terms of gold and nothing else. Since Jan. 31, 1934, the United States dollar has been defined as the equivalent of 15.238 grains of gold. All other free-world currencies are defined in terms of the dollar. All values in the free-world's system are expressed in terms of the dollar and hence in terms of gold.

Not one of the communist countries yet has a currency that is acceptable to all the others as a medium for multilateral trade. This hardly matters because the goods they exchange in bilateral trade are initially valued in terms of dollars, although for reasons of prestige the dollar amounts are usually expressed in terms of Russian rubles. This hardly matters either, because the Russian ruble, which at present is nonconvertible into gold, is nevertheless defined as having a gold content of 0.987412 grams of fine gold. This, by a curious coincidence, turns out to be almost exactly the same as 15.238 grains, the gold content of the United States dollar. Thus gold is the basic meas-

14

uring rod of all the world's money, free world and communist world alike. There is no other.

The hereafter of our wherewithal depends very much on whether people believe that gold is a "barbarous relic," or, on the other hand, the one immutable repository of all value, or something in between. In ways that have never really been understood or even investigated with any thoroughness, peoples' deep-seated beliefs about gold are what made the classic gold standard what it was, the gold exchange standard what it is, and will make any future currency exchange standard what it will be. When these standards break down, such beliefs are one of the most important, if not the most important, reasons for the failure. If it is to succeed and prevail, no such standard can ignore these beliefs.

The International Monetary Fund (IMF), the World Bank, and the General Agreement on Tariffs and Trade (GATT) are links in a paper chain that leads away from gold. So are such things as fixed and "floating" exchange rates, special drawing rights, and Eurodollars. These in turn are linked to the paper dollars you try to exchange at Orly and at Heathrow and the mortgage financing for your new home that your friendly banker could not find for you in 1969, even though you offered him "points" and an interest rate of 9½ percent!

For better or for worse, gold—not dollars, not pounds sterling, not German marks, not even special drawing rights—is still the bench mark of the world's money. No pronouncements by uninterested laymen such as Peter Davis, or blasé jet-setters such as Charlotte Ford Niarchos, or eminent economists, or the U.S. Secretary of the Treasury, or Charles de Gaulle, or even Pierre-Paul Schweitzer himself, will change this very much. Nor will the fact that since the Ides of March in money of 1968, the price of gold in free markets has soared to over $44 an ounce, and crashed to $34.80 an ounce, change this very much.

Some time before the time when beautiful women save their brightest smiles for gifts of bracelets and necklaces of brass and nickel and paper, and care nothing for jewelry glittering of gold, these beliefs about gold will change, but probably not so very long before.

You may agree with Peter Davis that what goes on in gold, like high society, does not affect your life. But you are wrong. For many people, particularly those who have it, money is a means of keeping score in life. What happens to gold, to the gold that your money

15

stands for, to your money that the gold stands for, and to the monetary reserves of each country by which they each keep score too, undeniably does affect your life.

How to Go on Living Like the Richest Country in the World Although Bankrupt

We have become accustomed to assuming that the United States is an unimaginably rich country, which it is—and that our gold reserve is an almost incomprehensibly large sum, which it is not. Twenty years and more ago, when we held more than $20 billion dollars of gold reserves representing about two-thirds of the whole world's monetary gold stock and had few external liabilities, the latter assumption was not so far off. But today, by startling contrast, the $11 billion or so of gold reserves that we have left represents only about one-fourth of total world monetary reserves. Some experts contend that of our $11 billion, $4 billion and more is mortgaged or pledged or otherwise unavailable because it is held to fund commitments of various kinds to other countries, to the International Monetary Fund, and to various international "swaps" arrangements and gold payment guarantees.

The total reserve assets of the United States at the end of 1969 were about $16 billion dollars. In addition to gold, these reserves included about $3.4 billion dollars in convertible foreign currencies and $1.64 billion worth of automatic rights to borrow currencies from the International Monetary Fund.

At the same time there were dollars outstanding in foreign hands of over $41 billion, a sum approaching four times more than the gold reserve. Of the $41 billion of paper dollars in foreign hands, more than $10 billion were in the hands of official foreign institutions, foreign governments and central banks and the like. According to long-standing treaties, statutes, the articles of agreement of the International Monetary Fund, and oft-repeated pledges of United States Presidents and Secretaries of the Treasury, all $41 billion of these foreign-held paper dollars, not just the ones in the official foreign institutions, are convertible into gold from the United States gold reserve at the rate of one ounce of gold for every thirty-five paper dollars. But all of these pious paper pledges are more or less meaningless in reality. The Treasury has asserted the power, if not the right, to refuse to honor them, in its discretion, and has exercised that power.

To put the United States Treasury's gold reserve position of $11 billion covering potential paper dollar claims against it of $41 billion dollars in perspective, each of the two largest New York City commercial banks alone shows asset reserves on its balance sheet of more than $21 billion.

If foreign holders of paper dollars thought of the Treasury's gold reserves the way a commercial bank's depositors think of its asset reserves, they might very well decide in all prudence to demand gold for their paper dollars. If the Treasury acceded to their demands there would immediately be a run on the Treasury, a U.S. bankruptcy, and a great many unsatisfied, unhappy, perhaps bankrupt foreigners, to say the least. Many foreign countries and a good many foreigners as well, not just currency "speculators" and "gnomes of Zurich," think there is a similarity between the reserves of the United States Treasury and those of a commercial bank. This is one reason why world monetary crises have been breaking out more and more frequently, in 1967, 1968, and 1969.

What if, for example, Germany took notice of the "bankruptcy" of our gold reserve, worried that she already held a surfeit of U.S. paper dollars, and refused to let anyone cash American Express travelers' cheques for marks anymore? What if Switzerland or Italy or Mexico should refuse to accept any more American paper dollars for a case of Blue Nun riesling or a Fiat automobile or a Mexican shawl, and demanded gold instead? There might conceivably be a run on the bank, but there are reasons why it is more likely that there would not. But more of the two-tier gold system, special drawing rights, and Eurodollars later.

Nobody knows how much gold the Soviet Union has, but it could easily be more than $11 billion dollars worth. What if she declared that the ruble was freely convertible into gold, and invited all the countries of the free world to be her trading partners? What if she priced her products to under-sell ours in all our world markets and paid for what she bought with gold?

Suppose the Soviet Union had accumulated $11 billion worth of paper dollars by selling small amounts of her huge annual gold production through the London, Zurich and Hong Kong banks, and she presented those paper dollars through a Zurich bank at the

Federal Reserve Bank of New York and demanded $11 billion in gold bullion for them. Would Alfred Hayes, the director of the New York Federal Reserve Bank, hand over all the gold we had left? If he refused, and word of his refusal got out, would all the other countries that held paper dollars demand gold too, and start a run on the Federal Reserve Bank? Or would it close and declare itself bankrupt? There is no reassuring answer to these questions.

NOTHING BUT GOLD AND SILVER COIN IS CONSTITUTIONAL TENDER FOR THE PAYMENT OF DEBTS—U.S. CONSTITUTION, ARTICLE I, SECTION 10.

The United States Constitution provides that "no state shall make any thing but gold and silver coin as Tender in Payment of Debts."

Suppose you go to a state bank in Minnesota, give it your note and a mortgage on some land you own, and borrow $14,000 that is credited to an account in your name on the bank's books. Then you default in repayment and the bank forecloses on your property and tries to sell it.

A lower court in Minnesota recently held that the bank could not recover on its mortgage because "creation of fiat money or credit upon the books of the bank consitutes the creation of fiat money by bookkeeping entry." It went on to say that Federal Reserve notes were not "legal tender" and Congress could not make them so because to do so would violate the constitutional provision just quoted, making only gold and silver coin legal tender in payment of debts. If this decision were widely followed, and the "gold clause" were not amended, the whole credit structure of the free world could topple. Gold still has its believers, and when they take a stand on the literal meaning of the unamended text of the U.S. Constitution it is not easy to dislodge them.

"GOLD CONTINUES TO BE THE BASIC ELEMENT IN THE WORLD MONETARY SYSTEM"

The International Monetary Fund is seeking to replace gold as a monetary reserve element through the creation of credits for use by each country's monetary authorities. These credits are called Special Drawing Rights, or SDR's. But in referring to the creation of Special

18

Drawing Rights—often called "paper gold"—through the International Monetary Fund, even the Managing Director of the Fund, Pierre-Paul Schweitzer, has admitted:

> Gold is a traditional means of international settlement and a point of reference for the values of national currencies. The value of Special Drawing Rights is guaranteed in terms of a weight of gold. More than one-half of all monetary reserves consists of gold, and it continues to be the basic element in the world monetary system.

This book says no more and no less. Observing the role of gold in the world money system through history is the best way to come to a working understanding of the money system itself, regardless of what the role of gold within the system may ultimately turn out to be.

FRAYING GOLD THREADS IN THE TAPESTRY OF
THE WORLD'S MONEY SYSTEM

The following chapters sort out, identify, and trace some significant strands that are woven into the vast tapestry of the world money system, and that will form the pattern of the tapestry in the future. Some of the strands twist away from the pattern, or form a false pattern, or do not carry the weight of the fabric, or may break and let it tumble down in shreds. The tapestry is not finished. The gold and silver filaments that have held it together most of the time since civilized man began to weave it are fraying and disappearing. Whether the fabric will fall apart, or some new synthetic miracle threads will be invented to hold it together, is a mystery hidden in the real hereafter of the wherewithal, as distinguished from the future of money.

1

MONEY PAST AND PRESENT AND THE LONG WAR BETWEEN THE MIDASES AND THE PURSIDES

*Money is one of those concepts which, like
a teaspoon or an umbrella, but unlike an
earthquake or a buttercup, are definable
primarily by the use or purpose which they
serve.*

RALPH G. HAWTREY,
Currency and Credit (1928)

On the island of Yap, one of the Caroline group in the Pacific, currency takes the form of large stones, the biggest of which, some twelve feet across and weighing five tons, represents an extremely static and safe form of deposit. Monetary transfers are effected through the use of smaller stones with a central hole that allows them to be slung on poles and moved from place to place.

At the other end of the spectrum we read of the development of a "cashless" or "checkless" society run with such inventions as "electromoney," "electrocards," "electrofunds," and "touch-tone banking." These catchwords reflect the latest stage in the evolution of the means of moving funds. They envisage the eventual disappearance of the use of coins, paper money, and checks, together with the possibility of effecting settlements between debtors and creditors almost instantaneously.

A BUNDLE OF ABSTRACTIONS AND A POCKETFUL OF DREAMS

The word "money" is a loosely bound bundle of a dozen or more separate but related abstract ideas. It is also a pocketful of dreams.

Money is the medium in which prices are expressed, debts discharged, goods and services paid for, and bank reserves held. It is the unit of account in which records are kept, costs computed, and values compared. It is a means of stating the price of goods and services, and of expressing debts, taxes, salary and wage agreements, rent, in-

21

surance obligations, and innumerable other contracts. It is a reserve of ready purchasing power. It is the only completely liquid asset.

In the context of the money supply, money means the circulating medium. It includes demand deposits and common money and currency, bank notes and coins. The word is also used more broadly to embrace money that does not enter into person-to-person circulation, such as the standard money, often gold, that may be held as the basic monetary reserve without at any time entering into general circulation.

A capsule history of the evolution of money is suggested by the numerical order of the definitions of money in Webster's *New Collegiate Dictionary*:

1. Metal, as gold, silver, or copper, coined or stamped, and issued as a medium of exchange
2. A sum (definite or indefinite) of money
3. Wealth reckoned in terms of money
4. Any form or denomination of coin or paper lawfully current as money—chiefly plural
5. Anything customarily used as a medium of exchange and measure of value, as sheep, wampum, gold dust, etc.
6. Any written or stamped promise or certificate, which passes as a means of payment, as a government note

Webster's assigns first place to the earliest ascertainable meaning and puts later meanings in the numerical order that semantic development has shown to be most probable. The technical senses follow nontechnical senses. In a way it also implies a ranking of various forms of money according to the willingness of the vast majority of mankind to believe in its soundness and accept it unquestioningly, with the best placed first. The kind of money that the "average jetsetter" and most other members of Western society use today to the exclusion of almost all other kinds is credit and checking-account money, which ranks last on the list.

In money development the historic progression from tangible words—that reflect the commodity origins of money such as "drachma" which originally meant a "handful" of iron nails and "pound" for a pound of silver—toward abstractions like government and credit-card money, is of profound significance. A bank note was originally a promise to pay some sort of asset, such as gold or silver (that is, commodity money). Now, in many modern countries, debt money is without any pretense to commodity backing or to convertibility into any form of asset money, or into any currency of any country other than the issuing country.

CATTLE MONEY IS NOT DIVISIBLE INTO SMALL CHANGE, BUT MAY INCREASE BY REPRODUCTION

Hundreds of different objects have served at one time or another as money, commodity money, including such things as slaves, gunpowder, and the jawbones of pigs. If the heaviest money ever used was the stone money of Yap, the lightest was the feather money of the New Hebrides. Salt money circulated among the natives of Ethiopia for centuries side by side with the gold and silver coins of the slave traders. Tobacco, leather, hides, furs, olive oil, beer and spirits, slaves and wives, copper, iron, gold, silver, rings, diamonds, wampum beads and shells, huge rocks and landmarks, and chewing gum and cigarette butts have all served as a medium of exchange. So have cattle, from which the words "capital" and "chattel" are derived, as is the Latin stem of "pecuniary." In *Economics*, Professor Samuelson observes: *

> Each has some advantages and disadvantages. Cattle are not divisible into small change, but while being hoarded, such "money" is likely to increase by reproduction, giving the lie to the doctrine of Aristotle that "money is barren."

The ox of Homeric Greece, the elephant of Ceylon, and the skull money used on Borneo during the 19th century cannot have served widely as a medium of exchange, although they may have been used as a basis for comparing the wealth of persons and tribes, and from that have become the standard for measuring other values as well. In the social system of Borneo, human skulls enjoyed unique prestige. It became customary to relate pigs or palm nuts to skulls when comparing their values for purposes of actual exchange. Thus skulls served as the standard, and pigs and palm nuts as the medium of ex-

* Samuelson, *Economics,* 7th Edition, McGraw-Hill Book Co., 1967.

23

change, just as in modern society gold serves as the standard (at least until quite recently) and silver coins (also until recently) and paper money as the medium of exchange.

In the evolution of the money material, there seems to have been a tendency to move from the more useful substance to the less useful and more ornamental. This may account for the frequent use of coins as ornaments and the issuance of coins with holes in them for stringing. It also, of course, helps account for the popularity of gold and silver, two of the most ornamental of all elements.

VEINS OF PRECIOUS METALS IN THE MONEY SYSTEM

Ancient writers such as Herodotus in the 5th century B.C. ascribed the invention of coinage and money, as distinguished from objects of barter, to the Lydians. King Croesus of Lydia reputedly struck coins of pure gold and pure silver. There is evidence of even earlier coinages in Lydia and Ionia made from electrum, a natural mixture of gold and silver, which the Greeks called "white" gold. Some of the earliest pieces found at Ephesus date from the 8th century B.C.

Gold was the great currency of Asia, of the later Lydian kings, and of most Indian dynasties until the 12th century. But silver was the currency of early Greece, the Republic of Rome, and of Europe generally from the 9th to the 14th centuries. Gold is not found in European coinage until the coinages of Philip II, Alexander III, and Lysimachus of Macedon, but silver is found in the Roman and Byzantine empires and their successors until the 8th century. It was revived in the 12th century in the commercial currencies of the Italian republics, and from the middle of the 14th century it also became the standard of the northern countries of Europe. At various times and places, copper, bronze, and lead have also been used as coins, and so have nickel, aluminum, and bronze.

From the 5th until the 13th century the besant of Byzantium, which had been derived from the Roman gold solidus, and the Arabic dinar were used in international trade and for hoarding purposes from Western Europe to Central Asia. With the progressive decline of the economic as well as the cultural level of Western Europe, there was little demand for gold coins. Charlemagne sanctioned the abandonment of the gold standard and established instead a monetary system based on the denarius, or silver penny, 240 of which were cut from a

24

pound weight of silver. Thus the denarius became the only important current coin. Its multiples, the pound (libra) and the shilling (solidus), were not represented in circulation by real coins, but were "monies of account," that is, numerical expressions for 240 pennies and 12 pennies respectively, later reflected in the British monetary system. The Italian republics of Florence and Venice issued coins made of gold, called florins in the case of Florence and ducats or sequins in the case of Venice. Finally, in the 16th century, large heavy silver coins came into use, variously known as dollars (thaler in German), piastres, or pieces of eight; and the dollar, of course, eventually became the monetary unit of the United States, Canada, China, and several Spanish-American republics.

GOVERNMENT MONEY, BANK MONEY, AND THE PAPER PROLIFERATION OF WEALTH

Demand deposits are now the most common form of debt money, and today at least nine-tenths of all transactions, by value if not in number, take place by check. A typical employee of a large organization will have his salary paid directly into his bank account after income taxes have already been withheld by his employer. His rent and dentist bills will be paid by check, his gasoline and hotel bills by a credit card. Except for petty cash, for lunches and carfare, he needs very little cash. Broadly speaking, modern man would rather deal in money that is intrinsically worthless and not see the commodity or even paper money at all than be bothered much about money that has intrinsic value.

THE MORE INTRINSICALLY WORTHLESS MAN'S MEDIUM OF EXCHANGE, THE RICHER HE IS—AS LONG AS FAITH ABIDES

The tendency to evolve from the simple barter or exchange of one intrinsically valuable thing for another to the use of an arbitrarily selected thing as a medium of exchange, such as money, is basic to human nature and is observable across the whole sweep of human history. Any old thing—it hardly matters what—will serve as the medium of exchange. In the things selected as the medium of exchange history shows a trend away from the use of things that are intrinsically valuable, such as cattle, toward things that are intrinsically worthless, such as paper and credit. The more use society makes of an intrinsically worthless medium of exchange the greater its wealth becomes. The human mind is capable of assigning much greater value to intangible hopes and fears than to tangible things. Over periods of time consider how much more most of us pay for insurance policies and stocks and bonds than for automobiles.

Acceptance of intrinsically worthless money depends on the social behavior of the people who use it; on their memory; on history; on the convenience of using it instead of some other form of exchange, because it serves as a convenient reckoning device like poker chips; and on many other things. Like a poker chip, the value of a standard unit of money results from the fact that other people will accept it at the same standard value. Poker chips are accepted at face value during the evening of the game, so their acceptance is limited and temporary. Standard money is usually acceptable over a much longer period of time, but during inflation for example, this time span grows shorter and shorter.

You object. You point out that this explanation of the source of value of noncommodity money involves circular reasoning. It amounts to saying nothing more than that noncommodity money is accepted because it is accepted because it is accepted. Your objection is sustained. You are right.

A Rose Is a Rose, and Paper Money Is Accepted Because It Is Accepted, Because It Is Accepted

As long as money was predominantly commodity money its value was easily explained in terms of the value of the commodity used as money. Even money that was no longer convertible into gold or some other commodity could be explained as having value in terms of the prospect of future redemption in some valuable commodity. But after the international gold standard collapsed in the decade of the 1930's, much of the world continued year after year to use money with no commodity value whatsover. It was not convertible into any commodity, had no prospect of future convertibility, and was theoretically worthless outside the issuing country. Nevertheless, inside those countries people still continued to use the local money just about as successfully as the people who lived in countries whose paper money was still convertible into gold.

The Soviet Union, China, and most of the other countries of the communist world have completely nonconvertible money—debt money that has no value outside the borders of the country. The same is true of countries such as modern Egypt, whose currency has little or no value outside its borders but is perfectly satisfactory as a local medium of exchange. Hardly anybody in such a country seems to mind the fact that he cannot get gold, except in the Moussky in the form of crude Bedouin nose clips which contain as much gold and as little workmanship as possible. The ordinary fellahin is too busy worrying about not starving to death, or the Israelis' next raid, to worry about what really is behind his money.

Once money has become established in a country and the government has made it legal tender, the government can usually remove whatever commodity basis it may once have had without causing a ripple of concern about its acceptability. The United States Government decreed that $1, $5, and $10 silver certificates, which were formerly redeemable in silver metal, would not be accepted in exchange for silver after June 24, 1968, but the passing of that date had no influence whatever on the general acceptability of silver certificates or Federal Reserve notes as legal tender. It is a logical absurdity but a historical reality that even without a responsible government or bank behind it, noncommodity money can continue to command a high degree of acceptability for long periods of time. Counterfeiters have always flourished, today more than ever before.

As long as a country is self-sufficient in its agriculture and grows enough to feed its people, and its factories produce enough manufactured goods to satisfy their wants, the country has no need to obtain goods from other countries, so there is no reason why it cannot have completely nonconvertible debt money and still exist perfectly satisfactorily. Unfortunately, however, no such country exists on the globe in the 20th century. All countries and all people in all countries to a greater or lesser degree have desires and demands that cannot be fulfilled by the resources to be found within one country alone. Therefore arrangements must be made for each country to exchange its currency with other countries.

Professional economists insist that people neither know nor care, and need not know nor care, whether their currency is in the form of silver certificates, Federal Reserve notes, or copper or silver coin. So long as each form of money can be converted into any other at fixed terms, the best is as good as the worst. In their view the only good reason for basing a country's money on some valuable commodity is that this provides a necessary safeguard against the government's or private lenders' overissue of money. In this way the commodity aspect serves as a limitation upon the governmental authorities in the regulation of the money. Or so economists quite logically insist.

Such logic ignores the illogical history of how peoples' faith in noncommodity money grew up over the centuries out of their faith in its commodity backing, not out of their beliefs in the money management activities of governmental authorities.

As long as the money structure was directly tied to gold or silver or some other commodity, the volume of money was limited by the physical character of the commodity. But the intrinsic character of government money and debt money includes no self-imposed limits to its issue, so the prevention of abuse in the issuance of such money depends entirely upon the exercise of restraint by or upon the issuing authority. The satisfactory functioning of noncommodity money is therefore partly, but not wholly, dependent on the strength and responsibility of the government or the bank that issues it, and on reasonable stability of economic conditions within the country where it is supposed to serve as money.

The silver in a silver dime was recently worth about seventeen cents and the silver in a silver quarter about forty-three cents. When we accept a piece of money, whether it be an increasingly rare silver quarter or a copper-clad one with red and silver milling around the rim, most of us do not stop to consider whether the quarter is convertible into silver, or has silver reserves behind it, or has an intrinsic value in silver in excess of twenty-five cents in paper money. Some of us do.

These days more and more people have become collectors of all pure silver coins. If I were to analyze my own motives, I would realize that I am willing to accept a silvered bronze quarter in exchange for something of value that I have to sell, because I have no doubt that I will be able to pass this quarter on to someone else in the same way. Thus the value of my quarter is the reflection not of the value of the silver or bronze in it, but the value of the goods and services that the people who use the same money find they can get for it when they choose to pass it on to others. This value is not directly dependent on governmental authority.

28

On the other hand, when I find a quarter that is all silver, not a common clad one, and I put it in a jar in my top bureau drawer and do not pass it on, this is just my own aberration and does not necessarily mean that pretty soon bus drivers are going to stop accepting clad quarters in payment for fares or that I am going to stop paying fares with them. I am acting on two logically inconsistent ideas at once: belief in noncommodity money, but a stronger belief in commodity money.

The spectacular role of gold and silver in man's money system during much of history has obscured the less palpable but more general truth that the richer a man or a society has become the less intrinsically valuable, the more intrinsically worthless, the medium of exchange behind his wealth becomes. But little as the medium of exchange behind the wealth may be worth, its presence nevertheless satisfies a basic human need to know or believe that some commodity or other that has tangible value is still embedded somewhere in the bones of the system.

Are the professional economists right in ignoring completely the quixotic fellow who pops silver quarters into the jar in his top bureau drawer and glows with inner satisfaction when he fobs off clad copper ones on the bus driver? Are they right to consider only the other fellow, the one who could not care less what his quarters are made of? Is he the only man of the future in money?

NEITHER ISIS NOR OSIRIS: THE LOST SECRET OF ANCIENT EGYPT

Professor John K. Galbraith in *The Affluent Society* observes, "To most people, money and credit, the way they are conceived and extinguished, and the fact that pieces of paper of little intrinsic worth can be so valuable, remain a great reservoir of mystery." The most significant features of modern economic society are the use of vast amounts of elaborate machinery, large-scale factories, large stocks of finished and unfinished materials, and an almost incredibly elaborate degree of specialization and division of labor. All of this machinery, these materials, and this specialized pool of labor is marshaled to perform vast public and private works through capital raised through the banking system and the organized capital markets. Professor Samuelson concludes that without the great facility for marshaling all these resources provided by our modern money system, the necessary specialization and division of labor would be impossible. The flow of debt money—that weightless, colorless, invisible abstraction—is thus "the life blood of our system."

Yet for more than 2000 years ancient Egypt marshaled huge amounts of capital for building vast pyramids, temples, and tombs; arranged a complex division of labor; and developed a degree of specialization in sciences, arts, and crafts that was the wonder of the world ever after. All this was apparently done without making any use of money as we know it.

The step pyramid of Sakkara and Zoser's funerary temple, which the first genius known to recorded history, the architect Imhotep, set around it, obviously called for vast amounts of capital and labor and an elaborate degree of specialization. So did the great pyramids of Gizeh, built by Cheops and Chephren about 2800 B.C. From earliest times Egypt's agriculture provided more food than her people needed, and Egypt was the granary for the whole surrounding world. On the walls of her ancient tombs and temples, paintings and reliefs show the fellahin performing specialized tasks in ways hardly more primitive than they perform them today. These sophisticated works of art show us wheat and spelt being cultivated for bread, barley for beer, the vine for wine, bees for honey, and palms for dates, and the domestication of asses, oxen, sheep, goats, pigs, horses, donkeys, dogs, cats, geese, ducks, and the other domestic fowl we prize today. Ancient Egyptians were masters at making arms and armour, and of architecture, shipbuilding, sculpture, and painting. Their pottery and ceramic glazes have never been equaled. Their furniture, metalwork, plate, and jewelry have been copied to this day, and jewelry inspired by Egyptian models can be found around the necks of Charlotte Ford Niarchos and other beautiful women of the jet set. It remains one of the most striking and sobering mysteries in Professor Galbraith's whole reservoir how such a vast and orderly deployment of capital, such an elaborate degree of specialization, and such an intricate division of labor could exist for more than 2000 years without what we know as money.

No coinage was known in Egypt at all until the time of the last native monarchy in the 4th century B.C., twenty-five centuries after the first pyramid was built at Sakkara, although it is probable that to some extent gold and silver rings took the place of coined money somewhat earlier. In the 4th century B.C. a few gold "staters" were struck in imitation of Greek coins, but with Egyptian devices on them. Weights and measures were well known from early times, and commerce with other countries was well developed. But even without money as we know it, the elaborate division of labor and concentration of capital that the high Egyptian civilization achieved did not prove to be impossible. No other civilization in the history of the world remained so stable for so long.

It is tempting to speculate about whether those ancient Egyptians whose serene faces stare at us from the walls of their tombs and temples led happier or more successful lives than we, in their blissful ignorance of the money that we consider the lifeblood in the veins of our system. Those serene faces at least remind us that it is not beyond the genius of the human mind to organize and maintain a high civilization for a long time wthout the use of government and debt money. More profound a mystery than the meaning of their faith in Isis and Osiris is the secret of how the ancient Egyptians did it.

THE ETERNAL FASCINATION OF GOLD

There is no mystery at all about how the ancient Egyptians felt about gold, though. They loved it.

The Egyptians of 3500 B.C. knew the art of using beaten gold in quantity, and covered the tips of their temple columns (*stelae*) with gold leaf, which caught the first rays of the rising sun before they became visible at ground level. The flash signaled the precise moment for the morning sacrifice, whether human or otherwise. It symbolized the polarization of night and day, of black and white, of the good Osiris and his evil brother Seth, of sun and moon, of gold and silver. The Egyptians applied gold leaf lavishly to sarcophagi like that of Tutankhahmen, to royal furniture, and to pets such as birds, dogs, and cats of the departed, to express the ideas of the richness of royalty and the attributes of deity.

Gold has been treasured in all ages and places for its brilliance, durability, and natural beauty, which is preserved in its pure form without any tendency to tarnish, rust, or oxidize like silver and other metals. In Far Eastern countries, single sheets of gold are beaten out between pieces of rice paper and applied by the faithful to statues of Buddha. Gold has challenged the artist in all ages as a medium evoking excellence and rarity.

31

When it gets to GOLD, even the bleak gray prose of the *Encyclopedia Britannica* lights up with a gorgeous gleam.

Gold is an extremely dense, valuable, bright yellow metal, with a resplendent luster. Because of its brilliant appearance, unalterability, and occurrence in the native condition, gold was one of the first metals to attract the attention of man. It was known and highly valued by the earliest civilizations, Egyptian, Minoan, Assyrian, and Etruscan, and from all these periods ornaments of great variety and of beautiful and elaborate workmanship survived; many of them being as perfect as when they were first made several thousand years ago. The making of gold from base metals by means of the philosopher's stone, and discovery of the elixir of life were the chief aims of the alchemists of the Middle Ages, and many of the advances in early chemistry were the direct outcome of such experiments. The chemical symbol for gold is Au; its atomic number is 79 and atomic weight 197.0. In this atomic age the transmutation of base metals into isotopes of gold is regarded as scientifically possible.

"To a Shower of Gold, Most Things Are Penetrable"
—*Thomas Carlyle*

Gold had an aura of divinity throughout the ancient world. According to one of the most popular Greek legends, Zeus sired Perseus in a shower of gold. Perseus, the son of the shower of gold, slew the Medusa and founded the renowned House of Persides and Company.

As Ovid, Apollodorus, Simonides, Hesiod, and Pindar tell the story in the various fragments that have come down to us, an oracle forewarned Acrisius, the King of Argos, that he was fated to be killed by his grandson. Acrisius' only child was his daughter, Princess Danäe, who was beautiful beyond all other women in the land. He locked her into a brazen dungeon dug deep into the earth so that she could not have intercourse with any man.

Although Zeus had come upon Leda in the form of a swan, on Europa in the shape of a bull, on Ganymede in the guise of an eagle, and on Semele in a bolt of lightning, he descended on Danäe through the open casement of her dungeon in what might be termed the most extravagant of all his disguises: He came upon Danäe in a shower of gold.

As a red-figured Attic vase painted in the early 5th century B.C.

(now in the Hermitage Museum in Leningrad) shows her, Danäe in her dungeon is unwinding the long fillet that binds her hair when suddenly she stops and gazes upward, inspired by the revelation of the great god's presence. Down through the open casement large lozenges of gold are falling upon her open loins.

The issue of this unique union was the infant Perseus. He was cast away in disgrace with his mother forthwith. He grew to heroic young manhood, and, to make short work of a long story, he found a highly qualified guide in Hermes, obtained a polished bronze buckler from no less than Pallas Athena herself, set out to find the Medusa, and by taking aim at the magic monster's mirror image in Athena's shield, succeeded in cutting off the serpent-tressed head without becoming ossified or petrified himself.

Perseus and his wife, Andromeda, begat a daughter, Electryon, who in turn begat the father of Hercules, the strongest man who ever lived, and surely one of the stupidest. Who else would have taken onto his own back Atlas' burden of carrying the world on his shoulders?

For Perseus, carrying the severed head in his wallet or purse was not the bloody mess it might otherwise have been. His was a magic purse that would stretch or shrink to just the right size for whatever he had to carry in it. So rich or poor, Perseus always had a full purse.

From time to time in the following discussion of the hereafter of the wherewithal, the epithet "Pursides," derived from Perseus, his ever full wallet, and his issue, is applied to people who still believe, basically, in the divine nature of gold and its unique relationship to the affairs of men and the gods that govern economics. The Pursides are still a big family almost everywhere in the world, but not in the central banks of the most economically sophisticated countries or the economics faculties of the leading universities. The most prominent examples of the family alive today are probably former French President Charles de Gaulle, his successor Georges Pompidou and their chief economic adviser, Jacques Rueff. In their keeping the "grandeur" of France and the Pursides faith in gold and the gold standard are but different facets of the same immutable reality.

Some of the speeches that President Nixon's Secretary of the Treasury, Mr. David Kennedy, made before he took office contain some observations that suggest there may be some Pursides' blood in his economic pedigree, too, but since he took office nothing more has been heard of this. Nevertheless, it would be a mistake to forget altogether about his Pursides past.

YOU CAN PUT IT IN YOUR TEETH BUT YOU CAN'T EAT IT
—King Midas and the Surfeit of Gold

William McChesney Martin was chairman of the United States Federal Reserve Board for so long that he himself seems like a character out of *Bulfinch's Mythology*. Echoing Keynes, he has scornfully called gold "a barbarous relic." He may be regarded as the commander in chief of the present-day economic camp opposed to the Pursides. The views of Dr. Arthur Burns, Mr. Martin's successor as chairman of the Federal Reserve Board, have so far not appeared to be very different from Mr. Martin's.

Mr. Martin and his camp followers, who usually include whoever is the current United States Secretary of the Treasury (since they come and go faster than Federal Reserve Board chairmen), hold that gold is just another overpriced nonferrous metal, good for little but for filling cavities and frivolous female adornment, not fit for such supposedly serious things as monetary and fiscal affairs. Somewhat paradoxically, however, they dislike seeing it leave Fort Knox just as much as any woman hates to melt down her wedding band. As for Zeus and Danäe's affair and its issue—Perseus, Hercules, de Gaulle, Pompidou, Jacques Rueff, and the rest of the Pursides—Mr. Martin and his followers repudiate their prattle with polite, pained, incredulous disdain. Their classical symbol is King Midas.

Were he not the gentleman he is, Mr. Martin might remark that although the radiantly beautiful Danäe, like many a lady of pleasure since, may have had a heart of gold, the shower of gold upon her loins was not a visitation from Zeus, the king of the gods, but merely the conventional expression of gratification that her nameless gentleman caller flung down upon her after squirming back out through her casement window.

Mr. Martin and his minions who regard gold as just another nonferrous metal, like any other commodity, and turn deaf ears to all the Pursides' mystic prattle, will hereafter sometimes be called the "Midases," after the ancient King of Phrygia who nearly starved to death from the surfeit of gold and who was not an attentive listener.

You will recall that in return for some favor or other, Bacchus told

34

King Midas that whatever wish he made would come true. Midas wished that whatever he touched would turn to gold. When Midas went to dine, the food he placed on his lips became a lump of the metal. To keep from starving, he implored Bacchus to take the favor back. Bacchus told Midas to wash himself in the source of the River Patoclus. King Midas did so and lost his near-fatal gift. Forever afterward the sands of that Babylonian River glistened with gold, and Midas, although poorer, was wiser.

But not much wiser. Later Midas was chosen as one of the umpires in a musical contest between Apollo and Pan, the rustic god who could indeed render pleasing tunes on his reed pipes. But when Apollo struck his silver lyre, no sound on earth or in heaven could surpass the beauty of the melody, except only the choir of the Muses. Midas, however, preferred Pan's country music, and Apollo's appealed to him no more than, say, the prattle of a Pursides.

The chief umpire, Timolus, the mountain god, gave the palm to Apollo, but Midas honestly preferred Pan and so he voted, although ordinary prudence might have suggested that it was dangerous to side with tinkling Pan against glorious Apollo, regardless of personal tastes. Why fight city hall? Indignant Apollo changed Midas' ears to asses' ears, saying that he was merely giving the right shape to ears so dull.

Midas had a cap especially made to hide his hairy, pointed ears, but he could not conceal them from his barber. Although the barber swore an oath never to tell, the secret so weighed upon him that he dug a hole in a field and into it said softly, "King Midas has asses' ears."

Thus relieved, the barber filled up the hole, but in the spring reeds grew up where the hole had been, and when the wind stirred them the reeds whispered the buried words aloud: "King Midas has asses' ears." This reminded all men not only of what had happened to poor King Midas, but also that when the gods are contestants the wisest course is to side with the stronger.

The human belief in gold is a mystical belief, like belief in a god, not a "rational" belief, like believing in the ability of men like Mr. Martin or governments like that of Britain to manage money smoothly and efficiently without the aid of anything beyond themselves, like gold. Yet there is no denying that the human race still contains a good many mystical believers, and a good many believers in gold who have little faith in men like Mr. Martin. One of the principal characteristics of modern Midases is that they continually turn asses' ears to the golden music of the Pursides, and ridicule the strong emotional beliefs of the believers, with scornful references to "barbarous relics" and such.

Perseus or Midas, which is the stronger god of the money system? Is gold the divinely ordained basis for our money, or are men like Mr. Martin and their governments the measure of all things, including gold and money?

Most government officials like Mr. Martin and most professional economists today are Midases. They believe that the country's and the world's economic system can and should be run on exclusively economic principles, with as little interference as possible from the Pursides' beliefs about gold, or partisan passions of nationalism or politics.

ECONOMIC MAN, THE WOODEN IDOL OF THE MIDASES

One reason the predictions and prescriptions of the academic science of economics turn out wrong so often is that they are based on an awful abstraction called "economic man." Here is a paraphrase of the *Encyclopedia Britannica*'s description of this wooden idol of the Midases:

Economic man, *homo economicus,* is the term employed, often with ironical significance, to describe the "abstract man" who acts and reacts exclusively from economic motives. The entire structure of the science of economics, if science it be, is based on this imaginary human, if human he be. If he is a purchaser, economic man will always prefer the cheaper of two products of equal quality, or, if the price is equal, that of better quality. If he is a worker, he will seek the kind of work that is least laborious and most remunerative. If economic man is the owner of an object, he will not part with it or lend it without money in return.

Economic man is real man stripped of all characteristics other than the purely economic; he is impelled by no motive other than that of interest. He is not rational except in the basest sense. His aim is always to buy low and sell high.

Economists have not spoken out clearly about his love life, but it seems likely that economic man would prefer an occasional call girl to a wife, as cheaper, although if his income rises, and hers stays the same, a realization of the tax savings available through filing joint income tax returns would compel him to make an honest woman, or, rather, an economic woman, of her. Economic woman would, presumably, continue to entertain gentlemen callers even after the marriage. Such a woman may be beyond even professional economists' powers to conjure up awful abstractions.

It would seem that if economic man were concerned with his own economic interest and had several jars full of silver quarters at a time when spot silver is $2.50 an ounce, he would keep on holding them for their silver content, and buy more. He would refuse to hold long-maturity bonds, or paper currency, which in recent years has depreciated in purchasing power by more than 5 percent a year. Yet economists never cease to assure us that "money is accepted because it is accepted because it is accepted."

So when economists tell us that the economic man of their invention will always accept a paper currency that has no commodity basis and no gold limit on its quantity in circulation, a serious question arises as to the intellectual capacity of professional economists and Midases in general to follow a rigorous pattern of logical thought. Fortunately, one hardly ever sees a real live economic man, or woman, on the sidewalk or in the zoo, or even in a bottle of formaldehyde.

THE FORGOTTEN MAN—REMEMBERED

> Wealth comes only from production, and all that the wrangling grabbers, loafers, and jobbers get to deal with comes from somebody's toil and sacrifice. Who, then, is he who provides it all? The Forgotten Man, delving away in patient industry, supporting his family, paying his taxes, casting his vote, supporting the church and the school. But he is the only one for whom there is no provision in the great scramble and the big divide. Such is the Forgotten Man. He works, he votes, generally he prays—but he always pays. All the burdens fall on him, or on her, for the Forgotten Man is not seldom a woman.—William Graham Sumner, *The Forgotten Man* (1883).

Like the constituency which is said to have elected Richard M. Nixon President, the forgotten man is usually unyoung, unblack, and unpoor.

To Professor Sumner's unforgettable thumbnail sketch of the forgotten man we may add, for purposes of our argument, that many a forgotten man is also a Pursides who believes in the central role of gold in the world money system.

Unless he be a latter-day Thoreau, no forgotten man in any country can live his life today isolated from the economic conditions that exist within his country, and no country today can maintain its economic system in isolation from the world economic system. When interest rates rise in the United States, British bank rates go up too, and mortgage money gets scarcer and costlier for American and Briton alike.

Pursides Versus Midases—The Hundred Years' War Between Gold and Paper

Perseus and Midas furnish us with two useful symbols for thinking about and understanding the past and future of money. The Pursides who believe that gold is the immutable, unchanging, and mystically ordained source of all money value, and the Midases who believe that it is not, represent two fundamentally opposed and tenaciously held polar viewpoints in the world of money as it has always existed and will continue to exist for a long time to come.

Contrasting the two leads toward a truer understanding of the March 1968 money crisis. It also highlights other world money crises that have waxed and waned in the past and will come and go in the future. It helps explain statements by high public officials involved with money matters that would otherwise seem conflicting or downright disingenuous. When placed within the context of the long war between the Pursides and the Midases, all such economic propaganda blasts, alarums and excursions, trial balloons and reconnaissance patrols, are understood more easily for what they really are.

For a while in 1968 a fairly even but unsteady balance between the two opposing forces seemed to exist. From the time of the British pound devaluation of November 1967, through the worldwide gold panic of the following four months until the Ides of March in Money, the Pursides held the upper hand. The "two-tier" gold system that the Midases put into effect that March weekend was a powerful counterblow by which they evened the match. In the

French riots of May and June 1968, the Midases struck more smashing blows at one of the Pursides' strongest bastions. And when the United States adopted the 10 percent income tax surcharge and $6 billion spending cut at the end of June, the Midases clearly took the offensive. Yet such later developments as the record-breaking United States "peacetime" 1968 deficit of $25.5 billion, the increasing rate of inflation in 1969, the surprising deficits in the United States' export-import trade figures, the slowness of the British balance of payments deficit to improve, the continuing success of South Africa in selling its gold at above $35 an ounce on the free market, and the franc-mark exchange rate crises of November 1968, May 1969, August 1969, and October 1969 showed that the Pursides had by no means been put to rout and were still capable of winning rounds. But the Midases still seem to hold the upper hand.

Money, People, and Governments in the Framework of the International Economy

The economic man who supposedly could not care less what his money is made of, the other fellow who drops silver quarters in the jar in his top bureau drawer, his son who squirrels away silver dimes, the comrade of a totalitarian state whose life's chief end is to serve the state by raging with the Red Guards, and the bored citizen of our affluent society and his wife who buy what the TV commercials tell them to buy and think what *Time* tells them to think—these are the basic units, the lowest common denominators, the building blocks, and blockheads, of the world economic system.

In a sense they are all forgotten men and women. Professional economists, government officials, money managers, and international organizations always forget that they never do quite what they are supposed to do. Being human, still, they always—well, almost always—tend to do something a little bit otherwise. This is why, despite the economists' blueprints, macroeconomic algebraic equations, governmental forecasts, international economic organizations, and all such pother, we still have booms, busts, economic crises, and expectations of inflation. And horse races. This is why the long war between the Pursides and Midases is not yet over, and why it is still necessary to speculate on the future of money.

39

2
THE IDES OF MARCH IN MONEY—1968

Caesar (to the soothsayer): The Ides of March
    are come.

Soothsayer: Ay, Caesar, but not gone.
                Julius Caesar, Act III, Scene 2.

*Great economic and social forces flow with a
tidal sweep over communities that are only
half conscious of that which is befalling them.
Wise statesmen are those who foresee what
time is thus bringing, and endeavor to shape
institutions and to mold men's thought and
purpose in accordance with the change that is
silently surrounding them.*
      JOHN, VISCOUNT MORLEY, *Life of*
      Richard Cobden, closing paragraph.

REGULAR INTERNATIONAL MONEY CRISES, LIKE VERNAL AND AUTUMNAL EQUINOXES

During recent years, international money crises have erupted regularly at least every six months, in the spring and in the fall, like the vernal and autumnal equinoxes. Sometimes a few crises occur at once, and between major crises minor ones pop up. In early November 1967 a flight from the British pound to gold forced the pound to its official "floor" of $2.376. This spurred selling of pounds for gold and forced Britain to spend her remaining gold and foreign currency reserves to support the pound. This further depleted her reserves, bringing on new waves of pound selling, which led to the devaluation of the pound from $2.80 to $2.40 on Nov. 18, 1967.

The same October and November, noting that United States gold reserves were declining, that the United States trade surplus was more than offset by the Vietnam war and other foreign expenditures, and fearing that the United States would soon renege on its solemn, oft-reiterated pledge to sell an ounce of gold to anyone who presented 35 paper dollars, foreigners were furiously selling paper dollars for gold, mostly through the London gold market. It remained illegal for Americans themselves to own gold, unless they were dentists, jewelers, or numismatists, or users of their wares.

As we have seen, on Jan. 1, 1968, the United States imposed mandatory controls on most direct investment abroad, and proposed the tax on foreign travel to stop the gold drain. None of this did much good, and in March 1968 the gold crisis reached its climax. In May and June, strikes and riots in France brought on a minor, or in between, franc-mark crisis; and in November, right on schedule, a major franc-mark crisis broke out as the flight from the weak franc pushed it to its floor—20.145 cents—and the mark to its ceiling—25.1899 cents. As the crisis went on, fear of franc devaluation downward and mark revaluation upward grew stronger and added to the speculative excitement, which President de Gaulle eventually snuffed out by announcing that franc devaluation would be an "absurdity." Six months went by. Currency dealers and other economic experts who had become used to the rhythm began looking around for another crisis, then predicting there would be one. Sure enough, another franc-mark crisis came along in May 1969, which was even more exciting than the one before. If you keep the rhythm well in mind and look for more such international currency crises with the turning of the seasons, you will be ready with the rest of the economic experts when the crises arrive.

Of these international money crises that now come and go so rhythmically that we think of them as routine disasters, the one of March 1968 can be singled out as one of the most fateful episodes in the entire history of the world's money.

It was a focal point in the vast tapestry at which strands of gold and silver from the past met and vanished. Out of this focal point new patterns are emerging; but because so many of the gold threads are gone, it is too early to tell whether they re-create the symmetry of the old one or create an entirely new one. The 1968 Ides of March in money is both a case history of how the world of money works and an event of great historic importance whose meaning and consequences may not be fully understood for generations to come.

41

During 1967 it had come to be realized around the world that foreign pound sterling deposits in British banks exceeded more than $10 billion, while Britain had gold and dollar reserves of only about $2 billion with which to pay off the depositors if they should all demand their money at once. As Britain continued to pile up deficits in her foreign trade balances, these $2 billion of reserves fell lower each month. Awakening public awareness of a gap this wide, and worsening, may bring a run on any bank, and the Bank of England was not spared. There was a flight from the pound to gold. The Chancellor of the Exchequer, Mr. Callaghan, assured the House of Commons during debate that there would be no devaluation of the pound. A few days later, on Nov. 18, 1967, Britain devalued the pound from $2.80 to $2.40.

By unilaterally cutting the value of her pound sterling obligations to foreigners 14.3 percent overnight, Britain rather neatly reduced her overall pound sterling debts. But this did not whet foreigners' appetites to keep on holding what sterling assets they had left. On the contrary, it made them want to get rid of what they still had as fast as they could without bringing general ruin down around their own heads. Like most big depositors who discover their bank is shaky, Britain's foreign creditors were torn between the desire to pull out immediately with partial losses and the desire to hold off for awhile and hope that the shaky bank could lure in more depositors, build up its reserves, and get back into business on a solid and secure basis and eventually be able to pay off all depositors in full.

A device widely used in international finance to protect foreign depositors and lenders against currency devaluation in the country where the deposit or loan is made is the "maintenance of gold value" clause. In the case of the pound, this would be a pledge to honor foreign claims on paper pounds sterling by delivering a fixed value of gold metal in repayment of the deposit or loan, at the depositor's or lender's request. One bright spot in Britain's otherwise bleak economic picture was that she was not heavily committed to such "maintenance of gold value" clauses. Repudiation of such a pledge to pay off in gold would have destroyed whatever confidence in sterling remained after the devaluation.

During the preceding year it had also become widely known

around the world that foreign-held dollar claims against the United States gold payment commitment were up to about $35 billion, while the United States gold reserve had fallen to about $10 billion or so. The United States had long proudly pledged, and foreign holders of paper dollars had truly believed, that the dollar was "as good as gold." In theory, at least, the U.S. was committed by law to surrender gold bullion from its gold reserve to any foreign holder of paper dollars, private or governmental, who demanded the gold for his paper. But in the weeks following the November devaluation of the British pound, it was also becoming widely known that the United States had borrowed a record $1.8 billion from foreign central banks to defend the dollar by supplying foreign currencies, instead of gold metal, to foreigners who wanted to get out of paper dollars and were willing to accept foreign currencies instead of gold itself. Obviously, like Britain, the United States was afraid of losing all that remained of the once seemingly inexhaustible reserves.

AN "INEXHAUSTIBLE" GOLD POOL—AND AN IRRESISTIBLE SPECULATION

As a practical and mechanical matter, the actual exchange of the paper money for the gold was carried out through the London "gold pool." This was an informal arrangement that nine leading free-world nations—including Britain, France, Italy, and the United States—had set up in 1960 to permit the treasuries of those countries to sell gold anonymously in proportions allocated among the nine countries through five ancient London gold-trading firms so as to maintain the free market price of gold at a figure close to the official price of $35 an ounce. By March 1968, when France's secret withdrawal from the gold pool became known, the United States was supplying more than 59 percent of all the gold sold through the pool. In the preceding months foreigners had been turning in hundreds of millions of paper dollars for gold bullion: In January 1968 alone, foreigners had cashed in more than $400 million in paper dollars for gold metal.

In the five months between the British devaluation in November and the following Ides of March, nearly $2.5 billion worth of gold had drained out of the United States and other countries' monetary reserves through the London gold pool. This was nearly 2½ times more gold than all the gold mined in California during the twenty-five years after the great 1849 gold rush. It was almost 9 percent of all the combined gold reserves of the remaining seven countries. The United States alone lost around $1.5 billion worth.

Who bought it all?

Monetary officials and economists alluded darkly to "speculators" and "hoarders" and "gnomes of Zurich." A forgotten man of Pursides' lineage in France or Italy or Great Britain or Germany, who had suffered but survived many a dramatic currency devaluation in his own lifetime and feared more, who got rid of paper dollars or his own country's paper money for gold, would have said that the buyers were other prudent investors like himself. No prudent man would put all his eggs in one basket of paper money. Losing his faith in paper money, he believed the the price of an equivalent amount of gold would at least remain stable; or having faith in the political ability of his government to keep his paper money stable internally, he believed that the price of gold would rise in terms of other countries' paper currencies.

By such a man's lights, with devaluations and rumors of more devaluations in the air, the one who did not exchange some of his paper money for gold would be the one who was the "speculator." Paper money can be devalued, but it can also be banked at interest while gold cannot. The "speculator," would be the man who put everything he had in paper money at high interest, instead of prudently diversifying into a gold hedge.

By mid-March 1968 the torrent of paper money being presented in London for gold had become a flood. A wizened old bullion dealer at Mocatta & Goldsmid Ltd., one of the five London gold-pool firms, one that had been in the gold-trading business since 1684 (ten years before the Bank of England itself was chartered), described the gold trading as "frenzied," as a "panic," as a "rampage." A page-one banner headline in the *London Morning Star*, a communist newspaper, called the rush to trade paper for gold a "A Mad Stampede." It saw this good news as but additional confirmation of the fatal social disease Karl Marx had long ago said would kill off capitalism.

The gold-buying spree had catastrophic consequences for the pound. At N. M. Rothschilds & Sons in St. Swithin's Lane the pound sank to a new low of $2.38975, and there were no buyers at all for pound sterling futures. In accordance with the fixed exchange-rate

44

rules of the International Monetary Fund, the Bank of England threw more of its precious foreign currency reserves onto the market to buy pounds to hold the price above the prescribed minimum. The dollar also weakened in continental currency markets, which another dealer described as "a shambles." At the gold pool itself the trading sessions were monetary anarchy.

During the months before the Ides of March on the free markets of Paris and Zurich and elsewhere than London, the gold price had risen from the official United States price of $35 an ounce to nearly $44. But as long as the United States and the London gold pool stood ready to sell or buy at $35 an ounce, how could a speculator, trader, or investor lose by buying in London at $35 and selling in Paris at $44? Spot silver, whose price had remained at about $1.29 per fine troy ounce in the eye of the fiercest political and economic storms of more than 100 years of United States history, shot up to $2.50, nearly double its historic norm. In the more distant futures contracts, silver was approaching $3 an ounce. Gold and silver, those two historic thermometers of the capitalist world's money system, were registering near-fatal fever levels.

A Pledge to Redeem Paper—to the Last Ounce of Gold

The historic week began on Monday, March 10, with a deceptively quiet communiqué from the Bank for International Settlements, datelined Basel, Switzerland, reporting on the deliberations of the free world's chief monetary officials who had met there over the preceding weekend. The central bankers' communiqué reaffirmed the determination of the national central banks of the countries that contributed to the London gold pool to continue their support of the gold pool based on the fixed price of $35 per ounce of gold. The United States and the other countries would let the "speculators" have all the gold they wanted rather than give up the system. The central banks would continue to sell gold as long as their gold supply lasted. To the last ounce of gold.

William McChesney Martin, Chairman of the U.S. Federal Reserve Board, who had attended the meeting as head of the United States delegation, reminded reporters that President Johnson and Secretary of the Treasury Henry Fowler had given many previous emphatic assurances that the dollar would not be devalued in terms of gold. He pronounced himself "very satisfied" with the results of the weekend meeting.

But Mr. Martin's soothing bedside manner did not cure the gold fever. As the week wore on, the rumor spread that Mr. Martin had paid a high but still secret price to obtain the European central bankers' agreement to this open-ended pledge of the United States' and their own entire remaining gold reserves to purchasers from the London gold pool. According to the rumor, the central bankers had demanded and Mr. Martin had agreed that by July 1 the United States would adopt a 10 percent income tax surcharge, make tangible progress toward reducing her deficit in international payments, reduce her domestic deficit, and generally put her economic house in order. If the United States failed to "shape up," then the foreign central banks would no longer hesitate to present their own outstanding paper-dollar claims, and they would demand full payment for them in what remained of the United States Treasury's gold metal. This threat, and Mr. Martin's pledge, were not public knowledge at the time.

"EACH STATEMENT OF REASSURANCE CARRIES LESS ASSURANCE"

On Wednesday, March 13, in an editorial entitled "The Gold Drama," *The New York Times* thundered:

> There is little to be gained by further reassurances from defenders of the system. The blunt truth is that they are no longer believed. Now fear and suspicion are feeding upon themselves, so that the fever for gold grows with each fresh denial of change from Washington and each fresh rumor that change is in the making.
>
> Distrust has now spread to the system itself. If the drama is not to end in disaster, Washington must take deliberate and constructive steps to defend the dollar.

It was widely recalled how the Chancellor of the Exchequer had assured the House of Commons in positive terms, like Mr. Martin's, that there would be no devaluation of the pound; a few days later devaluation had occurred. One European banker discounted the soothing reassurances that the President, the Secretary of the Treasury, and

Mr. Martin had given, saying, "Each statement of reassurance carries less assurance."

Anyone who is interested in applying the lessons of the past to the money of the future should cut out that comment and preserve it in his wallet. It may be expanded into a general postulate about money: When a high government official who is involved in his country's fiscal and monetary policy gives a public reassurance in positive terms on a controversial matter involving money, the chances are excellent that his government's policy is about to change in a direction contrary to the one indicated by the reassurance. The more emphatic the reassurance and the more often it is given, the more likely it is to prove untrue in the end. The official himself is not necessarily a liar in his private life. It just happens to be his job to mislead the world.

CRISIS AND CONFUSION AS THE BUSINESS OF THE WEEK

As the week wore on, the soothing reassurances of Mr. Martin and the other central bankers wore off. The gold panic worsened. It began to look as if the system would not even manage to wobble through to the next weekend.

An Italian government financial spokesman helped hurry the crisis along by letting it slip out that, in order to prevent Italy's losing all her own basic gold reserves, the United States had quietly agreed to cover Italy's, as well as France's contributions to the London gold pool with still more gold from the United States Treasury. In foreign-exchange trading there were the usual reports of the British pound falling to new low levels below $2.39 and of the Bank of England desperately throwing in more of its ever-dwindling dollar reserves to support it.

Confusion and crisis being the business of the week, the U.S. Federal Reserve Board could not be expected to wait idly in the wings without getting into the act. On Thursday it chimed in with some "fine tuning": It announced that in order "to strengthen the international position of the dollar and to curb inflationary pressure in the domestic economy," it was raising the discount rate, its basic lending rate, from 4½ percent to 5 percent. This brought the discount rate to the highest level it had reached in nearly forty years.

Top officers of money-market banks suavely adjusted their profit projections upward; shrugged off anguished outcries from the forgotten men who happened to be demand borrowers; and, assuming a tolerant, long-suffering air, issued the bankers' usual public criticism of Federal Reserve Board action as "too little and too late." Not to be outdone by the big boys below the border, Mitchell Sharpe, the Canadian Finance Minister, called for a suspension of gold trading in Canada, and increased the bank rate from 7 to 7½ percent. For the forgotten man, it was a rough and costly week everywhere.

In Saigon, the United States high command did its thing by announcing a huge operation named Quyet Thang, translated "resolved to win," a maneuver designed to regain the initiative which had been lost to the Viet Cong "Tet" offensive. More than 50,000 U.S. and South Vietnamese troops were sweeping between Saigon and the Cambodian border in the biggest operation of the war. They killed 215 enemy soldiers, seized 22 suspects, and uncovered three arms caches, while losing 11 killed and 94 wounded. The South Vietnamese command, as usual, said its troops had suffered only light casualties. For the first time in the war, sections of Saigon itself were included in the battle plan of an allied search and destroy operation.

Secretary of the Treasury Fowler, working to redeem Mr. Martin's pledges to the Basel central bankers by their July 1 deadline, argued in desperation before the Senate Finance Committee that a tax increase—the 10 percent income tax surcharge—would be needed within thirty days to preserve the nation's economic stability and "to maintain the international monetary system as we know it today." The Senate Finance Committee briskly voted down the tax surcharge proposal forthwith, twenty to one.

New York State chose the same week to announce its plan to raise the minimum pay of state employees 10 percent, or at least $600 a year, as part of a $100 million program to be financed by a big increase in the state income tax. As the forgotten man sat down to figure out his 1967 Federal, state, and city income tax returns, and thought of what all his public servants, international, Federal, state, and city, and his soldiers, sailors, and airmen, were doing to him, and how much he was paying them to do it, he barely had strength enough left to wince weakly.

The private sector also helped keep the week's chaos from cooling. The Dow Jones Industrial Average declined 11.32 points. Top-grade utility bond yields reached the 6.60 percent level, long-term U.S. Government bonds dropped nearly a full point, and yields on intermediate maturity Treasury issues moved above 6 percent. Yields on tax-exempt state and city bonds also moved upward to 4.62 percent on the bond-buyer's index, the highest point they had reached since March 1, 1934. Analysts described bond trading as "chaotic."

COLLAPSE OF THE CENTRAL BANKERS' FOUR-DAY BLUFF

On Thursday, March 14, four days after Mr. Martin's and the other central bankers' soothing reassurances, President Johnson peremptorily ordered Great Britain to close the London gold pool to stop the gold panic until the central bankers could get to an emergency meeting in Washington on Saturday to figure out what to do about the mess.

More of the usual soothing reassurances from the highest United States officials popped out as the penny dropped. Mr. Fowler and Mr. Martin quickly explained that the closing of the London gold pool, ". . . does not affect the United States' undertaking to buy and sell gold in transactions with monetary authorities at the official price of $35 an ounce."

Fine. O.K. But wait a minute. Where did that little phrase *"in transactions with monetary authorities"* suddenly come from? Just four days previously Mr. Martin had stated that the United States' commitment was to give an ounce of gold to anybody who presented thirty-five paper dollars, to the last ounce of gold. This sudden shrinkage from the old commitment to exchange gold for anybody's paper dollars to "transactions with monetary authorities" only caused a fresh new stampede among all nongovernmental holders of dollars left outside the officially constituted pale.

In no mood to take orders from President Johnson, President de Gaulle ordered the Paris bullion market to stay open on Friday, and the price of gold there soared to $44.36 an ounce.

REMOVING THE 25 PERCENT GOLD COVER FROM PAPER CURRENCY IN CIRCULATION

For many years there had been a law that required 25 percent of the United States paper currency in circulation to be backed by gold metal in the gold reserve. In his January 1968 State of the Union message, President Johnson had recommended removal of this last statutory limit on the amount of paper dollars in circulation. He argued that this would free our entire gold supply of $10 billion or so to pay off holders of paper dollars, and would show "speculators" that there was a huge, practically unlimited gold supply available to meet all their demands. This would quickly bring down the price of gold by increasing everybody's confidence in the full, free, unlimited gold convertibility of the United States paper dollar to the last ounce of gold.

President Johnson's ingenious argument was good enough for the Senate. On Thursday, March 14—the same day the President closed down the gold pool to save the last of our gold—the Senate passed by an unexpectedly close thirty-nine to thirty-seven vote the bill freeing the currency from the last vestige of limitation on the amount of paper dollars in circulation required to be covered by gold. The unexpected closeness of the vote suggested that a few senators, at least, saw that the realities of the menacing world money crisis which the President's winning argument had exposed as palpably false in every respect.

The President quickly signed the bill into law, and not a moment too soon: The Federal Reserve Board had been increasing the supply of paper money at such an unprecedentedly rapid rate that the very same day he signed the bill, the amount of United States currency in circulation topped the $40 billion limit to which the $10 billion gold-cover law had tied it. Now that all academic and governmental economists are talking knowledgeably about the vital importance of the money supply in determining economic activity, it is hard to believe that as recently as 1968 nobody said a word publicly about expansion of the money supply having anything to do with causing money crises and inflation, or limitation of the money supply being a way to cure these things.

AWASH IN A SEA OF PAPER MONEY, WITH NO GOLD BALLAST AND GOVERNMENT OFFICIALS SCULLING WITH THE RUDDER

The last legal limit on the amount of paper dollars the United States could print was the law that 25 percent of the paper had to be covered by the gold reserve. There was now no legal limit whatsoever to the number of paper dollars the government could print. Congress had removed this limit in order to set the entire gold reserve free to satisfy all private demands for gold at $35 an ounce and to preserve the free market in gold. The day it did so was the very day the free private market was closed down for good in order to save what little gold stock the United States still had left.

The forgotten man was confused, as usual, but not without some sound "gut" reactions. As he moved a sand-filled corrugated cardboard carton from a truck on New York's West 43rd Street into a building being renovated for the City University of New York, Joseph Rokovich said, "I figure our leaders know what they're doing— I hope ." John Wright, a guard at the Times Square branch of the New York Bank for Savings, was quoted in *The New York Times* as saying, "I'm not worried, but if this keeps on, maybe the dollar won't be worth anything."

Over the weekend George Brown, the unpredictable British Foreign Secretary, resigned in a huff because President Johnson had ordered Britain to shut down the London gold pool without consulting him. Mr. Brown had earned a reputation for spilling state secrets during convivial tippling and for frequently submitting and withdrawing resignations, so his latest resignation provided welcome comic relief after the high seriousness of the weekend.

The communiqué issued Monday by the hard-traveling central bankers who had hustled to Washington was a masterpiece of its kind: It was a calm bombshell. It said that the central bankers believed "that henceforth officially held gold should be used only to effect transfers among monetary authorities, and, therefore, they decided no longer to supply gold to the London gold market or any other gold market." Moreover, as the existing stock of monetary gold was sufficient in view of the prospective establishment of the facility for special drawing rights, "they no longer feel it necessary to buy gold from the market. They agree that henceforth they will not sell gold to monetary authorities to replace gold sold in private markets."

The communiqué added, "The decision, of course, involves no departure from the obligation of these countries to maintain the par values of their currencies established with the IMF."

In simplest terms, this meant that the United States had repudiated its pledge to accept paper dollars from anyone at all in exchange for gold at $35 an ounce. The last formal link between paper dollars and gold metal had been severed.

The United States and the other gold-pool nations had given up trying to hold the price of gold in the world's markets to $35 an ounce. This was explained as creating a "two-price" or "two-tier" system for gold: If a foreign central bank presented paper dollars to the United States the price was still $35 an ounce, but for anyone else's paper dollars the United States was not obliged to pay out any amount of gold. The dollar price of gold was whatever price the forces of supply and demand in the marketplace might decide it was.

The technique of dramatic construction could hardly be faulted. One week to the day after the central bankers had issued their forceful promise to stand behind the gold pool to the end (apparently in exchange for Mr. Martin's secret pledge), the monetary officials repudiated the reassurance.

And it is not likely that the "governmental authority" tier will enjoy much traffic. Suppose a foreign "governmental authority" now comes into the New York Federal Reserve Bank, turns in one billion paper dollars, and demands 28,571,428 or so ounces of gold? Have you ever seen the stony look that comes over a trust officer's face when the youthful beneficiary of a discretionary trust demands an invasion of the principal to buy an airplane? Any "governmental authority" so rash as to make such a demand might well be told politely to give back all Marshall Plan aid, pay up all war debts with interest, and also send back Hope Cooke, Princess Grace, and Jackie Onassis.

Instead of taking the next few days off, Federal Reserve Board Chairman Martin, who must have been travel weary by now, turned up making a speech to the Economic Club in Detroit, the country's capital of cost-push inflation. He let fly the observations that the two-price gold system was "a form of monetary gadgetry" or gimmickry, that "this country is overextended and overcommitted," that "it is time we stopped talking about guns and butter, and about the little war in Vietnam, and face up to the fact that it is a wartime economy." He went on to say that with the current budget deficit we could end up with "12 percent, 15 percent, and 20 percent interest rates before you are through," and that a slight slowdown in the economy, after four years of expansion, could result in a $50 billion budget deficit, "just like that." You could hear his fingers snap. Mr. Martin placed the problems of the dollar in a context he described as "a type of hysteria in the currency market" and "a distrust of all currencies." Then he stopped.

The following day an anonymous spokesman for the Federal Reserve Board took back his boss's description of the "two-tier" gold-price system as "gadgetry." Mr. Martin had meant to refer only to monetary devices used in the past, the spokesman explained, not to the excellent new agreement on gold and exchange rates among the seven financial powers that his boss himself had announced after the Ides of March weekend. The spokesman did not, however, dare substitute for his boss' word "gadgetry" any new characterizations of the "two-tier" system.

WHAT DOES IT MATTER IF ALL THE GOLD GOES?
WE WENT OFF THE GOLD STANDARD IN 1934

In school we learned that we went off the gold standard in 1934 amid much tumult and shouting and talk of constitutional questions. Why all the hysteria in the currency markets thirty-four years later? Why 20 percent interest rates and a $50 billion deficit just because we are selling off some of the "useless" gold? Why all these false reassurances, hysteria in high places, apocalyptic visions, and murmurous emanations by the Ides of March in money?

One simple fact seems uncommonly significant: The end of the 25 percent gold-cover requirement for the United States paper currency dollar, the end of the London gold pool, and the end of the United States' commitment to buy at $35 an ounce all gold offered, moved all United States paper money, dollar debt, and (because the dollar is a reserve currency) all the money of all the free-world countries much further away from any basis of value in gold, or any other commodity with intrinsic value in gold, or any other commodity with intrinsic value or usefulness of any kind, than it had ever been before in the 5000 years since man first invented money. Had paper money finally won the decisive victory over gold? Had the Midases put the Pursides to rout once and for all?

Out of the story of the Ides of March emerge three simple but important lessons. First, $35 will not necessarily buy anybody an ounce of gold, because the price of gold is what the market says it is —since then it has been $44 an ounce or more—and not what any government or group of central bankers say it is. Second, what economic officials say publicly is important because it means that soon they are going to take the exact opposite action. And third, where official assurances are forceful, and do not in fact prove false in the end, it is usually because the official speaking does not control the situation. Economic officials much prefer to be called liars than admit they do not understand the economic forces involved, or that those forces refuse to do their bidding.

The crisis waned, speculators turned to other things such as cocoa, tin, and pork bellies, and within a few weeks the world's money managers were congratulating themselves on having demonstrated conclusively how central bankers had finally gained the upper hand of gold. All summer and fall it looked as if they might have done so. Then in November 1968 a new franc and mark crisis erupted. Again the free market prices of gold and silver shot up to register a fever in the world's money system. For the average person life went on much as before. Many wondered what all the fuss had been about, and went out and bought more automobiles and appliances on the installment plan.

IS GOLD "THE BULWARK OF HUMAN FREEDOM" AND "THE SHEET ANCHOR OF INDIVIDUAL LIBERTY?"

Did it really matter that the amount of paper dollars that can be printed was no longer limited by any specific relationship between them and a finite commodity such as gold? Economists say no, and point to other paper currencies that had no fixed limit, such as the marks the German government printed in profusion in the early 1920's, or the assignats the French government issued in the 1790's, or the currencies of most communist and totalitarian countries today.

These exceptions are not exactly reassuring. Not one of the non-gold-backed currencies economists cite as exceptions has existed in a country at the same time as individual freedom in a political context of law and order with justice and respect for individual rights, including property rights. These precious social rights have existed only in countries, mostly in the West, that at the same time have also had some form of gold and silver backing for their paper currencies. This raises an entirely new, unexpected, but basic question.

Sir Roy Harrod, John Maynard Keynes' friend and biographer, asserts that gold is the "bulwark of human freedom," and "the sheet anchor of individual liberty." Can individual liberty as we have known it in the United States and Britain for the past 400 years continue to exist without a gold-backed currency? Before the Pursides surrender our money to the professional economists, the printing presses, and the central bankers, it is necessary to take a longer look at gold and at the Pursides' atavistic faith in gold.

54

How did the belief that gold is the divinely ordained basis of the value of all money value get such a strong grip on the forgotten man's imagination that when he thought the London gold pool was going to run out of it he stepped up the panic buying that brought on the Ides of March in money? And if gold is no longer of any significance as a reserve for money value, how did it get such a strong grip on the minds of U.S. Treasury officials that when the U.S. monetary gold reserve ran down to $10 billion Treasury officials repudiated all their pledges and the United States commitment to exchange gold for dollars "to the last ounce of gold," and simply refused to sell any more to anyone.

3

FROM THE GUILD OF GOLDSMITHS THROUGH ADAM SMITH TO JOHN MAYNARD KEYNES—PEELING AWAY THE LAST TIER OF THE GOLD STANDARD AND FINDING ANOTHER GOLD TIER, OR TWO, UNDERNEATH

I saw a money changer in the neighborhood
of the temple late yesterday afternoon, and it
did not seem to me that he was on his way to
catch an outbound train. On the contrary, he
was headed up the steps, cool as a cucumber.
"I wonder if the old place has changed," I
remarked as he passed.

HEYWOOD CAMPBELL BROUN

The Guild of London Goldsmiths existed before 1180, and was incorporated in 1327 under the mark of the leopard's head. Because of the necessities of their trade, goldsmiths became experts in the trading of gold and bullion, and by the 17th century they had come to dominate the London money-lending business. The merchants of the city had customarily deposited their gold bullion in the government's mint for safety, but in 1640 Charles I, unable to persuade Parliament to vote the money he needed for his army, seized 200,000 pounds sterling of the merchants' gold bullion from the mint. After that episode the merchants understandably were less eager for royal protection, and they looked for places where they could store their bullion beyond the reach of such "protection." The goldsmiths were private businessmen and had strong rooms for bullion storage, so the merchant community changed its old custom and began entrusting its money, bullion, and other valuables to the care of the goldsmiths. The goldsmiths' descendants are still very much in business today. Until the Ides of March in money, five of them were operating the London gold pool.

In acknowledgment of the merchants' deposits, the goldsmiths issued them "notes accountable" equivalent to a specific sum of bullion, and these gradually came to be accepted as money. As time went on, the goldsmiths realized that since there was always a substantial balance of gold in their strong rooms, it would be reasonably safe to use some of this gold that had been entrusted to them for safe-keeping to develop the money-lending side of their business.

Later, of course, the goldsmiths realized that there was nothing to stop them from issuing notes accountable that were not specifically related to specific gold bullion deposits, but simply contained their promise to pay on demand a given sum of bullion or money. Before long the goldsmiths found it more convenient not to tag each individual merchant's gold deposit so as to be able to give him back exactly the same bar of gold he had deposited. Instead, they gave him a receipt for an amount of gold, or money of a given value, which would not necessarily be the same bar of gold he had deposited.

LIMITS UPON CREATION OF BANK DEPOSITS AS A KEY GOVERNMENTAL CONTROL OVER THE QUANTITY OF MONEY

While 100 percent reserves are absolutely necessary if a bank is to be liquidated immediately and all depositors paid off in full, 100 percent reserves are not at all necessary if the bank is a "going concern," because new deposits balance withdrawals. Only a little ready money, perhaps less than 2 percent, is normally needed in the form of immediately available cash to pay off depositors upon demand. If a depositor should complain that his banker did not have all the money to pay him at once, the banker or goldsmith might reply, "Your money is safe. If you don't like my way of doing business, withdraw your funds and deposit them elsewhere."

By using fractional reserves of as little as 2 percent or less to support new loans the goldsmiths were able to create new capital and provide for the expansion of business. In practical effect the goldsmiths were able to create additional "money." This is a basic principle of modern commercial banking, of modern national banking, of modern international monetary banking, and indeed of all banking.

In modern banking in the United States, the Federal Reserve System requires member banks to keep substantial portions of their assets, such as one-seventh for example, in nonearning cash deposits with the Federal Reserve Bank. The "Fed" permits each member bank to count as part of its reserves the cash that it holds in its own vault. This legal reserve ratio imposed by governmental authority is one important means by which the Federal Reserve System controls the amount of new money that commercial banks can create by their everyday lending operations. Reserves of the magnitude of 7 percent are usually not necessary to protect banks against large withdrawals. The excess reserve represents the exercise of control by the national government over the creation and amount of money in circulation.

As time passed, national governments took over from the goldsmiths and the private bankers the coinage of money and printing of currency money, but most everyday lending and credit functions remained in the hands of private bankers. We are accustomed to thinking of money as something that only the government of a country can create. But it is easy to see how most of our "money"—bank deposits, loans, and the many other kinds of credit money—is created by banks and finance companies and other kinds of lenders, just as the goldsmiths created large amounts of money on a small base by issuing notes accountable.

THE OLD GOLD STANDARD: HOW IT CAME AND WENT

As we saw in Chapter 1, from earliest times the state or the sovereign would stamp a specified number of ounces of gold into coin form under the impress of the state to guarantee purity and weight. Often the edges of the coins were milled so that absence of the milled edges would disclose light weight and fraud.

In the 18th century restriction and regulation of trade was a commonplace feature of national and international life and went by the name of mercantilism. Movement toward free trade and free circulation of gold gained momentum in the 19th century and reached its peak in the third quarter of the century. But this period of virtually free trade turned out to be only a brief interlude in the long story of world economic development.

Queen Victoria's coins were about one-quarter of an ounce of gold (the "sovereign"), and President Buchanan's were one-twentieth of an ounce of gold (the "dollar"). The pound sovereign, being five times as heavy as the dollar, would have an exchange rate of, say, $5 to one pound. (The actual pre-1914 sovereign was worth $4.87, but for simplicity in examples $5 is substituted here.)

A fixed weight of gold was interchangeable with each country's nongold money at a rate of exchange fixed by the forces of supply and demand. This was the essential feature of the pre-1914 gold standard. If you wanted to import a Phaeton costing 1000 pounds sterling in which to drive from your house in Newport down to Bailey's Beach, you arranged for your banker to obtain $5000 and to have the $5000 converted into gold British sovereigns to pay for the Phaeton in Britain. Such a transaction between the United States and Britain seemed almost the same as it would have been if carried out entirely within the United States, but there were a few practical differences. Gold was inconvenient to carry around and ship across the ocean. So governments, like the goldsmiths, issued paper certificates that they pledged to redeem in gold metal. People had the right to exchange gold for these certificates, and these certificates for gold, and they often exercised that right.

Ocean transport was slow and costly, so if it cost two cents to ship an ounce of gold either way across the Atlantic, inclusive of insurance and interest costs, the exchange rate would depart a little bit from the official parity rate of $5 U.S. for one British pound sovereign. For example, the quoted price of a British pound in New York would have to rise above $5.02 before it would pay to buy actual gold bars in the United States and ship them to London to sell for the pounds there. When the exchange rate got down below $4.98, it would be cheaper to ship gold from London to the United States. The difference between $5, the official parity, and the $5.02 or $4.98 was known as the "gold points" around which the true mint parities of the pound and dollar were allowed to fluctuate.

The gold standard worked because each national government accepted the three necessary conditions: (1) The unit of national money was defined as a weight of gold, that is, gold was given a fixed price in national money; (2) nongold national money was readily convertible into gold; and (3) the price of gold in national money was related to domestic price and interest levels so that there was no incentive to convert nongold money into gold and export it for profit.

The first condition called for a higher price of gold on world markets than would be fixed by the free play of market forces without a monetary demand. This price had to serve as an incentive to gold production and assure a continually growing supply of gold for monetary usage. Through most of the 19th and early 20th centuries this condition was sufficiently satisfied to keep prospectors searching for new gold fields, and capital quickly flowed to develop new finds. When threats of a crippling shortage became most serious, the bounty of nature seemed to serve as a safety valve. As one gold field played out, another was discovered: California, Australia, the Yukon, Western Canada, the Transvaal Rand, and the Orange Free State. Gold output managed to stay high enough to satisfy industrial and hoarding demands, and to permit a slow increase in monetary stocks as well. As a result there was a growth in monetary gold stocks averaging just under 3 percent a year from 1850 to 1914—about one-fifth lower than the aggregate rate of growth in real gross national product during the period.

The requirement of convertibility for nongold money furnished a basis for confidence in all money. Anyone who preferred the commodity gold to nongold money—mainly paper, check money, or silver coin—could convert, if he wished. Gold could readily be obtained for payment in international transactions. The convertibility requirement also set an objectively determined limit—to be sure, a very broad limit—on the creeping creation of nongold money by national governments or banking agencies for whatever purposes they deemed expedient, or tolerated. This contributed to people's confidence in the money.

The accident of discovery or nondiscovery of new gold mines regulated the world supply of money. The fact that gold and the supply of gold were limited by nature, not governments, was at once the greatest virtue and the greatest vice of the system. The vice was that the supply of gold metal simply did not increase as rapidly as the need for more world trade increased, and as the need for money in the various gold standard countries increased.

The faster creation of nongold money than the addition of gold to monetary reserves during the heyday of the gold standard was so gradual that it was ignored for all practical purposes by the vast majority of people, and by governments as well. In fact, this faster growth of debt and credit money in relation to the growth of gold reserves and tangible wealth is what kept the variations of the price level under the gold standard within tolerable limits. So long as international convertibility of money into gold could be counted on as a matter of high probability, confidence in the gold standard and all currency was maintained.

The third condition of a gold-standard monetary system—national gold prices equated internationally with what money could buy or earn domestically—had broad implications for world trade. It yielded a system of stable exchange rates for the continuing interconvertibility of national currencies, and it reduced money costs and risks in trade and investment among countries. It also furnished the world with an integrated price system as a guide to international output and commerce, and fostered the development of specialization in accordance with the comparative advantages of each region's resources.

During the ascendancy of the gold standard, world trade flourished; world markets for new national products emerged; industrial production was progressively concentrated in ever-larger units at lower cost. The fruits of the industrial revolution became widely distributed over the face of the globe, and most widely over its gold-standard area. Pursides take and deserve great credit for this progress. But the Midases and Karl Marx and his disciples insisted that a "crunch" was coming.

An Automatic International Medium of Exchange
Independent of Governmental Action

Automatic operation was the essence of the true gold standard in its pristine theoretical form. Under it, anyone had the right to (1) tender gold in unlimited quantities to the monetary authorities and to receive an equal weight of gold in the coinage of the jurisdiction, (2) melt down coins, whose weight and fineness were specified and unchanging, into their raw gold content, and (3) export or import gold coin or gold bullion at will without any governmentally imposed charges.

Extraordinary as it seems today, in theory, at least, there was no central governmental control or regulation of the volume of money in any jurisdiction. Gold was of right money at a fixed price for unit of weight. The money of any one gold-standard country, through melting or redemption, free export and import of gold, and free coinage and free purchase of gold in the country of destination, was readily convertible at a fixed price into the money of any other. The international gold standard therefore gave the world an automatic international medium of exchange and unit of account that was wholly independent of the actions, legislation, or political vagaries of any single country that was a member of the system.

"YOU SHALL NOT CRUCIFY MANKIND UPON A CROSS OF GOLD"

Even in its heyday the international gold standard was sometimes threatened economically and politically. On three occasions in the mid-19th century the Bank of England temporarily suspended the convertibility of its bank notes, and narrowly avoided a fourth suspension at the time of the Baring crisis in 1890.

The automatic operation of the system could also bring disturbing changes in the supply of money available in any one country. If, for example, that country exported a large amount of gold, its supply of money, and its price level, would automatically have to go down. This could bring on a "panic" or depression in that country, although theoretically another country would be enjoying a "boom" at the same time, and the system as a whole remained in equilibrium. The Populist wave that threatened the dominance of gold in United States monetary affairs reached its climax in the famous cry of William Jennings Bryan at the Democratic National Convention of 1896: "You shall not press down upon the brow of labor this crown of thorn. You shall not crucify mankind upon a cross of gold."

Bryan lost the election, the Midases retreated to regroup, and public indignation in the United States never again came to boil over such a narrowly monetary issue.

Contrary to common belief, the gold standard was not a mechanism that had a long history in world monetary organization. The era of the true international gold standard was short—only from about 1816 to 1914. By 1900, Britain was no longer the workshop of the world as she had been in the middle of the 19th century, and other powers had exceeded her industrial strength; but she became the world's banker. The international gold standard rested basically on the ability of the Bank of England to keep sterling convertible into gold, and consequently to maintain complete confidence in the soundness of the currency.

World War I destroyed the system. The set of unique circumstances was removed, but until then, according to W. M. Scammell, "There can be no doubt that the international gold standard, as it evolved in the 19th century, provided the growing industrial world with the most efficient system of adjustment for balance of payments which it was ever to have, either by accident or by conscious planning." *

After World War I, John Maynard Keynes looked back on the prewar gold standard and wrote in *The Economic Consequences of the Peace*, "Very few of us realize with conviction the intensely unusual, unstable, complicated, unreliable, temporary nature of the economic organization by which Western Europe has lived for the last half-century." †

THE "AUTOMATIC GOLD STANDARD" AND THE "INVISIBLE HAND" OF THE FREE MARKET

The automatic operation of the classical gold standard and its complete independence of the actions of all governmental authorities paralleled neatly the automatic operation of the "invisible hand" by which every individual's pursuit of his own economic interest would result in promoting the best interests of society at large, according to the classical economic theories of Adam Smith. Indeed, they seemed bound together in one seamless web. It seemed an inevitable corollary to the truths about the general economic organization of the society of the world that Adam Smith had explained to nearly every-

* W. M. Scammell, "The Working of the Gold Standard," *Yorkshire Bulletin of Economic and Social Research*, May 1965, quoted in Anthony Harrison, *The Framework of Economic Activity*, St. Martin's Press, 1967.

† J. M. Keynes, *The Economic Consequences of the Peace*, Macmillan, 1919.

one's satisfaction in *The Wealth of Nations*. We are a long way from Adam Smith now, but all later economic studies are built in one way or another upon his thinking.

> Every individual endeavors to employ his capital so that its produce may be of greatest value. He generally neither intends to promote the public interest, nor knows how much he is promoting it. He intends only his own security, only his own gain. And he is in this led by an *invisible hand* to promote an end which was no part of his intention. By pursuing his own interest, he frequently promotes that of society more effectually than when he really intends to promote it.*

In Adam Smith's 18th-century model of the free competitive society, it was assumed that "the invisible hand" of the market assured a rhythmic sequence of expansion and contraction in economic activity. Expansion was accompanied by rising prices; contraction by falling prices. Movements in either direction were thought to be self-limiting. If prices were rising, one had only to wait; presently they would reverse themselves and begin to fall.

People and governments alike behaved in accordance with the laws of the market, and no particular individual or government had any control over the matter. According to Adam Smith, a continuous rise in the price level could not occur because the price level was self-correcting. Neither could a continuous decline. The laws of the market were "the invisible hand," whereby "the private interests and passions of men" were led in the direction "which is most agreeable to the interest of the whole society." Prices could not continually rise because the interaction of the market and individual initiative would force them down.

Suppose we have 100 manufacturers of gloves. The self-interest of each manufacturer will cause him to wish to raise his price above his cost of production, and thereby to realize an extra profit. But he cannot. If he raises his price, his competitors will step in and take his market away from him by underselling him. If all glove manufacturers combine and agree to maintain a solid front, an unduly high price will be charged, but in this case an enterprising manufacturer from another field, shoemaking for example, can move his capital into

---

* Adam Smith, *The Wealth of Nations,* Modern Library Edition (1937).

glove manufacturing and steal the market by shaving his price. If public demand for gloves is strong, the public will buy them up and glove prices will rise; shoe prices will fall as the public passes shoe stores by. As glove prices rise, profits in the industry will rise also; and as shoe prices fall, profits in shoe manufacturing will slump. Shoe factories will reduce their output. Workers will be released from the shoe business and move to the glove business, which is booming. Glove production will rise and shoe production will fall, but gradually the public demand for gloves will be satisfied and glove prices also will fall back into line.

In theory, the classic gold standard, like Adam Smith's model of the economy of the free market, was completely automatic in operation. This limited the responsibility of the monetary authorities— in most cases, central banks—to the simple matter of providing a mechanism of convertibility and a free market. This in turn created an aura of nonpolitical objectivity in governmental administration of the monetary system. It came to be considered a positive good for a national government not to meddle in monetary affairs, and to do nothing to interfere with the sacrosanct economic principles that would, in theory, work out the economic destiny of all the people of each country, and the world as a whole, if left strictly alone.

The classic, self-adjusting, freely operating gold standard of the pre-1914 century in its pristine theoretical form is one of those myths of economists, like Adam Smith's conception of a free market. Economists habitually construct such rigidly symmetrical theoretical systems after the fact to explain the success of practical working arrangements that "just growed" naturally out of the ingenuity of free individuals responding to the needs of commerce and the desire to make a profit.

Elliot Janeway provides a refreshing note of perhaps overreactive realism in *The Economics of Crisis*, when he implies that the classic gold standard was in fact managed, but not by a government: it was at least in part for the greater profit of J. P. Morgan and the House of Morgan. Mr. Janeway writes:

> Morgan's success symbolized that extraordinary operation, the pre-1914 gold standard. The old gold standard was never self-adjusting; and gold had never, in theory or in practice, embodied any intrinsically immutable value as a bench mark for

all other values (any more than did Marx's equally metaphysical concept, labor). The old gold standard was managed, but it was managed by men like Morgan. Above all, it was managed by the Bank of England, then very much a private organization. The Morgans of the world's financial centers achieved what no public agency, national or international, could have achieved at that time: a functioning system of international financial relationships that operate for the public on the basis of private relationships.*

But quiet, pragmatic intervention by powerful human forces such as J. P. Morgan does not fit neatly into professional economists' equations.

THE GOLD-EXCHANGE STANDARD GIVES CENTRAL BANKERS A FOOT IN THE DOOR OF THE MONEY MANAGEMENT VAULT

The upheavals of World War I destroyed the traditional gold standard forever. After World War I, world monetary leaders set out to reconstruct the gold standard in a form that they worked out at the International Economic Conference held at Genoa in 1922. They advised national governments to revalue their money in terms of gold according to the money's purchasing power in domestic goods and services. Countries had to reduce the volume of gold coin in circulation and otherwise economize on gold by holding foreign exchange—that is, currencies of other countries—in addition to gold, as monetary reserves to provide international convertibility.

Responsibility for maintaining convertibility was imposed on central banks. They had to keep a close eye on the amount of domestic money that the national governments and domestic banks created. Central banks also were supposed to cooperate actively with each other to keep domestic monetary expansion in close harmony among all countries with a view to the overall, as well as the domestic, stability of money purchasing power. This recognized that the link between domestic paper money and monetary gold stocks was looser than it had been before. It also openly acknowledged that the system was not automatic in its operation. It clearly imposed responsibility for the system's successful operation upon each country's central bankers.

* Eliot Janeway, *The Economics of Crisis,* Weybright & Talley, 1968.

By about the mid-1920's the system of fixed exchange rates among the major trading countries had been reestablished, under the guise that it represented a practical return to the prewar international gold standard. Countries added gold to their monetary reserves by cutting down on gold coins in circulation. They experimented with the use of foreign exchange—particularly sterling and dollars—as a supplement to gold in maintaining external money convertibility. This changed the gold standard into what came to be called the gold-exchange standard.

Countries on the gold-exchange standard did not keep 100 percent gold reserves and did not limit the issue of domestic paper money to the same or a greater value of gold. If a typical country held only one-fourth in value of gold behind its paper money, only one-fourth as much gold had to be mined to support the same world price level. Countries that did not have gold standards themselves, the Philippines for example, nevertheless kept their money exchangeable at fixed rates into another currency that was exchangeable for gold, such as the United States dollar. A country such as the Philippines would hold the money of the gold-standard country as her reserve. As long as countries could stay on such a "gold-exchange standard," the effect was much like the pure gold standard, but less gold was needed. Belief in gold as the ultimate reserve was as strong as ever, but the world was learning to carry on its day-to-day business with less and less of it. The god of the Pursides was not dead, but he was no longer quite as necessary.

For a time the reconstructed gold-exchange standard seemed to work. World trade revived and grew; the output of goods expanded everywhere—with one small ironic exception: gold itself. Costs of exploration and costs of mining were higher than in prewar years, and gold production dwindled. Nevertheless, during the political era of Stanley Baldwin in Britain and of Harding, Coolidge, and Hoover in the United States, the old idea that the economic system in general and the gold-exchange system in particular worked more or less automatically in normal times lived on and gained new disciples. Again it came to be considered a positive good for the national government not to meddle in monetary affairs and not to do anything to interfere with sacrosanct economic principles that would work things out for the good of all in the end. The forgotten man believed all this even more firmly than most professional economists.

THE CRASH AND THE DEPRESSION, AND THE DEMAND FOR A VISIBLE HAND

Suddenly, at the end of the decade, in October 1929, the unprecedented Wall Street stock market crash touched off a worldwide plunge into a terrible Depression. There followed a worldwide collapse of urban and farm real estate values and a precipitous drop in the prices of all goods and services. During three weeks of mid-1931, the United Kingdom lost one-quarter of her gold reserve. The new British government, formed at the end of that year, severed sterling's link with gold and abandoned the gold-exchange standard. Britain adopted tough new trade restrictions to defend her trading position. The United States abandoned the gold standard in 1934, and all but a few other countries followed. The universal Depression was without precedent in the history of capitalism.

Bank failures, unemployment, widespread misery, distress and starvation made the forgotten man in all countries forget his antipathy to government meddling in economic matters. Instead, suffering people demanded that their national governments expand their roles in economic life. The old idea that the government should keep its hands off the economy so that Adam Smith's "invisible hand" could put everything right suddenly switched to "Do something! Anything! Before we starve to death!"

The London World Economic Conference of 1933 convened amid high hopes of finding a solution to the monetary chaos and general misery, but adjourned in failure. Major countries banished gold coins from their national money. The post-World War I gold-exchange standard was dead. But the responsibility of free governments and central banks was no longer limited to the simple matter of providing gold and currency convertibility. The 1929 crash buried the idea that governmental activities that went beyond this were unwarranted meddling with Adam Smith's mechanically perfect model of the free capitalistic state. Governments that did not accept their new responsibilities and move fast and forcefully to demonstrate this to their people were quickly voted out of office, as Herbert Hoover's was in 1932. The electorate would no longer tolerate a hands-off governmental economic policy in any free country. Each country had to make its own recovery efforts by itself, learning as it went along to cope with the conditions that the chaotic international economic situation dictated to its domestic economy. People demanded a visible hand, and the hand they demanded was the government's, not J. P. Morgan's.

BRITAIN USHERS IN THE REIGN OF KEYNES

Even today in debates concerning the most serious economic questions—inflation versus a high rate of employment, high interest rates to foster saving and investment versus easy money, raising taxes as a way to slow excessive growth, and the like—one often hears blame for an undesired result laid at the doorstep of some such outworn abstraction as "government meddling." A glance at some British experience during the Depression era provides us with valuable insights about the agonizing process through which a free nation slowly comes to learn new and radical economic and social philosophies, translate them into political programs, and through forceful argument and adroit compromise accept them as governing law. In this as in so many other aspects of national economic life the British experience foreshadowed and provided significant precedents for later broadly similar developments in the United States. The last of such fateful British precedents for later United States experience has not yet been seen.

"ARE WE TO ACCEPT ECONOMIC DETERMINISM, OR HAVE WE FREE WILL?"

One day during debate in the House of Commons in May 1936, the opposition spokesman had asserted as a kind of dogma the Adam Smithian inevitability of the trade cycle involving large-scale unemployment during a long period of depression, with all its accompanying miseries.

His progressive views on economic and social questions had won Harold Macmillan, the youthful London publisher, election to Parliament as a Tory from the distressed industrial district of Stockton-on-Tees on the Northeast coast, which ordinarily voted overwhelmingly for Labour candidates. Macmillan was a Young Turk struggling to make his old-line party understand that the people were now in revolt against Adam Smith and were installing John Maynard Keynes in power, whether they knew anything about economic theory or not. In *Winds of Change* Macmillan describes how he rose in Parliament and challenged "this economic Calvinism," which the opposition spokesman had propounded.

"Are we to accept economic determinism, or have we free will?" Macmillan asked. "Can we apply human intelligence to make a solution of some of these problems or are they inherent in every system, capitalism, semi-capitalism, state capitalism, communism? Are these difficulties, two million unemployed and the ups and downs of trade, endemic or epidemic? That is the problem to which we should apply our minds." *

During the decade of the 1930's, Macmillan and others utilized legislative debate, pamphlets, and articles and economic tracts to bring the often abstruse economic ideas of John Maynard Keynes within the severe limitations in the forgotten man's ability to grasp difficult economic principles, and to bend them to the realities of national politics, and the practical limitations of free democratic government. Keynesian philosophy as expressed in Macmillan's eloquent parliamentary rhetoric moves us leagues and centuries away from Adam Smith and light years beyond the point of grumbling about "government meddling."

> All modern governments today, whether of the right or left, must be partners in production and they must plan together production and distribution. If we do that, we are going to do far more than by making speeches about democracy which we are so fond of making; about the great advantages it has over dictatorships. We shall be proving that in a parliamentary and democratic system we are able to organize the system of production more effectively than any other system, that we are able to use the powers of science and technology to develop wealth unknown before. In this new world, there is no conflict between government and industry: it is a partnership between all classes in the nation to achieve the only means by which we can carry these staggering burdens, and that is to make them relatively smaller by continual expansion of the national economy.
>
> I am not sure that the development of the social services in this century has not been the thing which has just saved capitalist society in this country—not saved it for political or what one

* Harold Macmillan, *Winds of Change*, Macmillan, 1966. Additional quotes throughout chapter 3.

may call humanitarian reasons, but saved it because it has been absolutely essential that the tendency to over-save in a growing healthy community, as England was from 1900 onwards, should be corrected by a tendency to force savings into circulation, into consumers' goods, which the social services have done. In this propensity to increase the rate of savings rather than the volume of expenditure on consumers' goods, savings must be forced into the creation of an active demand. How can that be done? In three ways. By more capital expenditure—and that the government is undertaking and must resolutely continue—by more consumption, and by reducing the security motive to save. By extending and not by retarding the social services, we shall be doing not merely a humanitarian thing, but what is a sound economic process from the point of view of capitalist society.

Level of Employment as the Measuring Rod of Currency Management

Here is how Keynes' policies on a practical political level would avoid inflation.

" 'What,' honorable members will ask, 'differentiates this from an inflationary policy?' Only this, that you must pursue this monetary policy, as I apprehend the government intend to pursue it—I trust so—with the criterion of the optimum level of employment. Having got the maximum rate of employment which could reasonably be expected, if you were to use the employment figures as the future measuring rod by which a currency is to be managed, I believe you should have a criterion which would preserve us at once from the difficulties either of the deflationary bog in which we were immersed ten years ago, or the equally dangerous inflationary position of pressing such a policy too hard."

Hammering Out Keynesian Economics on the Parliamentary Anvil

As Mr. Macmillan pointed out, "If the rate of savings, that is the rate at which purchasing power is withheld from consumption, is not equalled by the rate at which it reenters the market in the shape of expenditure on capital goods, there will be a depression because there is a reduction of purchasing power and a fall in prices. If through some cause, inflationary or other, the rate at which investment is being made runs ahead of true savings, there is inflation, a boom, and a rise in prices. As the income of a community increases it will spend more, but it will not spend as much more as the increase in its income. As it gets richer it will spend more, but as a community it will tend to save more still—so that there is, in the development of the national economy, a tendency to increase savings rather than expenditures on consumers' goods.

"UNEMPLOYMENT IS NOT IN ITSELF A HARMFUL THING— THE REAL PROBLEM IS NOT HAVING ENOUGH MONEY"

Still more important are the problems of poverty and growth, and of the quality of life of the people, as Mr. Macmillan explains.

"There is the problem of millions of people who are not living on the standard of life which ought to be provided by modern society. Unemployment is not in itself a harmful thing. When it is unemployment of the upper classes, it is called leisure. The real problem is that of not having enough money.

"What a strange thing it would be to a visitor from another planet who came and looked at this country and said, 'Yes, you have all these services. You have all these valuable things which are done for people. You educate your children free, but you do not feed them. Why do you educate them?' Well, because in Victorian times it was always regarded as respectable to give somebody free something which they did not particularly want. But to give a man food, to give him a house—oh, no, that pauperizes him; though how you can pauperize people who are already poor, I have never been able to understand.

"If we did not suffer as much in the great depression as the people of the United States, it was because we had a system of social insurance and they had none."

Mr. Macmillan contended that the real solution for oversaving and combating slumps is for government to spend more.

"When was this gloomy, dismal view invented that a legitimate public work must always earn its exact amount of revenue? On that basis Pericles would not have built the Parthenon unless he could have shown to his colleagues on the front bench that the revenue from tourists who had come to look at it would pay interest and sinking fund on it for all time. Even our medieval ancestors—obscu-

71

rantists, as I suppose the complete commercialist today would call them—built for us their abbeys, their cathedrals, their schools, their foundations, which we still regard as among the greatest of our architectural glories, and among which our youth are brought up and inspired and educated."

THE NEW DEAL HELPS BREAK THE CHAIN OF ECONOMIC FATALISM

In the United States Franklin D. Roosevelt was elected President in 1932 on a pledge to continue Hoover's policy of a balanced budget. But during the first 100 days after taking office, President Roosevelt pushed through fifteen major laws that led to vast increases in government spending; government intervention in business affairs, banking and finance, agriculture and resource development, industry and communications; and relief of individual poverty. Collectively, these laws came to be called the New Deal. The New Deal authorized the President to spend up to $3.3 billion on public works through the Public Works Administration. It was by far the most dramatic and sweeping national attempt to restore economic activity, and introduce social reform as well, anywhere outside of the totalitarian countries.

According to Arthur M. Schlesinger in *The Age of Roosevelt*:

> The NRA accomplished a fantastic series of reforms, any one of which would have staggered the nation a few years earlier. It established the principle of maximum hours at minimum wages on a national basis. It dealt a fatal blow to sweat shops. It made collective bargaining a national policy and thereby transformed the position of organized labor. It gave new status to the consumer. It stamped out noxious trade practices. It set new standards of decency in American life. It helped to break the chain of economic fatalism. It accustomed the country to the feasibility of government regulation and taught people to think in terms of national policy for business and labor.*

Even so, despite these heroic efforts, the United States did not reach a period of full growth, full employment, and full utilization

* A. M. Schlesinger, *The Age of Roosevelt*, Heinemann, Vol. II, The Coming of the New Deal (1960).

of resources until it plunged into World War II almost a decade
later.

Don't Talk About Keynes in the U.S.—Just Quietly Do What He Says So the Southern Bloc Won't Notice

The United States pragmatically evolved counterparts to most of
the British welfare-state institutions and programs, but no American
articulated the Keynesian philosophy behind them as clearly as
Harold Macmillan had done in Britain. It is amusing to speculate
about what would happen to any American politician who even today, more than three decades later, dared speak out as bluntly on the
economic theory behind these social reforms as Macmillan did in
Parliament so long ago. It would not be surprising if there were demands that any such forceful references to government planning and
partnership be turned over for scrutiny to the Subversive Activities
Control Board.

Even though a basic annual income of $1600 for a family of four,
which Mr. Nixon's 1969 national welfare reform proposal envisages
paying on the basis of an affidavit of need, is not enough to support a
family of four anywhere in the United States, it nevertheless demonstrates the nation's full acceptance of and commitment to the once
revolutionary principle that everyone—everyone who swears he
needs it—has a basic right to receive an income from the government
without working for it. This historic welfare reform plan, which
would require all recipients to accept jobs or training, contains a
built-in "work incentive" in that, before losing the right to any part
of the $1600 basic standard, a working recipient would be entitled to
retain the first $60 of his monthly earnings, plus half the remainder
of his earnings, regardless of whether he was engaged in the manufacture of shoes or gloves. On this basis a family of four would be
entitled to earn up to $3920 a year before losing 100 percent of the
$1600 basic standard, although this $3920 is still $1580 less than the
$5500 which the Bureau of Labor Statistics recently gave as its
minimum estimate of living costs for such a family.

When Mr. Nixon also proposed not only increasing basic Social
Security benefits by 10 percent, but also increasing benefits in later
years to keep up with cost of living increases, and also increasing the
amount of wages subject to tax to match rises in the consumer price

73

index, the world's greatest capitalist nation had moved a long way from the invisible hands of J. P. Morgan and Adam Smith.

Seeing such Keynesian economic policies in action show why it is not easy for free governments to prevent their debasement of currency by policy measures. It also suggests that it is now of over-riding importance that they do so.

Out of Keynes' radical economic philosophy grew the pragmatic regulatory and welfare policies that have made Britain a modern welfare state. Strict laissez-faire has passed into history. Nowhere on earth is it practiced today, although one may sometimes still hear it preached in the halls of the United States Congress.

IT IS EASIER TO PRODUCE VOTES WITH CURRENCY THAN WITH PRODUCTIVITY

The problem is universal. All governments are held responsible for the welfare of their people. The aspirations of the people often outrun their ability to pay for them, and nobody has yet found a way to create satisfaction for these aspirations without spending money. What this means is that if governments have a choice between achieving full employment and defending their currencies against inflation, they will almost always pick more jobs over a sound currency. Bank notes do not vote.

No government in a free country which left the economic welfare of its people to the private endeavours of each individual, pursuing his own interest, guided by Adam Smith's "invisible hand," to promote the higher end that was no part of his intention, would last very long today. And a country that followed such a hands-off policy would probably be a very bad place in which to live.

On the other hand, so would a country whose government by its own omnipotent hand directed all activities within the state toward no end other than the economic success of the state. Free governments, at least, are expected to lay hands on lightly to serve the general welfare of the people, and this does not mean exclusively economic welfare.

The aspirations of the people are a noble thing, and no one is against jobs. But it is easier to produce votes with currency than productivity. Central governments soon learn the utility of a deficit. It is convenient to take the views of the economists who followed Keynes and spend money during recessions. It is not convenient to

74

put some of the grain in the silo during the fat years. There is always something else to do with it.

What if more of the voters are borrowers than lenders and demand that the government inflate the money supply, reduce interest rates, and create more jobs? Will the truly responsive democratic government stand up in office against the demands of the majority of the voters for responsible limitations on the money supply and the rate of inflation? Can some way be found to slow or stop inflation? What about restraining the government from debasing the monetary unit by tying the amount of money to some objective standard such as gold?

DEVALUATION STRIPS AWAY A COUPLE OF GOLD TIERS, BUT A TIER ALWAYS REMAINS

By the mid-1930's world deflation had bottomed out, but at very low levels. Thereafter national—and clearly nationalistic—recovery policies such as the ones championed by Harold Macmillan in Britain and the New Deal in the United States, had gradually begun to take hold. World recovery progressed, but slowly. The shock of world depression, of widespread monetary devaluations, and of rampant nationalistic and mercantilist "beggar-thy-neighbor" policies imposed unbearable political and economic burdens on all countries. An international war threatened and gradually became inevitable. International disorganization defied all efforts by the major powers to reestablish a world economic order.

The 19th-century and early 20th-century gold standard had performed one of the most important functions that Adam Smith had assigned to the "invisible hand" of the free market: It had limited the power of governments to issue coin and paper money and create bank deposits to the amount that the public would willingly hold instead of gold itself. Gold could be obtained freely in exchange for other money.

Even after the United States went off the gold standard in 1934, everyone still believed that the United States dollar was convertible into gold by anyone (except private citizens of the United States who were not coin collectors, jewelers, or dentists) at thirty-five paper dollars for one ounce of gold metal. And this was true. The currencies of Britain, France, Belgium, and most of the other developed countries of the free world were convertible into dollars at relatively fixed

75

rates of exchange—$2.80 or $2.40 for a pound, 20 cents for the French franc, 25 cents for the Swiss franc, 25 cents for the deutsche mark, and so on. Therefore, in effect all other currencies were tied to a gold-exchange standard through the United States dollar.

For all anybody really knew and believed, notwithstanding "devaluation" we were still on a gold-exchange standard.

Money was accepted not just "because it is accepted," but because there was also that ultimate commitment by the United States to surrender gold metal for paper dollars, or other currencies that were convertible into dollars, at fixed exchange ratios.

When free domestic gold conversion was eliminated after World War II, some countries such as the United States replaced this privilege by legislation limiting the amount of paper money that could be issued to a percentage of the gold reserve held. Other countries imposed no formal metallic limit on the paper money they issued. But as long as free gold convertibility or a fixed paper money-to-gold ratio prevailed, or if there was a convertibility ratio between the currency of a country with no fixed ratio to gold and another such as the United States dollar that did have a fixed ratio, there was an ultimate limit upon the nongold government's power to permit unlimited issuance of paper money. Obviously, such limitations do not really limit the creation of bank money through loans and creation of new deposits, nor do they have any real effect on governmental creation of government employment, payment of government subsidies for production, increase of interest rates, increase of tax rates, and so on. Nevertheless, if public expectations are at once the strongest (and most unpredictable) factor that governs economic conditions, the public's belief in the limitations upon the money supply imposed by the gold standard or gold-exchange standard, or standard of convertibility, had an incalculable effect on the expectations of people themselves about the future of their money.

Pursides Make the U.S. the Haven for Three-Fifths of the World's Gold, Notwithstanding John Maynard Keynes

One might have thought that such blows as the collapse of the classical gold standard in 1914, the collapse of the gold-exchange standard in the worldwide economic collapse that began in 1929, the abandonment of the gold convertibility of sterling in 1931, the repudiation of domestic gold convertibility of the dollar in 1934, and with these economic catastrophes the repudiation of the economic philosophy of Adam Smith and the installation of John Maynard Keynes as the high priest of world money organization would have killed off all the Pursides and their faith in gold for good and all. But none of it did. In a way it seemed to make them stronger.

The Pursides had lost some big rounds, but they were still on their feet and on the move. Through this long period of economic uncertainty they made the United States the world's haven for money and for gold. The United States scarcely realized what was happening, and had no inkling of the ultimate consequences. By the close of 1939, United States official vaults held more than three-fifths of the then-existing monetary gold stock of the whole world. By taking in all of this Pursides' gold for dollars and foreign currencies, the United States, for better or for worse, had taken on the role of the Atlas of the world's money system.

Insofar as gold had anything to do with it, America had taken on its shoulders the crushing burden of supporting the world's money system that governs the economic well-being of the whole globe and all of its people.

4
_____

THE PIVOT OF THE FUTURE ECONOMIC GOVERNMENT OF THE WORLD— THE INTERNATIONAL MONETARY FUND AS A VALOROUS VISION AND A RECREANT REALITY

On July 1, 1944, while World War II was raging across the continents and oceans, 400 of the leading financial officials and economists of forty-four allied countries met at the rambling old White Mountain resort hotel at Bretton Woods, N.H. They nodded across the broad veranda toward the peaceful panorama of Mount Washington and the Presidential Range, unsnapped their attaché cases, and briskly set about planning the postwar economic future of mankind.

John Maynard Keynes led a British delegation of their ablest officials. The group from the United States included Harry Dexter White, Secretary of the Treasury Henry Morgenthau, his successor-to-be Frederick M. Vinson, Dean Acheson, and eight other fiscal and monetary experts. The French delegation included Pierre Mendes-France. Existing international agencies such as the International Labor Office, the United Nations Rehabilitation and Relief Agency, the League of Nations, and the United Nations Interim Commission on Food and Agriculture sent observers. And even the Soviet Union sent a six-man delegation. In the following three weeks, while the rest of the world watched the Allies sweep toward Paris, land in southern France, and island-hop across the Pacific, these men drafted the blueprint for world economic order under which we have lived ever since.

Their valorous vision ranks in significance with the invention of noncommodity money, the development of credit and bank money through the creation of loan and deposit accounts without full commodity backing, and the international gold standard and the gold-exchange standard. The International Monetary Fund, as they conceived it there, wove more tightly than ever before the future well-being of the whole world and its peoples into the vast unfinished tapestry of money. But the reality of the way the Fund has worked in practice since its founding has been modest indeed when compared with the size of its founders' original vision. Still, there is much to be modest about, and it is appalling to consider what the alternative might have been.

THE ATLANTIC CHARTER QUIETLY TRANSMUTES NATIONAL ECONOMIC OBJECTIVES INTO INTERNATIONAL ECONOMIC GOALS

The foundation for this framework of all future international economic activity was the Atlantic Charter. In 1941, during the darkest hours of the war, the United States and Britain agreed that thereafter the two governments would "strive to promote mutually advantageous economic relations between them, and endeavor to further the enjoyment by all people of access on equal terms to the markets and to the raw materials which are needed for their economic prosperity." The same year President Roosevelt announced the lend-lease agreement with Britain, and the 1942 Mutual Aid Agreement between the two countries incorporated the lend-lease principle. It provided that Britain need not pay for the goods supplied by the United States until after the end of hostilities, and also provided in Article 7 that final settlement of lend-lease should include:

> Provision for agreed action by the United States of America and the United Kingdom, open to participation by all other countries of like mind, directed to the expansion of appropriate international and domestic measures, of production, employment and the exchange and consumption of goods to the elimination of all forms of discriminatory treatment in international commerce, and to the reduction of tariffs and trade barriers.

The idea of "the expansion by appropriate domestic measures, of production, employment and the exchange and consumption of goods" through government action was a comparatively new idea as a positive objective of national policy. Indeed, in its time it was revolutionary. But after the reforms that Harold Macmillan and his like-minded colleagues had brought about in Britain, and the social measures of President Roosevelt's New Deal, neither government could argue any longer that the state should not try to influence the rate of expansion or the level of employment. It is now widely accepted, indeed axiomatic, that each country's national government is responsible for its overall level of national economic activity, continually higher standards of educational facilities, health services, welfare provisions, and all the rest. A high level of employment and growth in production are now major aims of every country's economic management, free and totalitarian alike.

The concept that all these things, including each country's national government itself, were to be influenced by appropriate *international* measures was still more revolutionary. The Atlantic Charter and the lend-lease agreement thus quietly changed the national economic objectives of each separate, sovereign nation into international economic objectives for the world as a whole. It made economic objectives an appropriate subject for positive action, international as well as national. This was a long revolutionary step forward, one that only a deep crisis such as the Allied wartime defeats of 1941 and 1942 could have forced upon proud and ancient sovereign nations. The crisis caused by the worldwide Depression of the 1930's had forced national governments to control and plan "free enterprise" in domestic economies with a "visible hand," when Adam Smith's "invisible hand" had failed to raise the people out of suffering and starvation. Now the crisis of world war forced the nations to acknowledge that there had to be some controls in the hands of some sort of international economic agency to relieve the economic sufferings of the separate individual nations themselves.

To Regain the Advantages of the Old Gold Standard, Without Deflation and Depression

In general terms the purpose of the International Monetary Fund as its founders conceived it was to regain the advantages of the gold standard without its accompanying disadvantages. Exchange rates from country to country were to be relatively stable, but international cooperation was to replace the previous automatic mechanism of gold losses and gold shipments from country to country. Individual countries were to be spared the need for making adjustments that in former times would have involved deflating themselves into drastic unemployment.

The fund hoped to lessen the need for import controls within a particular country. If Britain, for example, should need a short-term dollar credit, the fund could extend "purchasing rights" that would allow Britain to use "soft" British pounds to buy "hard" dollars, or some other currency, which the fund itself would hold. Then when Britain's balance of payments had improved, she would buy back, with gold or dollars, the pounds she had previously sold to the fund. The fund would try to set up rules and procedures, and exercise such influence as it could to keep a country from going too deeply into debt year after year. If a country piled up debts, the fund would apply financial penalties. While it would not force a country to create an internal depression in order to cut national income to a level where imports would fall within her means, it would permit the country to depreciate her currency by a maximum of 10 percent. This, in theory, would permit the country to restore trade equilibrium by cheapening and expanding exports and making imports more costly for the population. Thus imports would contract. This was a basic idea behind the fund.

SURRENDERING AN UNKNOWN QUANTUM OF NATIONAL SOVEREIGNTY TO A TECHNICAL, APOLITICAL, INTERNATIONAL ECONOMIC SOMETHING OR OTHER

There is no gainsaying the fact that no international plan or organization could pretend to begin to accomplish such broad objectives without requiring all of the proud and ancient sovereign nations that participated—the strong and weak alike—to surrender some unknown degree of their freedom of action, not only in the international economy but in their domestic economies as well.

Accordingly, the International Monetary Fund's planners took a rather complex, technical approach to solving what were and still are some of the greatest and most intractable problems of mankind—those of the world's peoples' food, shelter, clothing, and employment—in as completely apolitical a way as possible.

At first the fund was regarded as a technical organization with limited objectives and powers. Hardly anyone came right out and said so, but joining the fund was bound to require a surrender of each nation's precious economic sovereignty to the fund and to all other fund members to some unknown extent.

The fund's limited technical approach to solving the world's economic problems as it sees them has given it a kind of low visibility. This has permitted the fund to survive and become stronger without engendering violent opposition. The trouble has been that the low profile the fund shows to outsiders has served to excuse its managers from raising their sights any higher.

But no consideration of the hereafter of the wherewithal can be complete, or even very meaningful, without a careful look at the fund's beginnings, the role it has played, and, more important, the potential role which it has not yet found for itself a quarter of a century away from the drawing board.

THE KEYNES CLEARING UNION VERSUS THE WHITE STABILIZATION FUND

Two strikingly different sets of proposals for accomplishing the basic objectives were put forward at Bretton Woods. One was proposed by John Maynard Keynes on behalf of Britain, which was then as now a debtor nation whose economic survival depended largely on her successful efforts in international trade. The other was offered by Harry Dexter White on behalf of the United States, which was then the economic Atlas of the world, with about three-fifths of its monetary reserves of gold and largely self-sufficient, whose economic survival did not then depend to any very important degree upon world trade, and which was then, by contrast to her situation now, the creditor, not the debtor, of the world.

Most of the provisions ultimately adopted were from the White plan, more because of the vastly superior bargaining power of the United States than any inherent superiority of the plan. The White plan remains the basic constitution of the present fund. But most of the plans put forward since for improvement of the fund, expansion of its operations, and for reforming the international monetary system—the adoption of special drawing rights, the Bernstein plan, the Triffin plan, the Roosa plan, and so forth—are variations, adaptations, and refinements of basic ideas from the Keynes plan that was rejected at Bretton Woods. As was often the case with Keynes' ideas, they ranged too far ahead of their own time for instant acceptability.

A closer examination of the two plans and the dramatic conflict between their proponents is less important for what it tells us about history, important as that story is, than for what it tells us about what has happened to the United States' position in the world's economy since that time, and what the future holds for the fund and for our money.

THE PIVOT OF THE FUTURE ECONOMIC GOVERNMENT OF THE WORLD— KEYNES'S INTERNATIONAL CLEARING UNION

Both the Keynes and White plans provided for an international agency to have control over exchange rates; both provided for supplementation of national gold reserves by stocks of international liquidity; both gave the agency supervisory powers over actions by particular countries that might threaten international equilibrium; and both provided machinery for multilateral clearing of international payments.

In its overarching breadth yet essential simplicity, the Keynes plan for an International Clearing Union—which he saw as "the pivot of the future economic government of the world"—seemed to have great appeal to such latent idealism as then existed in the American mind. And it was even expressed in a style free from the usual jargon found in writings of economists. These two remarkable features may have doomed it from the start.

A National Overdraft, or Rubber Checks That Don't Bounce

The objectives of the Keynes plan were broad, its underlying pattern was simple. An International Clearing Union would administer a pool of international currency of whatever amount suited the needs of world trade. This pool or "quantum" would be capable of deliberate expansion and contraction in order to preserve an appropriate level of world demand.

The quantum was to be the aggregate total of each country's overdraft, and the overdraft that each country would be allowed was stipulated according to a formula. For example, the formula might be fixed initially by reference to the sum of each country's exports and imports on an average of three or four recent years, and might be 75 percent of this amount. This quantum total was to be expressed in a unit of an international currency known as a "bancor," whose value would be defined in terms of gold. Members would accept bancors as the equivalent of gold for the purpose of settling international balances. Each member state would agree to accept payments from another member by transfers of bancor credits on the books of the International Clearing Union. Countries with balance-of-payments surpluses would have credit balances; countries in deficit would have debits. Each member would also continue to hold and use all of her own separate gold and currency reserves for whatever purpose she chose—meeting deficits, carrying on foreign wars and aid programs, and anything else. By leaving each country's own gold reserves intact and free, the plan discreetly stayed out of the cross fire of the long war between the Pursides and the Midases.

The International Clearing Union of the Keynes plan simply projected on a grand scale the familiar principle that underlies the smallest closed banking system—the necessary equality of debits and credits. No credits could be removed from the system. They could only be transferred within the system, so there was no danger of its becoming insolvent.

The union could make overdraft facilities available to its members just as a bank making a loan to a borrower might simply create a deposit in his favor at the same bank, but stipulate that the proceeds of the loan could be transferred only to the credit of another member of the system. In the International Clearing Union it would be just as if a bank had loaned money to a borrower on condition that the borrower would leave the money on deposit with the same bank, and not withdraw it except to transfer it to the account of another depositor at the same bank. The second depositor would not withdraw the amount he had received from the first except to transfer it to the account of still another depositor at the same bank.

No initial deposit of gold or currency was required from members. The assets of the International Clearing Union would be book figures only, and the union was responsible for the accounting. This had the advantage of making the quotas of members (and of course the total resources of the union) flexible and capable of being increased by agreement if the general level of prices were to rise, or the volume of international trade should require an increase.

One of the key provisions of the union was designed to help stabilize deficits and surpluses in the foreign trade balances of member countries. If a country had a deficit in her trade balance, she was allowed to draw upon one-quarter of her quota in the union within a year if she so wished, without any conditions being imposed. If the country's debit balance against her quota exceeded one-quarter of her quota on an average for two years, the country could make no further drawings against her quota except with the approval of the union's governing body. If the deficit country increased her debit balance to more than half her quota, the governing body of the union would have the power to require the country (a) to devalue her currency, or (b) to institute control of her outward capital transactions, or (c) to surrender part of her national reserves of gold and currencies to the union to liquidate her debit balance with the union. If the deficit country's debit balance exceeded three-quarters of her quota, the union had the power to demand that the country take other prescribed action to alleviate her deficit, on pain of being denied further access to the resources of the union. In no circumstances could a country's debit balance exceed her quota.

On the other hand, if a member country acquired a credit balance with the union (through transfers of quotas of other countries) greater in amount than half her quota, the credit balance country was required to consult with the union's governing body as to "what measures would be appropriate to restore the equilibrium of her international balances," although the country retained the ultimate power of decision as to what to do. Presumably the union would suggest ways in which the surplus country might reduce her credit balances. These might include an expansion of the country's domestic credit and demand so as to encourage imports from deficit countries and discourage exports to them, or the upward revaluation of her currency unit, or the removal of restrictions (such as tariffs) on imports, or an increase in investments abroad.

As a further suggestion along this line, Keynes's plan provided that a credit balance in the union in favor of a member who did not use it for a certain period of time, should automatically be canceled. Thus, for example, if a country continued to export more heavily than she imported, she would lose her accumulated credits unless she spent them prior to a given date. To a country such as the United States, which in those days was a creditor country and had a large surplus in foreign account transactions, this seemed much too drastic. Now, of course, she would welcome it.

A Relaxed View of Exchange Rates

On the subject of exchange rates, which nowadays seem the chief preoccupation of the International Monetary Fund, the Keynes plan envisioned a system of stable rates that were variable according to need, but this part of his plan was not explicit. In the case of a deficit country whose debit balance exceeded half her quota, the union might require a stated reduction in the value of the member's currency if that seemed to be the proper remedy. On her own initiative a deficit country whose debit exceeded a quarter of its quota was permitted a "once-for-all" reduction of 5 percent in the value of her currency without obtaining the express approval of the union. Thus deficit countries virtually surrendered independent control of their own currency exchange rates, apart from the right to the once-for-all

85

5 percent devaluation. Creditor countries were under no direct compulsion to revalue their currencies if they piled up surpluses for too long.

Where Technicians Would Meet in Secret, Away from the Nationalistic Whispering Galleries of Washington

Keynes saw the Union as "of a purely technical and nonpolitical character . . . where central bankers might meet and, in secret, exchange advice and ideas." It would be operated by international civil servants with executive offices in London and New York, but with a minimum of political interference. It was a great disappointment to Keynes when at the first subsequent meeting of the fund at Savannah in March 1946, it was decided that the fund's offices should be located in the heart of what Keynes described as "The nationalistic whispering gallery of the Embassies and Legations of Washington." * Keynes hoped the union would be a world institution that would grow in prestige and powers with the years, acquire new functions, and "become the pivot of the future economic government of the world." This kind of talk and thinking probably doomed it from the start with the United States Congress of the day.

Perhaps a more subliminal reason for the rejection of the British plan was the fact that in Britain everyone was used to the idea that if there is not enough money in your checking account to cover checks, the bank is pleased to advance the money you need and charge you an appropriately high rate of interest on the overdraft. British banks are pleased to extend overdraft privileges. By contrast, in most places in the United States, unless you have made advance arrangements for overdraft privileges, an overdraft on your checking account is still a criminal offense, or at least will activate your banker's demand for immediate cash.

Just a Little Old International "Stabilization" Fund—The White Plan

The White plan was more modest. It countenanced no "overdrafts." The Keynes plan had been criticized as a scheme that would lead to inflation, and the White plan seemed designed

* Memorandum by J. M. Keynes on Savannah, quoted by Sir Roy Harrod, *Life of John Maynard Keynes*, London (1951).

to avoid this criticism. It called for the establishment of "an international stabilization fund with resources and powers adequate to the task of helping to achieve monetary stability, and to facilitate the restoration of international trade." Unlike the Keynes plan, which required no initial contributions from members, the White plan required each member to contribute a specified amount or quota to the fund, the aggregate total of the quotas being at least $5 billion. The amount of each country's quota would be determined according to an agreed formula that would give weight to such factors as the country's holdings of gold and foreign exchange, the fluctuations to which the country's balance of payments were liable, and her national income. Voting power in management of the fund was to be pro rata with the size of the quota, so votes were heavily weighted in favor of the United States. Political supremacy in the fund was equated with the size of the contribution. Deficit countries such as Britain regarded this as a manifestation of the then-prevailing attitude of the United States that the fund was merely another way for the United States to make dollar handouts to the deficit nations of the world.

Unlike the Keynes plan, there was no automatic initial access to withdrawal rights from the fund. In every case of a withdrawal, the fund had the right to place restrictions upon supplying currencies to a deficit country. A country that reduced or eliminated her deficit could buy back the fund's surplus holdings in her currency for gold or other approved currencies.

The British considered it essential that part of the burden of adjustment for deficit countries should be shared by the surplus countries, and that some form of sanctions be applied to a surplus country to force corrective action that would permit a deficit country to cure her own deficit. Provisions of the White plan for adjusting disequilibrium between deficit countries and creditor countries were roughly similar to those under the Keynes plan. However, unlike the more flexible provisions of the Keynes plan, the White plan permitted a change in exchange rates only when essential to correct a fundamental disequilibrium in the currency, upon approval of a weighted majority of member votes. The international unit of account in the White plan was called the "Unitad," not the "bancor" as in the Keynes plan. The Unitad was a unit equal to $10 worth of gold.

87

Britain's Postwar Blocked Sterling Balances, and Today's U.S. Gold Reserve Deficit to Foreign Paper Dollars

During World War II "blocked" British pound sterling balances accumulated in other countries as a result of Britain's desperate wartime purchases of primary commodities, equipment, and services. The White plan proposed that the International Monetary Fund purchase these blocked sterling balances from the countries where they were held, on condition that after three years had elapsed both the debtor country, Britain, and the former creditor country should each begin to repurchase 40 percent of the total from the fund at the rate of 2 percent per annum. There would be no restriction on the convertibility of the amounts purchased by the creditors.

Now, more than twenty-five years later, there are $41 billion or so of United States dollar balances in foreign hands; theoretically, even under the two-tier gold system, these are still exchangeable on demand through foreign central banks for the $11 billion of gold reserves still held by the United States Treasury. As one example of what might be done through the International Monetary Fund to forestall or ameliorate future crises and panics and runs on the dollar, the White plan's provisions for working off Britain's war-incurred blocked sterling balances serve as a suggestive precedent for reducing in an orderly way the disturbingly large foreign dollar balances in the hands of foreign central banks. Since the Ides of March in money these foreign held dollars are blocked balances in terms of gold, in view of the United States Treasury's subsequent highly conditional and subjective standards for exchanging gold for foreign held dollars at any price.

Gold As the Basic Medium of Exchange in Both the Keynes and White Plans

Perhaps the most significant feature of both the Keynes and White plans is that neither eliminated gold as the basic medium of exchange. In Keynes's Clearing Union gold was the unit of account. The value of the bancor and of all member currency units was defined in terms of gold. For the countries that owned gold and wished to use it as such, gold was also a form of international liquidity. Gold could be turned in to the union in exchange for bancor balances, but national central banks were also allowed to retain separate gold reserves and ship gold among one another for official settlements, provided they used it for settlements at the official parity. This protected gold producers, gold investors, and gold hoarders, but also left the way open for some form of future demonetization of gold if that should ever be about to come to pass.

Under the White plan gold was part of the quota deposit each member country was required to make. The fund had the power to accept gold deposits from member countries, and had to hold a 100 percent reserve against all such deposits, redeemable in gold or in any member's currency. Also, the fund might buy scarce currencies for gold, but only with the gold quota deposit of the country whose currency was scarce. Midases should take note that no one, not even Keynes, sought to displace gold from the central position it had enjoyed for centuries in the world's monetary arrangements and in the faith of its forgotten men and women. Instead, gold and the Pursides' belief in gold was set squarely behind the basic unit of value in both plans, thereby reinforcing faith in the new monetary arrangements with the age-old faith in gold-backed money.

The Keynes plan, in sum, envisaged the international equivalent of what every nation had evolved for itself sooner or later: it was to be a central bank of central banks, an international clearinghouse on whose books the reserve assets of national central banks would count as deposits. The aim of this plan was the flexibility and liquidity that well-managed central banking—in theory, if only occasionally in practice—can always bring to a national banking system.

The White plan, by contrast, basically re-created the discredited gold exchange system of the 1920's. The International Monetary Fund was to be added as a hedge against a short-term recurrence of any whipsawing financial crisis and as an "iffy" long-term compromise with Keynes's far-sighted concept.

THE WHITE PLAN AS THE BASIC CHARTER OF THE FUND

In general, the White plan, as described in the preceding paragraphs, formed the basic blueprint of the fund. The articles of agreement adopted in 1945 remained substantially unchanged in form thereafter until the adoption of special drawing rights in 1969.

Nonetheless, even in the White plan's limited form, the articles of agreement of the International Monetary Fund represented something radically new and important. For the first time in world history, all countries that accepted and ratified the fund agreement surrendered a measure of their monetary and economic independence of action. Each ceded to an international body the right to make the final determination of the value of national money in relation to the value of other countries' money and in relation to gold. Each consented to fixing a value for her money in consultation with the fund, which, in turn, had the responsibility for protecting the interests both of all other participating countries and of the particular member whose money was involved.

Each member obligated herself (1) to maintain a monetary reserve position in gold or foreign exchange sufficient to support her spot exchange rate vis-à-vis the money of each other member within a range of one percent of parity; (2) to advise the fund should any change in parity become necessary for reasons of fundamental disequilibrium in payments; and (3) not to change parity for corrective purposes by more than 10 percent without giving notice to and obtaining concurrence of the fund.

White's Uptight Exchange Rates As the Finical Hangup of a Fiddle-end Fund

Narrowly fixed exchange rates had not been envisaged by the Keynes plan. They leave a deficit country with no automatic corrective mechanism to prevent deficits or surpluses from accumulating until they reach the crisis level, at which time the drastic step of devaluation of the currency becomes the only way out. As *The Economist* of London said as far back as 1953: "If there is to be a crisis-proof system of international trade, it will have to include some such 'thermostatic' control. And if the nations are not prepared to move back to the gold standard and submit their domestic policies once more to its disciplines, they will have to move in the direction of much more flexible exchange rates."

The Wall Street Journal blamed the franc-mark crisis of November 1968 partly on the system of narrowly fixed exchange rates: "Plainly something is wrong with the pound and the franc, and something is very much right with the mark. The disparity is aggravated by fixed exchange rates which effectively conceal, for speculators and everyone else, exactly what these and other currencies are really worth. Working in the dark, a great many people can come to fear that the trouble is worse than it actually is."

There is no doubt that the purpose of the strict rules that the fund took from the White plan was to create an international system of fixed exchange rates between national currencies. Participating nations were given quotas in the fund. These were determined by the size of their economies, their participation in world trade, and the amount of gold they held. On the basis of these quotas they made subscriptions to the fund, 25 percent in gold and 75 percent in their own national currencies. In return, they received drawing rights that allowed them to "purchase" from the fund whatever foreign currencies they needed to supplement their normal reserves for balance-of-payments purposes; they would pay for these drawings by putting in more of their own currency. These quotas were created to permit individual countries to "stabilize" temporary imbalances in their payment obligations to other countries.

SCARCE-CURRENCY PROVISIONS—RESPONSIBILITY FOR MAINTAINING TRADE AND INVESTMENT AT A HIGH LEVEL SHOULD BE SHARED BY ALL

"Scarce-currency" provisions of the fund agreement are intended to recognize that a sustained surplus in the balance of payments of a leading member country, such as Germany in recent years, accompanied by deficits in the balance of payments of another country, such as Britain, is a threat to the stability of the fund and to the rest of the world's economy. The fund can refuse to approve a currency parity whose maintenance might involve recourse to the fund by others on a scale prejudicial to the fund and to other members. Or the fund may recommend a change in the parity of a currency, or ration the residual supply of the scarce currency to the other members. It may also borrow scarce currency from the member whose currency is scarce. Although there have been many occasions where recourse to these provisions might have been useful, they have never been effectively invoked by the fund.

The fund is permitted to penalize a nation that is in protracted payments surplus if she refuses to adopt appropriate policies. One penalty allows other nations to discriminate against the exports of such a country. At first glance this would seem to go against the whole "spirit of Bretton Woods," but the rationale is that protracted surpluses, no less than protracted deficits, can do great harm. In effect, the country that acquires the surplus is not putting her reserves to creative use through the export of capital or other means. The aim of the scarce-currency provisions is to revive the lost adjustment mechanism of the nineteenth-century gold standard, which, as already noted, tended to put pressure on both the debtor and the creditor. The fundamental philosophy of the Bretton Woods agreement was that responsibility for maintaining trade and investment at high levels for all should be shared by all.

Congress Defines the Dollar's Value in Terms of Gold, and Mortises a Gold Hinge into Money Movements

A year after the signing of the Bretton Woods agreement and just a month and a half before the Japanese surrender, Congress passed the Bretton Woods Act. This authorized the President to accept membership in the International Monetary Fund.

But Congress made two important reservations. It had come to look upon President Roosevelt's 1934 devaluation of the United States dollar in terms of gold as a breach of faith with the domestic and foreign public, and as a serious blow to United States international prestige—an action not to be repeated again solely on executive initiative and responsibility under any circumstances. So Congress made it mandatory for the United States to advise the fund that it would continue the existing gold parity of the dollar. Second, Congress prohibited the President or any person or agency on behalf of the United States from proposing or agreeing "to any change in the par value of the dollar . . ." or from approving "any general change in par values" under the fund agreement "unless Congress by law" should authorize such action.

Thus Congress in effect froze the dollar in terms of gold, and tied the whole world's monetary system to gold. No Pursides could have asked for more. If the United States could never make a change without congressional initiative, what change could there ever be? If Congress were to debate the monetary price of gold in its usual deliberate fashion, offering lengthy hearings and expert testimony on all sides of the question, the whole international monetary system would disintegrate from uncertainty while the debate was progressing. Thus by an apparently irreversible solemn act of Congress, the value of the dollar in terms of gold, and gold as the bench mark of all currency values, has been legally mortised into the world's money system.

THE RECREANT INVISIBILITY OF THE FUND

The "pivot of the future economic government of the world" quietly settled down to its work, as it saw it, and just as quietly evolved into just one more international financial bureaucracy—albeit with more prestige than most. As the fund busied itself over the years keeping exchange rates fixed between member countries and keeping itself profitable, most of the other, broader powers the founders had placed in the grand design of its articles of agreement atrophied from disuse. A responsible employee of a large international bureaucracy is more likely to be seen walking on water than he is to act under possibly nonprofit-making powers for whose exercise there may be little or no administrative precedent. The valorous vision evaporated into a recreant reality that was little more than a currency stabilization fund. In this limited role the fund has not prevented worldwide financial crises from erupting with increasing, or at least equinoctial, frequency.

At times like these, when crises smite the real world's monetary system, the International Monetary Fund's low profile becomes as inconspicuous as Adam Smith's invisible hand. At such times the suffering nations of the free world are calling out to it for courage, strength, and leadership, and more help from a visible hand.

5

WHAT WE HAD "JEST GROWED"— SO DO WE REALLY NEED FIXED CURRENCY EXCHANGE RATES?

*Some years ago in London the late Baron
Rothschild was asked by a friend to explain
the international financial system, gold and
so on. He replied, "My dear chap, there are
only two men in the world who understand the
international financial system—a young
economist in the Treasury and a rather junior
man in the Bank of England. Unfortunately,
they disagree."*

EDWIN L. DALE, JR., in *The New York Times*

Why do we need fixed exchange ratios between national currencies? Does it really matter whether exchange ratios between currencies are fixed or floating? Why, indeed, did we need a gold standard, and a gold exchange standard?

Classical economists such as Adam Smith and David Ricardo and Karl Marx do not insist on such a mechanism. Indeed, to the extent that fixed rates prevent price (the exchange ratio of a currency) from performing the important function (of equating the quantity supplied with the quantity demanded) which Adam Smith assigned to it, "pegged" exchange rates run counter to his doctrines. No automatic adjustments of international currency values through fluctuations of currency prices in the free market can occur as long as the International Monetary Fund establishes and enforces relatively fixed exchange ratios between national currencies. Is there any logical necessity for the International Monetary Fund to operate as a currency stabilization fund?

AN INTERNATIONAL MONEY SYSTEM GROWS LIKE CRABGRASS

History shows that an international monetary system has a tendency to grow like grass and live a life of its own. It "jest grows,"

94

usually with very little resemblance to the elaborate models that economists abstract from it after the fact to explain it.

Nobody drew a blueprint in advance for the classic gold standard that the world lived by in the pre-1914 century. It "jest growed." Yet in retrospect it was a remarkable technical invention. So good, in fact, that after World War I no one could think of anything better than to resurrect it in the form of the gold-exchange standard. After World War II when the Bretton Woods planners laid the foundation for a new postwar international money system, they sought to build on the best features of the old gold standard. We have all lived under their system ever since.

They did not attempt to make all national currencies freely convertible into gold. They did not try to keep the amount of money issued in all countries in the world tied to a fixed ratio based on the amount of gold metal available for shipment to settle international transactions. What they did try to preserve was the system of fixed exchange rates between national currencies. These rates, for better or for worse, are now fixed firmly in the articles of agreement of the fund itself. (However, some of the poorer countries are allowed, with the permission of the fund, to let their exchange rates fluctuate on a temporary basis.)

Fixed Exchange Rates for Flourishing World Trade

If you want to buy a Rolls Royce Silver Cloud in London, you can still be reasonably certain that the $12,000 it will cost will be about 5000 pounds sterling, or will be at least until the next devaluation.

Is it necessary to maintain these exchange rates indefinitely at such rigidly fixed parities? Theoretically, exchange rates among currencies could fluctuate freely from day to day, as prices do on the stock market or commodity exchanges. But if they did, an American importer of British cars, Italian woolens, or Japanese steel would have more difficulty putting a price on his product. He would not know from one day to the next exactly how many dollars the product would cost him. And if he could not be certain, he might not import at all. The same question arises for importers everywhere, and without importers there would be no world trade. Steady, known exchange rates seem to be important if not essential to the orderly conduct of international trade, investment, and travel, and the whole system exists to make possible these orderly international transactions.

Currencies are exchanged from country to country mostly by private individuals and businesses and banks, and to a lesser degree by the action of central banks and governments and international bodies. The supply and demand created by the sum of all the separate decisions to sell and buy come together in a market that operates in all the main financial centers: the foreign-exchange market.

An American importer of British cars needs pounds to pay for them. A British tourist in the United States needs dollars. An Englishman purchasing an American security also needs dollars. So does an English importer of American machinery.

How the Fixed Exchange Rate System Works

If on a given day the demand for dollars on the London market exceeds the supply of dollars, the price of the pound drops and the price of the dollar rises. But the system of fixed exchange rates provides that in day-to-day trading, price fluctuations of a currency are limited to a narrow band of one percent above or below a defined "par value." In practice, most major nations have limited this trading range to three-quarters of one percent either side of par. No currency can fluctuate more than one percent on either side of the par value that the country concerned has officially established for its currency with the fund.

Thus as the pound falls against the dollar and nears its "floor"—currently $2.38—the British government, through the Bank of England, must intervene. It must buy pounds with dollars that it has in its reserves.

This is serious for Britain. When Britain must spend dollars to buy pounds, the Bank of England—hence the country—loses "reserves." If Britain runs out of reserves, she can no longer support the price of the pound, and at that point the pound must be devalued—made officially cheaper. That is what was done on Nov. 18, 1967, when the pound was devalued from $2.80 to $2.40.

Why was the demand for dollars larger than the demand for pounds? The answer is that Britain had a deficit in her balance of payments. The combination of her exports and imports, plus the inflow and outflow of tourism and investment and the costs of foreign

96

aid and troops abroad, added up to more outpayments than inpayments. The pound fell on the world markets because more pounds were offered than were demanded by individuals, businessmen, or banks of other countries. That is the meaning of a "weak" currency, in the international sense, and it happens primarily because of a balance-of-payments deficit.

This is one reason the system of fixed exchange rates cannot work automatically merely because the agreement of the fund sets fixed parities. Each member nation of the fund must fulfill two additional responsibilities. First, each nation must have reserves with which to support her currency in international transactions. Second, each nation must ultimately balance her international payments or else run out of reserves and face devaluation of her currency. But only in the event of a "fundamental disequilibrium" in a nation's balance of payments is a change in par value to be contemplated. There is evidence that the founding fathers at Bretton Woods expected that these changes in par value would be easily accomplished, with little disturbance to the system.

But the practice of the fund has been to hold foreign exchange rates far more rigidly in place than appears to have been contemplated at Bretton Woods.

The essence of the system is the universal legal commitment of all the nations to exchange currencies with one another at fixed exchange rates among currencies. In its first twenty-five years of existence, the International Monetary Fund has seen its principal job as keeping these ratios more or less permanently fixed. As long as each sovereign nation has her own separate currency, exchange-rate rules make it possible for private individuals, banks, and businesses within nations, and the nations themselves, to do business with one another across national borders. Fixed exchange rates make it possible to exchange one separate currency for another, and one product of one country for that of another, at relatively fixed, permanent, and stable rates.

Since the end of World War II, world trade has doubled every ten or eleven years, and the system of fixed exchange rates has probably contributed a great deal to that expansion. Germany set free the deutschemark for only a short time in 1969, and Canada, the one leading country that tried a floating exchange rate on a long term basis, gave up the experiment after a few years.

But the valid objection remains that a country may struggle along for years attempting to preserve the fixed value of her currency, as Britain has often been forced to do, when that currency is basically overvalued. The recent history of the British pound—ending in the devaluation of Nov. 18, 1967, and its continued weakness much of the time since then—is an example of this.

Furthermore, countries resort to various protectionist measures in order to preserve the fixed rate, such as export and import controls and taxes, restrictions on capital outflows, and restrictions on foreign travel by their nationals. Also, fixed exchange rates tend to encourage high interest rates, because many countries take restrictive measures to keep their currencies strong, such as raising interest rates to increase the profits of lending institutions and to hold money deposited from abroad within the country.

THE FRANC-MARK EXCHANGE RATE CRISIS—NOVEMBER 1968

The franc-mark exchange rate crisis of November 1968 was an example of the kind of economic crisis that the system of fixed exchange rates can produce.

Because of the basic strength of the German economy—stable domestic prices, virtually no unemployment, a 1968 growth in gross national product of 5.5 percent and in productivity of 7 percent and a record foreign trade surplus of $4 billion—rumors became current that the mark would be revalued upward. Because of apparent weaknesses in the French economy—a domestic rate of inflation of 7 percent, huge domestic wage and price increases after the students' and workers' strikes of May and June 1968, and the beginnings of a deficit in the foreign-trade account—it was rumored at the same time that the franc would be revalued downward.

Among the lesser signs of crisis, Frenchmen streamed across the border into Switzerland and Germany carrying suitcases full of francs to exchange for Swiss francs and German marks. As speculation mounted, the Bank of France was forced to pour out its reserves of gold and foreign currencies to keep the franc from falling below its floor of 20¼ cents. At the same time the mark threatened to break through its ceiling of 25 cents. In three weeks before the crisis, 1.7

billion in francs were sold, until at the end it was costing France some $800 million a day in gold and foreign-currency reserves to support the franc.

After a week of black headlines the major money countries pledged a total of over $2 billion to help France support the franc. President de Gaulle refused to devalue it downward, and Germany refused to revalue the deutschemark upward. Speculators laid low and the crisis quieted down, but no one was sure that it would not erupt again soon. Advocates of floating exchange rates believe that this crisis would not have happened at all under a system of fluctuating exchange rates.

FREELY FLOATING RATES TO ELIMINATE IMBALANCES OF PAYMENTS AND EXCHANGE RESTRICTIONS

If inflation occurred within a country, a floating exchange rate would permit the currency to fall against currencies of other countries in foreign-exchange dealings, and provide an immediate indication of the loss of confidence in the currency.

Of course, freely floating exchange rates would involve many practical problems for exporters and importers, and possibly a good deal of government regulation. It is possible that countries would not permit their exchange rates to float downward against other countries' rates, and would resort to artificial controls to prevent this from happening.

But on the other hand, if foreign exchange rates were free to fluctuate there would seemingly be no need for such things as balance-of-payments problems, travel taxes, or foreign funds controls. Domestic tax increases would not be needed to right the imbalance. No doubt in time of crisis somebody would even figure out the right price at which Americans could cash travelers' cheques for francs.

The classic gold standard that served as a model for the present system used to perform this function, but was never so rigid and unchanging. Although gold is still the measuring rod of all values in the system, the present system of fixed exchange rates is not directly tied to gold, and it lacks the flexibility that free flows of gold once gave to the system. Essentially, the present system depends upon the willingness of the 112 or so member nations of the International Monetary Fund to abide by the rigid treatylike obligations they have assumed under its articles of agreement, and upon the confidence of private individuals, banks, businesses, and nations in the soundness of the system.

Insofar as the system is "accepted because it is accepted," it bypasses gold, but insofar as it is accepted because it is indirectly tied to gold, its soundness depends on how all these people, banks, businesses, and nations think and feel about gold. Thus the whole system remains in the cross fire of the old struggle between the Pursides and the Midases.

What Would Be So Terrible About Fluctuating Rates and a Free-Floating Price for Gold?

Prior to World War II, no exchange rates were fixed by treaty such as those presently in effect under the International Monetary Fund. Under the pre-1931 gold standard, however, the British were able to maintain a relatively fixed parity between sterling and other currencies by being willing to buy and sell gold at fixed prices. Under the pre-1914 gold standard they did this with some help from J. P. Morgan and his colleagues, as Mr. Janeway has disclosed.

But the floating exchange rates that followed Britain's abandonment of the gold standard in 1931, the subsequent United States change in the price of gold and abandonment of the gold standard as well, the "beggar-thy-neighbor" policies that each nation followed independently after abandoning the gold standard, and the collapse of world trade and investment during the 1930's suggest that adoption of floating exchange rates could lead to another depression.

The "Wider Band," "Crawling Peg," and Other Alternatives to Fixed Ratios

The conclusion that changes in the fabric of foreign exchange rates are inevitable and essential is only the beginning of trying to analyze present international financial problems. If fixed exchange rates are to change, how are they to change? Continuously? Occasionally? By what amount? Under what kind of international supervision, if any?

Some of the most knowledgeable economists—including Professors Milton Friedman of Chicago, Fritz Machlup of Princeton, and James Tobin of Yale—have urged that fixed exchange rates be abandoned nd flexible exchange rates adopted. They argue for letting the market determine dollar exchange rates without pegging quotations or requiring open-market operations of any sort. Others go further and suggest that the United States end immediately her standing offer to buy gold at $35 an ounce. Thus in addition to being made independent of foreign currencies, the dollar would also be made independent of gold, at least in theory.

Two less radical ways of introducing more flexibility into the present "uptight" exchange rates have been called, in the jargon of the international economists, the "wider band" and the "crawling peg," either alone or in combination.

Under the former proposal, exchange rates would be allowed to move within a band of, say, 5 percent above or below par, in contrast to the present one percent or three-quarters of one percent. Under the latter proposal, the par value of a currency under basic upward or downward pressure could be allowed to respond to that pressure, at predetermined time intervals and by predetermined amounts.

A Specific Solution for the Fixed Exchange Rate Problem— Good for All Countries and Currencies Except the U.S. Dollar

There is room for compromise if the Midases in charge of most governmental economic offices would only listen to the Pursides. The advantages to trade and business of fixed rates could be substantially preserved by permitting a somewhat wider range of fluctuations in exchange rates, such as 2 percent or 3 percent or 5 percent. Businessmen could cover these fluctuations in their foreign transactions by "hedging" operations, or the buying now of "futures" in the foreign currency; this would be a present purchase of the future of money.

The rates should not be completely free. Experience has shown that world trade flows more smoothly when there are somewhat definite ratios between important currencies. Some relaxation of rigidly fixed exchange rates would relieve the pinch of fixed exchange rates for all other countries, but not for the United States.

The Posture of the Monetary Atlas of the World

Two fundamental obligations—to maintain adequate reserves of gold and "hard" foreign currencies, and to balance international

101

payments to avoid running out of reserves—and what must be done to carry out these obligations, are clear enough in the case of France and Britain. But they are not at all clear in the case of the United States. No one has heard of the United States herself buying dollars in the foreign exchange markets to support the dollar as such. This is because the United States dollar occupies a unique position at the center of the free-world money system. The reason it occupies this privileged position, for better or worse, is primarily because of the dollar's unique link to gold. Historically, in money policies, the United States has remained the most Pursides of all major countries. This is the fundamental reason why the United States has become the monetary Atlas of the world supporting the whole system on her gold-backed dollar.

The Burden on the Back of the Gold-Backed Dollar

A Japanese selling to Sweden usually denominates his bill in dollars. An Italian wanting credit to finance a sale to Germany often borrows not lire but dollars from a bank in London (dollars which are known by the invented name of "Eurodollars"). All nations hold United States dollars as reserves. The dollar is used as a world-wide transactions currency and a worldwide "reserve" currency as well, even for transactions among foreigners that have no connection of any kind with the United States.

Certainly nobody planned it that way. Not even President Roosevelt when he took the United States off the gold standard in 1934 but maintained convertibility of the dollar into gold at $35 an ounce. It "jest growed." Ten years later, after the world had grown accustomed to it, the convertibility of the dollar into gold at the new rate was acknowledged in the articles of agreement of the International Monetary Fund. The act of Congress then mortised it in tight, and the United States and the world is now stuck with it, for better or for worse.

Under the fund rules and the practical workings of the system, other nations fix the value of their currencies in terms of the dollar. Their central banks "intervene" on the foreign-exchange market to support their currency against the dollar, and only the dollar. They gain and lose reserves as they are required to buy or sell dollars.

The United States, on the other hand, does not intervene at all. Instead, alone in the world, the United States stands ready in principle at all times to redeem in gold, at a price of $35 an ounce, the dollars held by foreign central banks.

When the United States has a balance-of-payments deficit, a two-part series of steps occurs. First, because of the surplus of dollars in foreign markets, foreign currencies rise against the dollar in the markets and foreign central banks become buyers, not sellers, of cheaper dollars. They gain reserves. Their balance-of-payments surpluses become the counterpart of our deficit. Second, some of them cash in some of those dollars at the United States Treasury for gold.

The United States, like other countries, loses reserves when she has a deficit in her balance of payments. But unlike other countries, the United States cannot settle reserve deficits by paying out dollars. She must settle up in gold. More than $12 billion of reserves, all gold, has been lost since United States payments deficits became serious (starting in 1958). About $11 billion of gold is left, even after the 1968 gold rush, but the process cannot continue indefinitely or even very much longer.

But what if it does?

Lately the United States, like France, has shown a high rate of inflation in her domestic economy, a leveling off of productivity, a deficit in her balance of payments, and a rapid depletion of gold reserves. Can she anticipate being caught in the same kind of money crisis that seized France? The answer is no. There would be a different kind of crisis, and it might be much worse than France's because of the unique relationship between the dollar and gold.

THE U.S. CANNOT FIX HER CURRENCY BY DEVALUING

Foreigners hold $41 billion or so in paper dollars as claims against United States gold reserves of $11 billion or so. If Britain or France were in a comparable position she would long since have had to devalue her currency. Indeed her position would have deteriorated well beyond the point where even a drastic devaluation could help much.

The United States cannot even attempt to solve her money problems by devaluing the way all other countries can. Technically, under the rules of the system, devaluation of the dollar would take the form of reducing its "gold content"—a unilateral United States action that would raise the official monetary price of gold. This would not materially affect domestic prices within the United States, except that prices of foreign goods would become more expensive by

103

the amount of the devaluation. The most obvious consequence of the United States devaluing the dollar by, say, doubling the price of gold, would be that the value of the paper dollars in foreign hands would be cut in half; their $41 billion or so would then be only $20 odd billion.

This would hardly gain new friends abroad. Under the rules, every other nation has the right to devalue right along with the United States on the same day, or the next day, or anytime later. But because the United States is so powerful in world trade, most other countries would be terrified, as well as angry, if the dollar's value were reduced against that of their currencies, thus making foreign exports costlier in the American market, and American exports cheaper in foreign markets. They could and probably would prevent devaluation in the real, or commodity, sense—a change in the dollar's worth against other currencies—by immediately devaluing their own currencies by a like amount.

Conceivably, all foreign holders of dollars would have grounds for legal action against the United States for their losses from such a devaluation if they could find a court to take the case. Their willingness to hold paper dollars has depended partly, at least, on the United States' oft-repeated pledge to redeem them in a fixed quantity of gold metal, and their reliance on this pledge would be the substance of their summons and complaint.

Thus a change upward in the dollar price of gold would not seem to help the United States in solving the problem of the gold drain arising from a deficit in balance of payments and domestic inflation.

As the dollar becomes more widely used throughout the world, more and more transactions between two foreign countries that do not involve the United States at all are expressed in United States dollars. This is the way the pound sterling was used in world trade in the 19th century. This fact tends to alleviate the problem of floating rates. When the millenium of money arrives there will be one worldwide currency for all trade, aid, investment, and tourism, and the entire problem of fixed and floating exchange rates will vanish.

A BRILLIANT VISION: ONE WORLDWIDE DOLLAR-BASED CURRENCY

If the United States cannot obtain enough gold, or export enough goods and services, to settle her paper-dollar obligations to foreigners,

104

the only way out appears to be to adopt a bolder, more brilliant vision: one worldwide currency, with both the dollar and gold as its basis.

Any large, drastic movement toward more flexible exchange rates (as distinguished from the modest changes proposed above), would make more difficult the eventual integration of the world economy. Each of the proposals to allow substantially greater exchange-rate flexibility has serious technical difficulties that would outweigh the presumed advantages. Within the present articles of agreement of the fund are provisions that have remained unused for a quarter of a century. These could alleviate most of the hardships brought about by the present rigid, unchanging, fixed exchange rates. But materially greater exchange-rate flexibility would lead to the formation of competitive world power blocs. Therefore a change toward substantially more flexible exchange rates might not be progress, but a retrograde step.

The long-range goal should be a single currency for the entire Western world. Any changes made in the international monetary structure should be taken with this goal in mind, and the International Monetary Fund should now take on the job. Rusty as they may be from disuse, the powers of the fund are enough to do most of the job. And as Maury Maverick once remarked about Yale, "Like a Stetson hat, it has the name." Besides, there is really no alternative.

THE GRAND DESIGN IN SMALL-SCALE OPERATION, AND OTHER MONETARY ALARUMS AND EXCURSIONS

The system can only work when the United States supplies liquidity by running international deficits, and every dollar of deficit that the United States runs injures confidence in the system.

PIERRE MENDES-FRANCE

World War II ended, and when peace of a sort broke out we found economic life under the grand design drafted at Bretton Woods not so very different from the way it had been before. The International Monetary Fund has existed ever since. Its practical operations have been quite useful, but have disappointed the high hopes of its creators. There is no reason why it should not now begin to fulfill its promise, and the need is greater than ever.

On Dec. 27, 1945, representatives of thirty countries took part in a signing ceremony in Washington. By the end of the year, thirty-five countries had given notice of their membership. New members were admitted later from countries that had originally been outside the United Nations. Italy became a member in 1947; Germany and Japan in 1952. In 1969 there were 112 members, including almost all the noncommunist countries.

INTERNATIONAL PUBLIC SERVANTS SHUFFLING PAPERS IN ANOTHER INNOCUOUS INTERNATIONAL BUREAUCRACY

In practice, the operation of the fund has not appeared to involve any real interference with national sovereignty. Although members are expected to submit to the rules of the new international economy, maintain stable exchange rates, discard foreign trade controls, and accept the fund's advice on certain courses of action, the only sanctions for failing to do so are loss of rights and privileges in the fund itself. None of the prerogatives that national governments claim—

106

such as the right to make a final determination of their exchange rate, or to control domestic credit, fiscal, monetary, and tax policies—are formally exercised by the fund. The formal panoply of national sovereignty is still scrupulously observed.

Directors are appointed by each of the five members having the largest quotas: the United States, Britain, Nationalist China, France, and India. Two are chosen by the American republics not otherwise entitled to appoint directors, and five by the members other than such American republics. Voting power on the board of governors and the directorate is pro rata with the size of the member's quota, and gives the United States approximately 25 percent of the vote. Thus the management of the fund in a sense is political rather than technical, since governors and directors regard themselves as political delegates rather than international economic technicians.

"MON GENERAL, THERE WILL NEVER BE ESTEEM FOR A COUNTRY THAT HAS A BAD CURRENCY"

The first managing director of the fund was the late Per Jacobsson of Sweden, who developed the concept of standby drawings and extra financial aid for underdeveloped nations, and helped stimulate new uses of the fund by coming to Britain's aid with a large loan after the 1956 Suez crisis. A number of orderly devaluations have occurred during the fund's existence. Unlike the self-defeating rounds of devaluation of the 1920's and 1930's, those under fund supervision have involved only small repercussions, with the exception of the British devaluations of the pound sterling in 1949 and 1967.

It is reported that Per Jacobsson once even persuaded President de Gaulle to take measures to strengthen the franc at a time when it was weakening, by saying, "Mon General, I do not think there will ever be esteem for a country that has a bad currency." Per Jacobsson's sucessor was Pierre-Paul Schweitzer, a French senior civil servant who had formerly been the number-three man in the Bank of France.

The five largest among the original quotas subscribed were the United States, $2.75 billion; the United Kingdom, $1.3 billion; China, $550 million; France, $450 million; and India, $400 million. In 1959 and 1966, members joined in enlarging fund resources substantially. By 1969 the total quotas of all members was about $20 billion, of which all but $740 million had been paid. The United

States' quota had grown to over $5 billion, and the United Kingdom's to $2.50 billion.

At the annual meeting of the fund in October 1969, Pierre-Paul Schweitzer, the Managing Director, announced that there would be a general increase in the quotas of all fund members, probably taking effect in 1970, and, in addition, that there would be many special increases for countries such as Japan whose quotas no longer adequately reflected the size of their economies. The overall quota increase will be between $7 billion and $8 billion, but arduous negotiations will be necessary before final agreement is reached on how this is to be distributed.

RESTRICTING "AUTOMATIC" DRAWING RIGHTS TO THE "GOLD TRANCHE"

At the first meeting of the fund in Savannah, Ga., in 1944, the members decided to make drawing rights on the fund only conditionally available. This restricted "automatic" drawing rights only to the first 25 percent of a nation's quota—this is the so-called "gold tranche" (literally, "slice"). Use of the other tranches—the credit tranches—was increasingly subjected to regulation by the fund, which scrutinized the member's "credit-worthiness" beforehand, like a gaggle of governesses. No such procedure had been envisioned at Bretton Woods.

In addition, all drawings had to be repaid within a maturity term of three to five years, instead of coming due automatically when the member's reserves increased, or, failing that, after consultation with fund to determine the method and timing of repayment.

These decisions changed the fundamental nature of the fund. Instead of being an organization that was to create a new kind of world money, it came to resemble the traditional type of banking institution, simply creating medium-term and provisional credits.

A FOREIGN AID AGENCY FOR HAVE-NOT MEMBERS

Another policy has had an adverse effect over the years. It was decided on an informal basis that the more highly developed countries that were receiving Marshall Plan aid should not at the same time be eligible to use the fund's resources. Since underdeveloped countries did not receive Marshall Plan assistance, the fund came to be thought of as an agency that served primarily the needs of these countries. As time has passed, however, underdeveloped nations, through political pressure, have been able to draw two tranches, without prior scrutiny of their policies, in cases where there is a "short-fall" in export earnings due to so-called "exogenous causes"—that is, causes beyond their control. The more developed industrial countries have no such privilege. While they have practically automatic access to that first gold tranche, they must submit to prior fund scrutiny and conditions when they draw additional tranches. Thus the fund has become widely regarded as a kind of foreign-aid agency and not, as it was intended to be, a source of liquid-reserve supplements for all of its members.

Within a decade following World War II the "miracle" of European and Far Eastern recovery was there for the world to see. Production and trade flourished as never before. Economic growth generally achieved unprecedented rates, and a new era of human enlightenment and welfare seemed to have burgeoned. If the new monetary system was not the proximate cause of this almost unbelievable development, it clearly had something to do with it.

By the huge amounts of postwar United States foreign dollar economic and military aid, first to governments in areas devastated and disrupted by the war and later to developing and less developed countries, and expensive foreign military ventures such as the Vietnam war, the United States placed vast sums of new money in foreign hands. This had even more to do with foreign economic growth.

AS A MONETARY RESERVE, THE DOLLAR IS NO LONGER AS GOOD AS GOLD

Financially, the free world's monetary-reserve growth took largely the form of dollar and sterling balances and hardly at all the form of gold. Moreover, when free countries' reserve growth did take the form of gold, the gold was largely drawn away from the monetary-reserve stocks of the two countries whose money had earlier been thought of as satisfactory foreign exchange for the monetary reserves of other countries, Britain and the United States. When growth of monetary reserves did take the form of foreign-exchange balances in dollars and sterling, these dollars and pounds largely represented payments deficits of the United States and Britain in the hands of aid recipients or foreign-trade creditors. Some Pursides here and there began to question the absolute equivalence of value between monetary reserve currencies and gold.

For fifteen years or so after Bretton Woods, the United States dollar served as an acceptable medium of exchange for an ever-growing number of international transactions, and as a store of value for international reserves as well. But in the 1960's the problems that Keynes had foreseen gradually began to surface. Pierre Mendes-France, a former governor of the Bank of France who had been at Bretton Woods, addressing a Cambridge University audience in 1966, put the matter succinctly: "The system can only work when the United States supplies liquidity by running international deficits, and every dollar of deficit that the United States runs injures confidence in the system."

If the United States had backed the Keynes plan in 1944 when she was the number one creditor nation in the world and in an immensely strong long-term position, her international assets (which for the most part were invested at long term) would have continued to expand and accrue ever-growing returns. But at the end of the 1960's the United States' short-term foreign debts far exceeded her realizable foreign short-term assets. Under the Keynes plan these short-term debts would have been switched to the account of the international clearing union. There they would have been the collective responsibility of all nations that had participated in the real wealth that the debt creation reflected. The most serious problems plaguing the dollar today would not exist.

Symptoms of Gold Fever

What was happening in the meantime to the world's continuing output of and demand for gold? In the years just preceding World War II, gold output had spurted. This reflected in part the increase in its real value during world deflation, and also reflected the stimulus of the 1934 increase in its dollar price from $20.67 to $35 an ounce. For a decade after World War II, gold output was well below immediate prewar levels. By the late 1950's, however, it had regained these levels and then exceeded them. At about this time, Soviet Russia began to release part of her rising gold production to the market.

All told, from 1950 through the early months of 1968, some $23.8 billion in additional gold became available from output and from Russian sales. Of this large sum, industrial uses, objects of adornment, and the arts took only an estimated $5 billion, and net additions to official monetary gold stocks roughly another $5 billion. Thus the amount going into Pursides' private hoards and speculative holdings aggregated something like $12.8 billion, of which as much as $3 billion apparently vanished into private holdings during 1967 and the early months of 1968 just before the Ides of March in money.

"Hoarding" or "speculation" or "investment" in gold on this scale had been a symptom of the growing lack of confidence in the durability of the existing nongold world monetary arrangements that the Midases had played such an important role in building. The Vietnam war, the Israeli-Arab wars, the Cold War, Soviet and Red Chinese aggressiveness, and the shift in the balance of overall world power toward the totalitarian countries evidenced by Russia's naval forces in the eastern Mediterranean and her military forces in Czechoslovakia, all contributed to this uneasiness. Many a forgotten man purchased gold coins, gold wafers, gold leaf, and gold nose clips. Those who could afford it began to buy standard gold bars, while the more speculative saw in the gold market an opportunity seldom presented elsewhere—a one-sided speculation, at some cost to be sure, but with no risk of substantial loss as long as the United States stood pledged to maintain a floor on the price and buy gold at $35 an ounce. Before long, private demands far exceeded supplies of new gold available for purchase, and a worldwide run on gold was in the making. In 1966 Soviet Russia ceased all gold sales in the free-world markets, and the aggregate amount of gold held as central bank monetary reserves actually began to decline.

Just before President Kennedy's election in 1960, there was a sudden surge of demand for gold on the London gold market, and its price there rose from $35.20 (its normal limit) to $40 an ounce. Only the joint efforts of American and British monetary authorities brought this splurge under control. But the traumatic effect of this on the newly elected President was such that shortly after his inauguration he pledged the entire United States gold stock to defense of the dollar through the London gold pool.

Another ominous event was the 5 percent upward revaluation in terms of gold of the German mark and the Dutch guilder in the early spring of 1961 to correct their presumed undervaluation vis-à-vis sterling and the dollar. And still another warning of trouble ahead was a heavy run against sterling in the spring of 1961, which gave rise to a sizable package of emergency credits from European central banks and prompted United States authorities to help the Bank of England until it could arrange an International Monetary Fund drawing adequate to defend sterling.

CREATION OF THE GENERAL ARRANGEMENTS TO BORROW

A succession of three large and alarming deficits in United States international payments registered new crisis points on the gold-fever chart. These prompted the International Monetary Fund, with United States urging, to negotiate an agreement with its ten leading members (the so-called Group-of-Ten countries) to establish special borrowing facilities outside of the fund that would complement the regular facilities which then existed. Under the agreement—formally known as the General Arrangements to Borrow—participants committed themselves to provide an additional pool of $6 billion of their respective currencies, upon due consultation, to finance concurrently, if necessary, maximum permissible drawings from the fund by the United States and Britain. Since the Group-of-Ten was in effect an exclusive club consisting of the high-income countries, this seemed to leave the International Monetary Fund as merely a kind of bail-out operation for the weak sisters who did not belong to the GAB (General Arrangements to Borrow) club.

SHIFT OF THE BALANCE OF MONETARY VOTING POWER TO EUROPE

Perhaps most significant of all for the United States was the fact that in the Group-of-Ten the European countries could outvote the United States. This symbolized the fact that the balance of monetary power in the free world was shifting from America toward the European countries considered as a unit. The United States, which was still legally obligated to pay for paper dollars in gold although she no longer had enough gold to cover all the paper dollars in foreign hands, could now no longer call the tune. Notwithstanding these United States legal obligations and this shift, the Midases were still calling gold a "barbarous relic," and they were not listening very hard to catch the tune that the European powers were now starting to play for themselves.

In spite of these warnings of rough international financial waters ahead, the monetary authorities of America and Britain, together with those of six other major trading nations, had backed the London gold pool to support the gold price within the market's parity with the United States Treasury's gold price.

The United States Federal Reserve System launched a program of foreign currency operations for the defense of the external convertibility of the dollar. And to facilitate the execution of such operations, it established a network of standby-credit (currency-swap) arrangements with the principal central banks abroad.

Lastly, the ministers of finance of the principal trading nations that were members of the International Monetary Fund, plus Switzerland, joined in authorizing their deputies to engage in a study of the world's future needs for monetary reserves and ways to assure their steady growth significantly. The finance ministers instructed their deputies to proceed with the study on the premise that a world price of $35 an ounce for gold would be adhered to indefinitely.

Of these three developments, the first, the gold-pool arrangement, was brought to an end by the "gold rush" of 1967 and early 1968 on the Ides of March in money. The second, the central-bank reciprocal credit network, continues to prove useful. It has expanded from a modest beginning in 1962 of $700 million of potential temporary credits between participating central banks (including the Bank for International Settlements) and the Federal Reserve System, to an impressive total of more than $9 billion. This expanded sum shows the concern among monetary authorities that resources in ample supply be promptly available to cushion large temporary flows of funds internationally and thus to help assure the maintenance of orderly exchange-market conditions. The third development—the product of four years of arduous international study, debate, and negotiation—was a concrete proposal for the creation of a new international asset to supplement gold in meeting the world's future needs for growth in national monetary reserves: special drawing rights, or paper gold.

If we call them rights to make overdrafts not punishable by criminal sanctions, and, indeed, not necessarily repayable at all, we are at once reminded of the British banking practice, and the original clearing union plan put forward by Lord Keynes at Bretton Woods. The quarter century it has taken to reach agreement on this aspect of

113

Keynes's 1944 plan only shows how effective a world war was in spurring economic reform.

In comparatively peaceful recent times it took economic officials four years just to agree on a twenty-five-year-old plan that had a great deal to recommend it when it was new.

7

THE WORLD BANK AND McNAMARA'S BAND, AND THE COMECON MARCHING ALONG BEHIND

Political institutions are a superstructure
resting on an economic foundation.

NIKOLAI LENIN

"I do not wish to seem overdramatic," United Nations' Secretary-General Thant has often told international leaders, "but the world has only about ten years left in which to avoid disaster by finding answers to the problems of pollution, overpopulation, and the arms race." The United Nations, the political superstructure of the world, finds itself fragmented into power blocs—the Communist bloc, the free capitalist bloc, the Afro-Asian bloc, and so on. Countries such as Red China, which is completely excluded from U.N. membership, are hostile to any action it takes. These conflicting political power centers and epicenters leave the United Nations in hopeless deadlock at precisely the times when it is most urgent for it to take meaningful action toward solving these three overwhelming problems. But U Thant's comment holds out no hope that any political solution will be forthcoming through the United Nations.

114

POLLUTION, OVERPOPULATION, AND CURBING THE ARMS RACE— PROBLEMS TOO BIG TO BE POLITICAL

Pollution, overpopulation, and curbing the arms race are menaces that go deeper than politics. Neither socialism, dictatorship, monarchy, communism, or democracy can be said to be wholly without blame for them, nor can any one national political faith claim it has solutions for them. Political debates in the United Nations pale into insignificance before them. That is why U Thant called upon the nations to subordinate their "ancient quarrels" of politics and launch a global partnership to solve these problems that overshadow politics.

A partnership is an apolitical economic association of two or more people to carry on business for economic profit. The end of the world in ten years from one or another of the disasters U Thant enumerated would be contrary to the interests of such a partnership's business.

Modestly carrying on day-to-day business and banking a modest profit, the International Monetary Fund maintains a profile of low visibility for itself but is the pivot around which some highly visible social, and indeed political organizations revolve, as junior but highly public partners: the World Bank, the International Development Agency, and the countries who participate in the General Agreement on Tariffs and Trade (GATT). Like the satellites of other great powers, those of the International Monetary Fund no doubt also help it reassure itself of its own importance, and keep down large-scale unemployment among economists and international officials, and discarded United States Secretaries of Defense.

THE WORLD BANK—NEVER A DEFAULT

The International Bank for Reconstruction and Development, now more familiarly known as the World Bank, was another significant part of the grand design the planners drew at Bretton Woods. In prosaic terms, the bank's capital is used for international loans for projects which are economically sound but for which private loans are not available at reasonably low interest rates. The leading nations of the world (except the Soviet Union) have subscribed about $21 billion to its capital stock in quotas determined in proportion to their economic importance, of which the United States' quota is about one-third. But the real importance of this truly international bank is greater than the loans it makes out of its subscribed capital: It also issues bonds and uses the proceeds to make loans, and has successfully floated bond issues in the United States, Switzerland, and elsewhere. The bonds are readily salable and fairly safe, because they are backed by the credit of all the member nations to the extent of 100 percent of their quotas in the bank.

INSURING PRIVATE FINANCING THROUGH THE WORLD BANK

In addition, the bank can insure private loans in return for a premium of one-half of one percent. Private individuals and banks then put up the money, knowing that the World Bank's credit is behind the loan. If a loan goes sour, the bank pays the loan out of its interest or premium earnings.

Highly developed as well as underdeveloped countries benefit because the proceeds of loans to underdeveloped countries often are spent in the developed countries. Examples of projects financed through the World Bank are loans to El Salvador for construction of a hydroelectric plant on the River Lempa, to Chile for the Lota coal mine on the Gulf of Arauco, and to Peru for an irrigation system in northern Peru. Such loans have also been used for a 100,000 kilowatt thermal power plant in Port of Spain, Trinidad; for quay cranes at Port Lyttleton, New Zealand; for digging high-grade manganese ore in Gabon; for a railway in Mauritania; for expanding the Apapa Wharves in Nigeria; and for developing the Indus River Basin in Pakistan. Projects that the World Bank has financed have changed the face of the globe. Over the years the bank has been a spectacular success. It boasts that it has never had a default. It vigorously denies the charge that through it the poor are taxed in rich countries to help the rich in poor countries.

THE INTERNATIONAL DEVELOPMENT AGENCY—
PRIDE IN ANY REPAYMENT

The World Bank in turn has its own satellite, the International Development Agency, which makes "soft loans" to underdeveloped countries for education, roads, hospitals, and the like. There is also a second satellite, the International Finance Corporation, which makes loans to foreign development banks for financing private investment projects. Through these organizations the onus of making a handout is widely delegated, and the onus of receiving one is altogether eliminated. There are no boasts that these have never had a default. Here there is boasting when a loan is repaid.

Shortly after being installed as the new president of the World Bank, former United States Secretary of Defense Robert S. McNamara, in a bold 1968 speech (which the *New York Journal of Commerce* reported apprehensively under the headline "McNamara's Band,") predicted that in the five years through 1973 the World Bank would lend nearly as much as it had in the entire previous twenty-two years since it began operations. The bank's rate of lending to Latin America will double, investment in Africa will triple, lending for education will rise three-fold, and loans for agricultural improvement will quadruple.

TYING ECONOMIC DEVELOPMENT LOANS TO MEANINGFUL BIRTH CONTROL MEASURES

Mr. McNamara coupled this dramatic expansion program with a lengthy and emphatic warning about excessive population growth. Pointing out that such growth nullifies hopes for raising living standards and creates unrest and wars, he said, "A treadmill economy tends to emerge, in which the total national effort will exhaust itself in running faster and faster merely to stand still." With scarcely a glance at his slide rule, he noted that if a country with a birth rate of 40 per 1000 (the actual rate in India and Mexico) could cut it in half in twenty-five years to 20 per 1000 (the rate in many developed and richer countries), its standard of living could be raised 40 percent in a single generation.

In a later speech on birth control which McNamara, a Presbyterian, elected to deliver at a solemn academic convocation at the University of Notre Dame, he left no doubt that he intended to shake up this world, and the other one at St. Peter's as well. "It may seem strange that I should speak at a center of Catholic thought on this awkward issue. I have chosen to discuss the problem," he explained, "because my responsibilities as president of the World Bank compel me to be candid about the blunt facts affecting the prospects for global development."

Without referring directly to the Catholic Church's opposition to artificial contraception, McNamara mentioned "certain precise and painful moral dilemmas," and predicted ominously that the population problem would be solved "one way or the other."

"Are we to solve it by famine? Are we to solve it by riot, by insurrection, by the violence that desperately starving men can be driven to? Are we to solve it by wars of expansion and aggression? Or are we to solve it rationally and humanely in accord with man's dignity?

"Providence, I think, has placed you and me—all of us—at that fulcrum point in history where a rational, responsible, moral solution to the population problem must be found. You and I, all of us, share the responsibility—a responsibility to find and apply that solution."

The population explosion has a place of growing importance in all economic studies and in the future of money as well, but more fall-out from it is beyond the scope of this book. If McNamara can make it go away and disappear as he did such other costly problems as the Edsel car and the RB-70 bomber, his assurance that the boys would be home from Vietnam by the end of 1966 will be gratefully forgotten.

But here is a money-saving suggestion for McNamara. If the vastly increased lending program that he announced helps "treadmill" economies to emerge in underdeveloped countries, and their national efforts exhaust themselves in merely standing still, such loans will not only lower the quality of life there but will lead to unprecedented defaults in repayment of the loans themselves. A larger volume of loans will only aggravate the problem if no steps are taken at the same time to foster adequate birth control methods in the area where the loan proceeds are spent.

Adoption of specific, meaningful, mandatory birth control methods in the loan applicant's area should be made a precondition to any more McNamara loans from the World Bank. Such a money message would sound louder and clearer in underdeveloped countries than a season of McNamara sermons in front of St. Peter's.

SPECIAL DRAWING RIGHTS TO FOSTER SOCIAL POLICIES

Unlike ordinary drawing rights in the fund, which are like loans or credits and must be repaid, "special drawing rights" or SDR's (of which more later, mostly in Chapter 14) will be permanent grants of an international money which cannot be extinguished except by formal fund action. Members will be free to use this "paper gold" without conditions as to their own monetary and fiscal policies, but they will be expected to use them to meet balance-of-payments difficulties.

No sooner were special drawing rights (SDR's) off the drawing board of the planners at the International Monetary Fund than several highly regarded economists—including Sidney Dell, a United Nations economist, and Professor Robert Triffin of Yale—offered the idea that it would be wrong to distribute the lion's share of them to Britain and the United States, and others among the richest nations. On the contrary, they urged that the SDR's be channeled to the underdeveloped nations. Under these proposals the World Bank would presumably sell the special drawing rights to governments of developed countries in return for their own currencies which would, in turn, be loaned to the underdeveloped nations.

By the terms of the legal amendment to the fund articles establishing SDR's, a direct link between them and aid to developing countries is ruled out, but since SDR's would increase the monetary reserves of rich countries, there remains hope that some will "trickle down" to developing countries through expanded aid programs of the richer ones.

THE GENERAL AGREEMENT ON TARIFFS AND TRADE

Although the General Agreement on Tariffs and Trade (GATT), created in Geneva in 1947, is for all practical purposes another international superstructure of the fund, not a separate and distinct entity like the fund itself. Rather, it is a set of rules for the conduct of trading relations among nations, and a framework through which the contracting parties (those who have accepted the conditions of the GATT) can discuss tariff reductions and related problems. By way of distinguishing the purposes of the fund from GATT in a phrase, the principal objective of GATT is the reduction of tariff barriers and discriminatory treatment between countries in international commerce, while the purpose of the fund is to promote exchange stability and maintain orderly exchange arrangements among members by establishing a multilateral system of payments for current transactions and making resources available to the fund's members in order to lessen disequilibrium in their international balance of payments. For practical purposes, the activities of GATT may be considered as part of the activities of the fund itself.

GATT's most important work has been the meetings to negotiate worldwide tariff reductions, held in Annecy in 1948, at Torquay in 1951, and at Geneva in 1956 and 1960–1961. All of these resulted in significant multilateral tariff reductions covering many thousands of items and many billion dollars of world trade. The United States Trade Expansion Act of 1962, which allowed the President to reduce American tariffs by as much as 50 percent, on the basis of reciprocal concessions, led to the later rounds of bargaining on tariff reductions through GATT known as the Kennedy Round.

The GATT agreement also forbids certain practices that are inimical to world trade, such as subsidization of imports and the use of tariffs to protect domestic industries, except "infant" industries. When the European Common Market was being formed, GATT was the body through which most of the rest of the trading world negotiated with the Common Market in an effort to persuade it to amend or ameliorate its restrictive policies against nations outside the Common Market.

Closer Economic Ties Between Communist Countries and the West

That the International Monetary Fund does not suffer from the same sort of deadlocks that the United Nations does is not particularly surprising: The fund's membership does not include the Soviet bloc.

The only communist member of the economic command post of worldwide capitalism is Yugoslavia. But in time she may be only the first of many communist members. Yugoslav Finance Minister Janko Smole has said: "You can't kill the idea of closer international monetary cooperation. It may be dormant for the time being, but it's far from dead."

He should know. Yugoslavia has opened her doors to foreign investment capital, built gambling casinos to lure Western tourists, permitted private citizens to build Adriatic seaside villas, and generally substituted profit for propaganda in economic planning.

Likewise, while other Soviet bloc countries were only just beginning to send out feelers to the fund, Yugoslavia became a full member of the International Finance Corporation, the daughter of the World Bank that helps countries find foreign risk capital for local undertakings. Yugoslavia is specifically seeking Western partners for joint ventures with domestic companies. One Belgrade official explained that "We believe our efforts will serve as a guide to the other Eastern European countries."

The payment record of Soviet bloc nations in trade and financial dealings with the West has been good. The Soviet Union, Poland, Rumania, and others receive high credit ratings from Western businessmen and show no signs of reneging on commitments with foreign firms. Furthermore, most of the Eastern European nations are members in good standing of the Bank for International Settlements, a multinational group that includes the central bankers of most industrialized nations. The Soviet Union remains aloof from the Bank for International Settlements (BIS), but other European communist countries, including Albania, participate in the organization's annual meetings and deliberations.

More importantly, as one European banker notes, "the communist banks' participation in BIS provides them with an open door for joining the IMF and generally strengthens their Western contacts."

Several Soviet Bloc members are expanding their banking ties with the West. Hungary's central bank established a Paris branch and is planning similar offices in London and Zurich. Bulgaria's Litex bank opened a branch in Beirut, and Moscow's Narodny Bank and Prague's Czechoslovenska Obchodni Banka also have branches there. Hungary's central bank has business connections with about 2000 foreign banking institutions, and not long ago sent a group of professors to Vienna to study the Austrian banking system.

Many Soviet bloc countries have sought to make their currencies convertible. Bulgaria and Czechoslovakia are actively seeking greater acceptability of their monies in international trade. The Russians claim that failure of Western nations to convert the ruble freely has been the principal stumbling block to Soviet membership in the International Monetary Fund itself.

Such goals can only be met by closer contacts with Western financial agencies such as the fund and the World Bank. In this respect, Yugoslavia has shown the way as well as the obvious benefits of such relations. As a member of the World Bank, Yugoslavia has received about $350 million in loans since 1949 and is currently negotiating massive new credits worth more than $150 million to help modernize industry and become more competitive in international trade. This is an example the other Red nations, equally intent on competing with the West, can hardly afford to ignore.

COMING ALONG WITH THE COMECON

The Soviet Union and her satellites are members of the Council of Mutual Aid (Comecon). This is, broadly, the communist equivalent of the European Common Market, except that the Comecon is dominated by the Soviet Union whereas the Common Market has no single permanently dominant partner. In their trade with each other since World War II, Comecon countries have operated on a bilateral basis and have had to balance separate deals completely by exchanging goods that are on agreed lists drawn up well in advance as part of each country's plan.

This system provides assured markets, but is too rigid for much development. The countries initially value in dollars the goods they exchange, although for reasons of prestige the sums are often expressed in rubles. Since each pair of countries exchanges goods of equal value, little or no money changes hands. The Comecon countries simply have no acceptable money with which to pay each other. Under the bilateral system this hardly matters. But with the growing need to do business also with the West, particularly to buy Western capital goods, Comecon countries find themselves with a chronic shortage of convertible currencies with which to pay for imports. This is not an unfamiliar problem in the West.

This is where the Comecon Bank, the Bank for International Economic Cooperation, comes in. It is a dim mirror image of the International Monetary Fund. It was created in 1964 to gain the advantages of multilateralism by creating a new currency called the transferable ruble, and to foster full convertibility among national currencies of the Comecon countries. The idea is that each Comecon country pays some of her own currency into a pool to back the transferable ruble. Then when one country runs up a credit balance in trade with a second, she is credited with transferable rubles. She can draw these in the currency of any of the member countries.

The three main conditions of operation of the bank are (1) all settlements between member countries of the bank are to be effected in the transferable ruble, which has a gold content of 0.987412 grams of fine gold, almost the same official gold content as the dollar; (2) funds in transferable rubles may be freely used by holders to pay for goods or other purposes in any other member country; and (3) each member country, when concluding trade agreements, envisages a balance of receipts and payments with all other member countries within the calendar year.

The initial authorized capital of the bank was 300 million transferable rubles (about $327 million). The subscription quota of each member was worked out on the basis of the exports in their mutual trade. The Soviet Union provides by far the largest portion, amounting to about 116 million transferable rubles. East Germany provides the next largest amount (55 million), followed by Czechoslovakia (45 million), Poland (27 million), Hungary (21 million), Bulgaria (17 million), Roumania (16 million), and Mongolia (3 million).

THE "TRANSFERABLE" RUBLE IS CONVERTIBLE BY SOVIET FIAT— BUT GOLD IS PREFERRED

The bank got off to a slow start, and is still operating on a relatively small volume considering the promising possibilities that exist for expanding Comecon trade. The main problem is that although the new ruble is fully convertible among the communist countries, it is still not accepted as directly convertible into the more or less gold-backed currencies of the West, which by Comecon standards, at least, are "hard" currencies. And it is hard currencies that Comecon countries, with their eyes on the rich trade with Western Europe, want to amass. The transferable ruble—despite its impressive title—is still not much more attractive as a trading currency than the zloty, the koruna, or the leu were before it.

Some Comecon members have suggested that the transferable ruble should be made truly transferable. This would mean backing it with gold or hard currency (the United States dollar or the deutschemark). This is where the rest of the world comes in. Such transferability would of course mean a vast increase in the possibilities for world trade, and the concomitant possibility for breaking down cold war political barriers. This brings us full circle again to the Pursides' ancient theme: all that is necessary is a convertible gold-backed currency, whether Karl Marx canonized it or not.

8

EACH SOVEREIGN NATION IS NOW BUT A PROVINCE OF THE INTERNATIONAL WORLD OF MONEY—AND MONEY TROUBLES

CANON CHASUBLE: *Were I fortunate enough to be Miss Prism's pupil, I would hang upon her lips [Miss Prism glares]. I spoke metaphorically. . . .*

MISS PRISM: *Cecily, you will read your Political Economy in my absence. The chapter on the Fall of the Rupee you may omit. It is somewhat too sensational. Even these metallic problems have their melodramatic side.*

CECILY: [*Picks up books and throws them back on the table*]: *Horrid Political Economy! Horrid Geography! Horrid, Horrid German!*

The Importance of Being Earnest, Act II

As Miss Prism said, these international money problems do have their melodramatic side. The inscrutable thoughts of President de

124

Gaulle during the franc-mark money crisis of November 1968 when he made his melodramatic radio broadcast announcing his "non" to the idea of letting the franc fall may have been a sensational surprise to all the world's statesmen, as usual. But they were perfectly scrutable to Cecily Cardew when she exclaimed, "Horrid Political Economy! Horrid Geography! Horrid, Horrid German!" Just so did President de Gaulle's exalted dreams of winning esteem with a hard currency join the rupee in the dust.

Less than forty years ago, a President of the United States observed that the United States tariff was "solely a domestic question," and as such inappropriate for international bargaining. No opposition paper or politician quarreled with his view. That era is long gone, never to return.

MAN'S PERSISTENCE IN REACHING OUT BEYOND HIS COUNTRY'S FINANCIAL HORIZONS

Man's persistence in reaching out beyond his country's horizons to exploit opportunities in other lands is amply documented by history, from the Phoenicians' investments in the tin mines of Cornwall to Fiat's automobile manufacturing plants in the Soviet Union. For many decades before World War I, international economic ties were vital to the economies that we think of today as "advanced." Migration was high, capital was flowing across international boundaries at impressive rates, and there were large movements of goods among these countries.

From World War I to World War II, the technology of international transportation and communication continued to advance steadily. World production went up about 40 percent in the interwar period, but nations managed to suppress the growth of world trade so that it increased by only half the rate of production. International investment enjoyed a period of growth in the 1920's but national restrictions were increasing.

In the 1930's many nations turned inward to test whether a proper mix of national policies could generate full employment and reasonable rates of growth internally. Each nation tried to fend for herself. There was a rash of competitive devaluations and export subsidies. National policies sought to prop up internal demand and float national economies off the shoals. Governments restricted trade and

125

controlled international capital movements, against the tide of integrating pressures created by the advances in transport and communication. But after World War II all this changed.

INTERNATIONALIZATION OF THE WORLD ECONOMY

Illustrations of the internationalization of the world economy, of the world of money, and with it the internationalization of money troubles, now abound. From 1953 to 1965 the volume of international trade in manufactured goods among the advanced countries almost tripled. More significantly, it outran the expansion of production by a very considerable margin. International air freight rose steadily by 20 percent or more each year. Arrivals and departures of international travelers in North America and Europe grew about 10 percent annually. Direct investment by United States interests in the other advanced countries rose annually by about the same percent.

By the early 1960's there had also been a wholesale dismantling of governmental restrictions on trade, payments, and capital movements among the more advanced countries of the world. There was a slow explosion in the international exchange of goods, people, ideas, and money.

AN ECONOMIC FAMILY OF MAN

The economy of any advanced country of North America or Europe imports a considerable part of its technology from outside its boundaries. At the same time, each exports a continuous flow to others. Each relies upon plants in other nations to provide a flow of critical products, and relies upon their markets to absorb substantial proportions of its products. Each draws on the savings of people in other countries for some purposes, and exports quantities of its own people's savings to satisfy the needs of others. Sanctuary is offered to business enterprises that frame their strategy in global terms, while some of its own nationals are expected to establish themselves in other countries in pursuit of worldwide trade.

When the rediscount rate is raised in New York, the cost of money rises in Brussels. When the United States runs a large budgetary deficit, inflationary pressures build up in Europe. When Sicily has an earthquake, dishes rattle in Holland.

126

The efforts of the Marxist countries of the Comecon to create a transferable, international ruble in order to weave stronger trade patterns with the Adam Smithian countries of the International Monetary Fund, and to join the fund itself, are striking illustrations of how the lives of all countries, including Marxist countries, are woven ever more tightly into the world economic tapestry, notwithstanding political hostility, nationalistic hostility, and ideological hostility to each other. It is ironic, too, that as the West dismantles the gold backing of its currencies, the Marxist countries seek gold backing for a truly transferable ruble. The vast tapestry is still shot through with gold threads, but perhaps more now in the East than in the West.

There is an inexorable trend toward the internationalization of all economic problems. What any one country does or can do in her domestic political sphere is more and more constricted by the consequences of her action upon her position in the international economy as a whole. By the same token, the action of any one country to solve her own domestic problems causes reverberations in most other countries on the globe. When Britain devalued her pound in November 1967 from $2.80 to $2.40, thirty-four other countries had to devalue their own currencies. This in turn touched off the gold panic that reached its climax on the Ides of March in money of 1968. Americans and others who had cash on deposit in London banks suddenly found they were 14.3 percent poorer. Britons who owned real estate in the United States were at least that much richer. When Britain cut back the Aldabra project and reimposed the twenty-five cent prescription fee and charges for dentures under National Health Service to save the pound from further international weakness, millions of myopic and denturic Britons had an economic bite added to their other woes, although ecology may have gained.

MAKING A PROCRUSTEAN BED

This is the meaning of the international economy. It is the whole of the economic relations between real people of the various real countries of the real world with each other. It is the flow of goods and services and the factors of production, labor, and capital, from one country to another. It takes in institutions—financial ones such as banks, commercial ones such as corporate businesses, national ones

127

such as the Federal Reserve System and the Bank of England, and international organizations such as the International Monetary Fund and the Comecon Bank, whose existence furthers these flows. The international economy is the framework within which all people and countries in the world pursue economic activity. In abstract terms, its interrelationships fall under five major headings: (1) people under free-world national governments, (2) relations between different free-world governments, (3) supranational organizations, (4) relations between communist governments, and (5) interrelationships between free-world and communist countries and supranational organizations. For some people and countries it is merely uncomfortable; for others it is a Procrustean bed: it stretches and it squashes.

While the international economy imposes Draconian laws on the kind of internal economic regimes some countries must adopt, it has relatively little effect on others. It imposes rigid limitations on the standard of living of a country that is not self-sufficient, such as Britain. It requires that over a period of time such a country reduce the value of her imports and the standard of living of her people if the amount of foreign sales that her economy is capable of making does not support the economy's prevailing internal level. It does not impose such severe limitations upon relatively self-sufficient countries such as the United States and Soviet Russia, because they still produce enough agricultural products and manufactured goods within their borders to supply most of their people's needs, although both countries become less self-sufficient every year.

A NATIONAL SOVEREIGN IS A PRISONER IN ITS OWN HOUSE

Each country must pursue national policies and ideals within this economic framework: the individual liberty, or servility, of the people; economic efficiency in the production and allocation of goods and services; full employment, or sufficient employment to maintain a decent standard of living for the people; the encouragement of the arts; the carrying on of necessary and unnecessary wars; and the improvement of the quality of life. Plans must also be made to accommodate ever-increasing pollution and population.

A government of a relatively free and open national economy is more and more helpless within its own house. Whatever happens in any economy—a general strike in France, the fall of a government in

Britain—becomes the pressing business of all others. By the same token, at a moment of economic crisis in any one country, each government feels compelling pressures to help douse the others' fires. The French criticism of British economic management before France's own May 1968 strikes did not exempt France from the need to assist the pound sterling in crisis. The wry American satisfaction at President de Gaulle's comeuppance in November 1968 did not permit the United States the self-defeating pleasure of failing to support the franc.

Today, formal international commitments among principal noncommunist countries of the world cover such subjects as tariffs, import and export licenses, and subsidies; the level of foreign exchange rates and the price of gold; the price and quality of international air service; the price of coffee, wheat, sugar, and tin; safety-at-sea standards, deep-sea fishing and whaling rights; dumping of oil at sea; and the international use of the ionosphere. There is a pooling of foreign-aid funds through the World Bank and through various regional banking institutions; a pooling of international technical assistance efforts through many U.N. agencies.

Through institutions such as the International Monetary Fund and Organization for Economic Cooperation and Development (OECD), there are well-entrenched habits of international consultation and international persuasion on "domestic" subjects of the most sensitive sort: on internal and international interest rates, on budgetary and fiscal policy, and on employment and income policy. Within the European Economic Community and the European Free Trade Association, both the commitments and the consultations go deeper still. What appears to be no more than a decent respect for the opinions of mankind is in truth the sovereign's realization that as a matter of survival there must be a willingness to expose critical national economic policies to the collective scrutiny of a jury of international peers. There is no escape.

Sovereign nations still bravely assert, usually for purely domestic political consumption, that "the vital interests" of any sovereign, as the sovereign perceives them, take precedence over any international obligation. But it is doubtful that any modern national sovereign would be strong enough to hold a position for a domestic "vital interest" against an international economic tide running against it. With perhaps 75 percent of the free world's gold production, South Africa, has the economic tide running with her, and so will probably swim successfully against the world's political tides for a long time to come.

Within recent years such ancient and august sovereigns as Britain and France, by not sufficiently curbing imports and by postponing devaluations, have tried for political reasons to stand against economic tides which were running the other way, and the verdict of history will almost surely be that the political stand could not resist the economic tide.

"NOTHING HAS ALTERED MORE SINCE MY YOUTH THAN THE RELATIVE STRENGTH OF THE BRITISH ECONOMY"

Some years ago, Dean Acheson remarked that "Great Britain has lost an empire and has not yet found a role." World economic tides have run against modern Britain more destructively than against any other major country of the world. Britain's experience serves both as a cautionary tale to show what the international economy can do to the greatest of governments, and as an inspirational tale to show how much gritty fortitude the forgotten Briton can bring to his country's endless economic battles, unrelieved by any of the elation of an Agincourt, an El Alamein, or even an Anguilla.

For Harold Macmillan this economic tide was the strongest of all the "Winds of Change" that he described in the first volume of his memoirs:

> Nothing has altered more since my youth than the relative strength of the British economy. In those days, the mysteries of exchange, balance of payments, inflation or deflation, the size of reserves, the rate of growth, were carefully hidden from the vulgar gaze. They played little or no part in the political controversies of the day. They were scarcely referred to even by the serious part of the press, and altogether neglected by the popular journals. Most businessmen spent their lives without thinking about them at all. If they exported their products, they did so for profit and not under the impulse of an officially inspired export drive.
>
> For Britain, two world wars have meant the outpouring of her wealth on such a scale that from the leading creditor nation of the capitalist world, she has become, at least in short term, a constant and embarrassed debtor.

Britain was once the monetary Atlas that supported the global
economy. That role has been surrendered, and the burden has been
shifted to the United States. It should not be surprising that now
America is beginning to feel some of the same economic tides that
have sucked away so much of Britain's economic foundations: unfavorable balances of payments in international trade, excessive currency balances in foreign hands, loss of monetary gold reserves, a
costly foreign war, and rising expectations in our domestic population for high-cost social programs.

From 1926 to 1931 the flow of gold from Britain to France alone
was equal to all the new gold mined in the world. After World War
II, when Britain had returned to gold at the old parity, she was
forced to adjust all her wages, salaries, and costs, which proved impossible. As the crisis approached, not only was the whole world in
difficulties, but British exports had become more expensive in terms
of money. "In the last analysis the fall of sterling in 1931 represents
the victory of economic forces over monetary action." *

Britain's loss of gold before her final abandonment of the gold
standard in 1931 suggests the recent running down of the United
States gold reserve. The Ides of March of money showed that national
governmental efforts can be too weak to prevent international economic forces from continuing to win victories over sovereign governmental monetary action.

In 1969, foreign-exchange reserves of the U.K. remained around
$2.5 billion, scarcely improved since the November 1967 devaluation.
Actually, this reserve position is a minus figure because of the huge
short-term borrowings and "swap" credits that have kept the pound
at its stated value in recent years. An austerity program of dimensions
that astonished most people when it was announced was not effective.
Britain's cost-of-living index rose about 4.5 percent in 1968, retail
prices even more, and export prices rose 7 percent. Britain needs a
large balance-of-payments surplus for several years to discharge and
to justify its present obligations, but has not yet been able to achieve
one of any significance.

* Sir Arthur Salter, Recovery: *The Second Effort* (London, 1932).

131

A Run on the Sterling Area Bank

Recently Britain had short-term debts to foreign countries of about $10 billion, of which about $6 billion was represented by the reserves that sterling-area members had on deposit in London and theoretically could withdraw on demand. But Britain had only about $2.5 billion of reserves on hand to meet the continual withdrawals.

World monetary officials made an agreement to provide $2 billion more of credits to enable Britain to work off some of the foreign claims against sterling balances in an orderly manner and avoid panic. Withdrawal of the reserves would signal dissolution in fact, if not in name, of the "sterling area" that once dominated world finance. It would leave the noncommunist world using only the dollar as a "reserve" currency to back the value of all other moneys, finance trade, pay international debts, and provide a psychological foundation for people continuing to believe that "money is accepted because it is accepted."

Withdrawals of sterling balances, of course, contributed to the continuing shakiness of the pound, which, in turn, led to more withdrawals, and so on. Weakness of the pound frightened sterling-area members into withdrawing portions of their London bank reserves, and accentuated the shakes. Weakness in the pound, in turn, caused distrust of other paper currencies, especially the dollar. The British reserves of $2.5 billion no longer convey the impression of overwhelming strength that helps postpone a run on a bank. The mystique of the Bank of England is no longer enough.

The French still seem likely to keep Britain out of the Common Market until Britain humbly accepts the stiffest economic terms France can impose. The European Free Trade Association, of which Britain is a member, is not a substitute. Nor is the North Atlantic Free Trade Area. The vestigial Commonwealth is not a substitute, nor is the "special relationship" with the United States.

The Sixpence Continues on the Wrong Side of the Ledger

As Mr. Micawber said in *David Copperfield*, "Annual income 20 pounds, annual expenditure 19 pounds, 6, result happiness. Annual income 20 pounds, annual expenditure 20-ought-and-6, result misery."

Today in Britain the sixpence continues on the wrong side of the
dger. Although exports of manufactured goods remain at a high
vel, Britain's finances and economy continue to run slowly down.
: Britain must continue to rely on financial support from other
ountries, misery in Britain can probably be postponed a few life-
mes, but ultimately seems inevitable. A new world role for Britain,
r even a way to reverse her steep economic decline for more than
iort intervals of favorable trade balances has not yet been found.

TOUCHES ON THE TILLER" OR "HAMMER BLOWS ON THE CONOMIC THERMOSTATS"

Recently, from no less an academic source than the Professor of
conomic Organization at Oxford, John Jewkes, came a surprising
ntidote for what Professor Jewkes diagnoses as Britain's Keynesian
conomic malaise:

> There is no great mystery about the cause of the present de-
> crepitude of the British economy. It is not because the people
> are lethargic, uncooperative, or indifferent to good living. It is
> because successive governments have created an environment
> which enfeebles the hope of personal advancement and the in-
> clination to save; fosters the belief that there are shortcuts to
> prosperity, and leaves so-called economic experts free to lay
> clumsy and disrupting hands on subtle autonomous mechanisms.
> These gimmicks, artlessly referred to by those who devise and
> operate them as touches on the tiller, but better described as
> hammer blows on the economic thermostats, do, of course, grad-
> ually become discredited.
> If the economic energies of the British people are to be re-
> leased, if there is to be a change of economic environment mak-
> ing recovery feasible, certain conditions precedent must be
> satisfied.
> First should come the sweeping away of the extraordinary
> clutter of departments and agencies in Whitehall devoted to con-
> trolling individual prices and incomes; and wrestling jealously
> with each other for status and even for employment.
> The correct way to prevent inflation is for the central govern-
> ment, by general measures, to restrict the total of public and
> private spending and keep competition active. To assist with the
> latter, the various agencies controlling monopoly should be ac-
> corded higher standing and be more adequately staffed. That,

133

too, should carry with it greater emphasis on the vital pa
played by smaller firms in creating industrial efficiency ar
should pinpoint the crippling burdens placed upon such cor
panies in Britain by recent legislation.*

Professor Jewkes goes on to propose that "taxation should be r
duced. This means reducing public expenditure. If, for instance, tl
'free' National Health Service were turned into a system of Heal
Insurance (with, of course, special provision for the poor) this woul
reduce public expenditure by 600 million or 700 million pound
The purpose would be not to cut down spending on medical servic
(the opposite is badly needed) but to reduce taxation, provide tl
people with control over more of their own spending, and thus i
duce economical use of the services.

"It would be a good rule if, when the government seems to ha\
run out of ideas or resources, the market and the price system shoul
be resorted to.

"In brief, any government which seriously intends to help th
people to restore their own prosperity should take to heart the wor
of a fine poet who, doubting the virtues of restraint in the literar
style of a contemporary, protested:

'They use the snaffle and the curb all right.
'But where's the bloody horse?' "

It is refreshing to hear a contemporary professor of economic
flailing away at "so-called economic experts who lay clumsy and di
rupting hands on subtle and autonomous mechanisms," with all th
gusto of a Little John laying a pikestaff on a sheriff, or a President c
the National Association of Manufacturers lambasting the New Deal
and telling us that Adam Smith of the "invisible hand" is alive an
well everywhere but in Whitehall, and remains Britain's best hand
riding economic jockey. But is is chastening to observe that nowher
does Professor Jewkes acknowledge that although the snaffle and th
curb may be Whitehall's, the directives that the "status seekers" ther
are obeying are handwritten on the wall by the ever more visibl
hand of the international economy.

* Professor John Jewkes, *The Wall Street Journal* of November 21, 1968 (ed
torial page article). Taken from *The London Daily Telegraph* commenting o
British economy.

An Economic Union with the Common Market, or the United States, to Loosen the Procrustean Bed

Another proposal for Britain's salvation would give recognition to the financial and economic backing the United States has supplied to Britain over the years, and increasingly in recent years. This would be a role for her as a Commonwealth, or eventually as a fifty-first state of the United States, economically integrated with the other fifty. Otherwise, what will the large population of the British Isles eat when the countries that supply her imported food will no longer accept her paper pounds for their products?

Economic union with the United States, or economic union with the Common Market countries? In either case Britain would lie more comfortably in an economic Procrustean bed much bigger than the one she is squeezed into now, unless, of course, Professor Jewkes' reveille can arouse the country to greet the new economic day unaided.

France Is Not Responsible for the Squalls That Brought Down the Pound and Threaten the Dollar (According to de Gaulle)—But Not Immune from Them, Either

Britain is by no means the only country caught in the vise of international economic forces. Across the channel her ancient Gallic enemy, ally, and rival suffered a reversal of economic fortune far more swift and striking, reflecting perhaps the contrast between the traditionally volatile Latin temperament of the Gaul, or de Gaulle, and the sangfroid of the Anglo-Saxon.

Three weeks before the November 1968 franc-mark money crisis, speculators began briskly selling francs in anticipation of the crisis. President de Gaulle dismissed the possibility of a devaluation of the franc as "the worst absurdity." As we have learned, each such reassurance carried less assurance.

An Uneasy Armistice Between the French Franc and the West German Deutschemark

After the franc devaluation in 1958 (the fourteenth in this century), central bank reserves in France built up steadily from $1.7 billion to roughly $7 billion in 1966–1967, including an increase in

gold holdings from $1.3 billion to more than $5 billion. This was pos
sible because of continuing balance-of-payments surpluses based on a
fairly good relative stabilization of internal prices and an inward flov
of capital. Early in 1968 as much as $1.5 billion of short-term fund
were in France, which was then considered a relatively safe haver
for liquid capital. But the dramatic events of that May and June de
stroyed this confidence, and foreign deposits began to move ou
rapidly. A gigantic run on the franc reduced reserves by at least 50
percent to no more than $3.5 billion. Much of the reserve so ardu
ously built up over the previous seven years was lost in six months.

The speculative run on the franc was exacerbated by a simultane
ous rapid growth in West Germany's trade surplus from burgeon
ing exports. In 1965 and early 1966, West Germany was in a situa
tion not greatly different from France's in 1968 and 1969. There
were rapid wage and price increases as well as adverse foreign trade
trends. West Germany stopped her inflation abruptly by applying
monetary and fiscal brakes to the economy. This led to a recession in
1967, but recovery in 1968 was made possible by the stability of both
internal and export prices. In 1968, consumer prices in Germany were
up about one percent compared to about 6 percent in France, $4\frac{1}{2}$
percent in the United States and about the same amount in Britain.
Inflation in the United States in 1968 and 1969 was a major con
tributor to the prosperity of German exporters. The mark was under
valued relative to the currencies of other major trading nations. Also,
there was growing evidence that the British austerity program initi-
ated early in 1968 was not working, raising serious doubts about the
stability of the $2.40 pound.

The immediate consequence of social unrest in France was a huge
general wage increase of more than 10 percent. From January to July
the official French wage index (1956=100) rose from 237.5 to 265.3,
or 11.8 percent. Prices increased much less than wages because of
controls, because of a normal lag, and because of some good productivity increases.

In three weeks the speculators sold $1.7 billion francs, and France
had to use her gold reserves to support the franc at parity. The world
currency markets finally had to shut down completely to stop the run.
Volatile funds poured out of France into Germany on the twin assumptions of franc devaluation and upward revaluation of the mark.

At a hastily called conference of international monetary officials

1 November, France threatened a massive devaluation of the franc
nat would have forced other currency devaluations. Germany offered
o impose export taxes that would make German goods less competi-
ive, but refused to revalue the mark upward. Demand for gold hit
ne highest level it had reached since the previous crisis on the Ides
f March of money.

Gold Is the Sun and the Dollar Is the Earth. The Earth Revolves Around the Sun and the Relationship Doesn't Change"

As tension at the finance ministers' meeting reached its height, the
West German Minister of Economics, Karl Schiller, snapped at the
United States Secretary of the Treasury, Henry H. Fowler, "Let us be
clear that the mark is not under-valued, but the dollar is overvalued."
Fowler responded with a stunning paean to gold and dollars, not
DR's: "Gold is the sun," he said, "and the dollar is the earth. The
earth revolves around the sun and the relationship doesn't change."
A stunned Schiller retorted: "Then I guess we're all little satellites
launched from Cape Kennedy."

After Fowler had characterized the German trade-tax concessions
s inadequate, Herr Schiller declared, "If the lopping off of one-
third of our export surplus is not a sacrifice, then it is obvious that
we have quite different concepts of social values."

The Germans refused to revalue the mark upward to save the
franc. The delegates consulted with their governments about new
positions, searching for a compromise solution. The forms of such an
accommodation gradually began to emerge. It included devaluation
of the franc and a loan of $2 billion to France as a support for its
currency. The French stalled. They insisted that unless the Germans
backed down they would undertake a massive devaluation that would
wreck the international monetary system. In the end, as we know,
de Gaulle refused to devalue the franc, but announced a program of
strict economic controls.

The speculators, and the world at large, regarded the ministers'
conference as a failure and the measures President de Gaulle adopted
s mere stopgaps, and nervously awaited the next crisis as sure to
come as an equinox.

Just a year earlier, in November 1967, President de Gaulle had
issued his own paean to gold in the international money system when

he said, "It is possible that the squalls that brought down the poun
and that threaten the dollar, for which France is not responsible, ma
ultimately lead to the restoration of an international monetary system
based on the immutability, the impartiality, and universality that ar
the characteristics of gold."

There is no evidence that the troubles of the franc a year later, an
the losses of his own gold, had budged President de Gaulle one cent
meter from these views. Indeed, perhaps the most significant thing c
all to come out of the November 1968 crisis was the surprising fac
that the United States Secretary of the Treasury, on the evidence o
his Copernican metaphor, was either a secret descendant of the Pu
sides or a brand new recruit to their ranks.

No devaluations occurred. Instead, tax changes in both countrie
affecting imports and exports of merchandise had the planned effec
of increasing the value of the mark for trade purposes by 3 percent t
5 percent, and of devaluing the franc, in merchandise trade, by
similar amount. Also, several forms of additional controls over prices
foreign exchange, and currency movements were added to the tap
estry of regulations already existing in France.

THE GREAT SOUTH AFRICAN POKER GAME IN GOLD

Mr. Fowler had told Herr Schiller at Bonn that "gold is the sun
and the dollar is the earth. The earth revolves around the sun an
the relationship does not change." In point of fact, since the Ides o
March in money and the advent of the "two-tier" gold system, the re
lationship between gold and the dollar had changed dramatically
Every business day the dollar price of gold in the free markets hac
traded in a range between about $40 to $44 an ounce, not $35. Hac
Mr. Fowler been bluffing? Did gold really revolve around the dollar
as in Ptolemaic astronomy?

One of the ways Treasury officials had been trying to maintain
the fiction of the $35-an-ounce price became known as the Grea
South African Poker Game in Gold.

It had been assumed that the success of the two-tier gold-price
scheme hinged on maintaining a narrow spread between the officia
price and the free-market price of gold. If the free-market price wen
much above $40 an ounce, the Treasury believed that first small cen
tral banks, and then larger ones, would convert their paper dollars to
gold, and precipitate another run on the gold bank at Fort Knox.

But the two-tier scheme conflicts sharply with the interests of South Africa, which is by far the greatest gold-producing country in the free world. Rather than sell all her gold output in the free market and thus depress the price, she wished to be able to sell some gold directly to the International Monetary Fund in exchange for convertible foreign currencies at the fixed $35-an-ounce price. So dispute raged over whether the International Monetary Fund is obligated, or merely authorized in its discretion, to purchase gold from its members at the fixed floor price of $35 an ounce.

The United States threatened to veto any fund purchase of South African gold. This would have compelled South Africa to sell all of her gold in the free markets, which were already overburdened by liquidations of speculators, and would have allowed the fund to take such gold as South Africa wished to sell at the so-called "club" price of $35 an ounce only after premium sales in the open market had pushed the free price nearer to or even below the $35-an-ounce level.

Since South Africa produces most newly mined gold, it is the only major source through which free-world monetary gold stocks can increase. Notwithstanding the Washington Ides of March pronouncement officially seeing no need for further gold acquisitions, the world's central banks still very much want to increase monetary gold stocks.

Even the managing director of the International Monetary Fund seemed to be playing this game. By delaying his decision to take South African gold at $35 an ounce, the fund finally forced South Africa to make a drawing on the fund; under normal conditions, South Africa could have tendered some of her vast gold holdings instead. World speculators in gold were thrown into a minor panic and they unloaded and drove down the price. During the Johnson Administration, Treasury officials had often asserted that they expected offerings of gold on the free markets to force the price *below* $35 an ounce.

What are the rules in this poker game? The Articles of Agreement of the International Monetary Fund, Article 5, Section 6, provide: "Purchases of currencies from the fund for gold: (A) Any member desiring to obtain, directly or indirectly, the currency of another for gold shall, provided it can do so with equal advantage, acquire it by the sale of gold to the fund. (B) Nothing in this section shall preclude any member from selling in any market, gold newly produced from mines located within its territories."

The weasel words in the above-quoted provisions are "equal advantage." The United States has argued that there is *un*equal advantage if South Africa sells gold at a premium in free markets and at the same time sells some to the fund at the $35 "club" price.

If South Africa sells some gold at a premium on the free market, even though it is a lower premium than she hoped for, it would appear that she could still sell her surplus at the official price of $35, thereby obtaining a "floor" as well as a ceiling. But United States Treasury officials have contended that the fund could refuse to accept all gold offered if the free market price fell below $35 an ounce. They seem to forget that if this happened their own $11 billion gold reserve stake in the game would lose more value than anybody else's.

South Africa was astute enough to take account of the hands held by her poker opponents. She played her strong hand cautiously, with due regard to the feelings of her opponents, who had been bluffing and losing with weaker cards. She gradually sold some of her gold on the free market, and some to the International Monetary Fund for foreign currencies. It became clear for all to see that for a while, at least until the free market price fell back to $35 in November of 1969, real control of the price of gold had passed from the United States, and the International Monetary Fund, to the Finance Minister of the Union of South Africa.

"We Live in Times when Silence Is Golden"—
At Least in South Africa

The two-tier gold system continued to stumble along from crisis to crisis, with gold prices remaining near or above $40 an ounce. The United States Treasury's efforts to bluff the official gold price back to $35 an ounce failed for a year and a half.

Pierre-Paul Schweitzer, head of the International Monetary Fund, is reported to hold the view that the articles of the fund require it to buy gold from member countries. But he qualifies this interpretation by saying that the articles would not be controlling if a majority of the weighted votes cast, and the board of the executive directors of the fund, held otherwise. With nearly one-fourth of the weighted votes in the fund, the United States would oppose official purchases from South Africa until she was forced to sell in the free market first.

When asked whether South Africa intended to sell her gold on the open market or to offer it to the International Monetary Fund for other currencies at $35 an ounce, South Africa's Foreign Minister,

Nicholas Diederichs, replied, "We live in times when silence is golden."

At the end of 1969 the game ended when South Africa officially won the right that most people thought she had always had under the rules of the fund: to sell gold to the fund at $35 an ounce when the free market price is at or below that level, or when she has a balance of payments deficit. But when the price in the free markets is at a premium, South Africa must sell her gold there, and not to official central bank buyers. So the fund has become the funnel through which South African gold moves into the world's monetary reserves. It has now become the duty of the fund to redistribute gold among those of its members who want it most.

"BRING MORE BUYERS TO THE MARKET, AND INCREASE THE DEMAND, AND THE PRICE WILL FALL": U.S. TREASURY ECONOMIC DOCTRINE, GOLD DIVISION

The United States has even sent up some trial balloons for the idea that gold might be freely available for hoarding and trading by American citizens. The reasoning behind this was that if a large American market for gold should open up, South Africa would start releasing her supplies of the metal generally, thereby pushing the price down closer to the official level. However, most knowledgeable monetary experts feel that opening up this new source of private demand for gold would not reduce the price at all, but would send it much higher. Adam Smith suggested 200 years ago that if you enlarge the market and increase demand for a scarce commodity, its price will rise, not fall.

HAPPY ENDING: AS THE TREASURY FAILED TO JAWBONE DOWN GOLD, AND THE UNITED STATES TRADE POSITION DETERIORATED, AND BY ALL ECONOMIC STANDARDS DISASTER LOOMED, EVERYTHING ACTUALLY GOT BETTER

In the 1960's the United States enjoyed annual surpluses of $5 billion to $7 billion in merchandise foreign trade; in 1968 the trade surpluses fell to less than $1 billion. Soaring imports and rising costs brought the country's foreign trade balance to the worst level it had ever been in the century.

Yet other things also happened in other places. Britain, France, and Germany imposed mandatory controls over business investing and bank lending abroad; the Soviet Union invaded Czechoslovakia;

141

Italy moved toward more socialism and growing social unrest; and by no means least, the United States stock market rose for a while as the major European currencies went through crises. The United States, viewed in isolation, might have plenty of money problems for the owner of large amounts of capital, but relative to alternatives it looked good. The German mark was exceptionally strong, but West Germany, after all, borders on the Soviet's Eastern European empire.

So in recent years funds have flowed into United States markets. Controls over outflows have worked well. The result has been the anomaly of the worst competitive performance by American industry in modern times, along with a surprisingly good overall balance-of-payments record.

The pressures of the international economy on sovereign nations are not necessarily destructive forces, but their unpredictability has got to be humbling to the most autocratic heads of state, and the most discrete of professional economists.

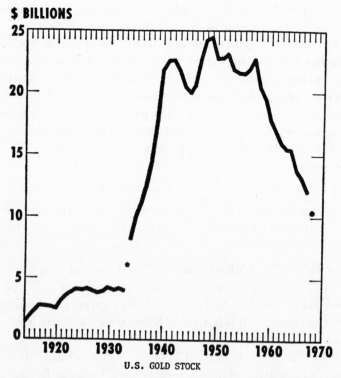

$ BILLIONS

U.S. GOLD STOCK

* Valued at $20.67 per fine ounce through 1933, at $35 thereafter.

142

9

THE UNITED STATES ECONOMY ONCE WAS AN ISLAND, ENTIRE OF ITSELF— NOW IT IS STUCK WITH THE ENTIRE WORLD, AND VICE VERSA

A creative economy is the fuel of magnificence.
EMERSON, *Aristocracy.*

GOLD RUSHES BACK TO WHERE IT RUSHED FROM, WITH A PUSH FROM HITLER

The international monetary system runs on faith. For the last quarter of a century the faith at the basis of the system has been the United States Treasury's pledge to redeem dollars held by foreign governments for gold at an unchanging $35 per ounce. The dollar's period of greatest strength occurred during the late 1930's, when gold flowed into United States coffers in torrents at a time when the economy was operating at only half speed. Probably the most important reason was the spectre of European war posed by Hitler's Germany. Capital fled to the geographically safest haven, the United States. More and more other countries valued their own money in terms of dollars and took to keeping a large part of their reserves in paper dollars.

HALCYON DAYS IN INNOCENCE OF INTERNATIONAL PAYMENTS PROBLEMS

For twenty-five years from 1933 to 1958, the United States, unlike nearly all of the other countries of the world, seemed blissfully emancipated from and innocent of any concern over her international balance of payments and the economic consequences of her domestic and foreign policies, either for her own citizens or the rest of the world's.

Just as their British counterparts had been able to do before them in the halcyon days Harold Macmillan recalled from his youth, American government officials and businessmen alike could plan their policies with no concern for their effects on or limitations imposed by the international economic order. Now the United States' halcyon days are gone forever too.

After World War II, other nations gradually followed the United States into currency convertibility and trade liberalization, and these relationships helped build a large world market for trade based on the dollar. Much of the capital that had sought a haven in the United States began moving back to Europe.

For the years since 1958, and for the foreseeable future, the position of the dollar has changed dramatically. America has serious and basic gold and balance-of-payments problems. In 1950 the United States gold stock stood at about $24 billion while foreign short-term claims against the dollar, and the United States gold that the dollar represented, were about $8 billion. Lately, the United States gold stock has stood at around $11 billion and foreign claims against the dollar and its United States gold backing at about $41 billion.

A World of National Governments in Economic Shackles

Practically no decision that affects United States domestic policies can be taken without consideration of the effect it will have on the United States' balance of payments, and on the willingness of foreign countries to continue to hold their demand notes on our gold instead of demanding gold for them. If our interest rates are put low, to encourage domestic growth, foreign dollar investments in the United States will be withdrawn to other countries where rates are higher. If lowering our domestic taxes increases our domestic budget deficit, this in turn will increase foreign holdings of paper dollars, and foreigners will turn in more paper dollars for gold. If the United States government permits inflation and other forms of debasement of the domestic dollar, this, too, will cause foreign holders to turn in more dollars for gold. When the United States wished to escalate the war in Vietnam, it had to heed the criticism of countries such as France who felt that the increased expenditures debased her large holdings of paper-dollar balances. Without regard to the politics or morality of the war, criticism of it became justifiable on solely economic grounds. It was a grisly luxury we simply could not afford.

It is no longer possible for the United States to consider economics from a purely national domestic standpoint; all economic decisions must be made in light of the position of the United States in a world of national governments linked together by economic shackles that clamp more tightly every day.

ADJUDGED BANKRUPT BY THE GOLD-EXCHANGE STANDARD WE IMPOSED UPON OURSELVES

In recent years, faith in the dollar has eroded because in seventeen of the past eighteen years the United States has spent, lent, or given away more money than she has earned abroad. Compared with the vast size of the United States economy, which is larger than all of Europe's together, this balance-of-payments deficit seems trivial because it has averaged a mere 0.004 percent of the gross national product. But now, with the deficit in foreign hands about $41 billion and the gold stock at about $11 billion, if all the holders of paper dollars demanded gold at once there would not be enough to pay even one-third of them. Proud as we are, strong as we are, the time has come when we must ask forbearance from our creditors or be adjudged bankrupt by the gold-exchange standard we have imposed upon ourselves, and whose benefits in the form of a universally acceptable dollar we have taken for granted for so long.

RETURNING THE DOLLAR TO SOUNDNESS IN THE WORLD ECONOMY

Dr. Othmar Emminger, a governor of the Deutsche Bundesbank and one of Europe's leading central bankers, has warned that in the unanimous opinion of European financial officials, a two-pronged attack on the problem of the dollar is essential. For the short term, he said, balance-of-payments controls must be fully implemented. For the long term the United States must achieve "effective restraint on inflation," which in practical terms would have to be accomplished through budget processes. Promises of European financial officials that they would not present paper-dollar demands on United States gold stocks are less unqualified than before. A German source said that they would never do that "unless we gave up hope that you will ever reach equilibrium," the point at which dollars are no longer pouring out of the United States faster than they are coming back. "When would that be?" he was asked. "I don't know," he said with a shrug. "We have had hope for such a long time already."

145

While the United States dollar has been spared the direct consequences of the most recent world monetary upheavals, its position has basic and seemingly continuing weaknesses. Its current strength depends in large measure on favorable popular psychology, and on upheavals in other countries that cause capital to flee to American shores. But continued inflation, recession, or other economic blows in America could quickly reverse the favorable direction of these flows.

"An Outside Element, Artificial and Unilateral, Weighing on Our National Patrimony"

While European capital investment flowing into the United States has been helping to make up for the declining surplus in the United States' export-import trade balance, there has been a rising political outcry abroad about the effects of American economic penetration of foreign economies. By 1950 more than 400 American companies had $1 million or more in foreign direct investments, and the number and amounts have increased steadily ever since. By no means all Europeans have viewed this enormous export of American capital and the $41 billion of paper dollars which are held abroad as a desirable thing.

In his best-selling book, *The American Challenge*, J. J. Servan-Schreiber, founder and publisher-editor of the French weekly newsmagazine *L'Express*, has written, "Fifteen years from now it is quite possible the world's third greatest industrial power, just after the United States and Russia, will not be Europe, but American industry in Europe." * His book has had an extraordinary impact in Europe.

President de Gaulle, the retired commanding general of the Pursides, seemed to be talking about this economic penetration, and not so much the question of gold itself, when he issued his own famous and often-quoted paean to gold in a November 1967 press conference.

"It is true that there is an American foothold in some of our business enterprises. But we know that this is due in large part not so much to the organic superiority of the United States as to the dollar inflation they export to others under cover of the gold-exchange standard."

President de Gaulle went on to point out that "it is quite remarkable that the total of the American balance-of-payments deficit for the last eight years is precisely the same as the total for American investment in Western European countries."

* Atheneum, 1968.

146

He added, "There is obviously an outside element, artificial and unilateral, weighing on our national patrimony. And it is well known that France would like to see an end to this abuse, in the interests of the whole world, even in the interests of the United States, for which the balance-of-payments deficit and inflation are just as deplorable as they are for everybody else."

Yet on the deepest level President de Gaulle was really talking about gold after all. In the beginning, at least, American multinational corporations derived their ability to achieve the economic hegemony to which Servan-Schreiber was pointing with alarm not so much from any inherent or intrinsic superiority of their own, but from the vast gold reserve that had once been behind the dollar they used, and the residual psychological gold reserve that still remains behind it.

Servan-Schreiber's book demonstrates, with a combination of irrefutable statistics and a fine Gallic polemical style, the strong likelihood that Europe is well on its way to becoming a permanent satrapy of the American economic empire. Starting with a rather matter-of-fact examination of American investment in Europe, he finds an economic system that is in a state of collapse. He concludes, "It is our own."

THE DECLINE OF THE UNITED STATES IN FOREIGN TRADE

It is ironic that the chorus of alarm about United States' business penetration of other countries is at its height when penetration of the United States market by other countries is also at its height, and growing faster than ever.

To Servan-Schreiber the United States might respond that she finds a once-great favorable merchandise foreign-trade balance in a state of collapse: "It is *our* own."

For many years now the United States has depended on a large surplus in its merchandise trade with the outside world to offset by several billions of dollars a year the chronic deficits in other parts of her balance-of-payments account, such as foreign aid, military costs, and tourism. This surplus has helped maintain the world's confidence in the ultimate soundness of the dollar and has helped stave off foreign demands for gold, just as a going business that is currently profitable can usually get its bank loans renewed. But toward the end of 1967 and in 1968 this once large merchandise trade surplus all but disappeared.

As anyone who looks around these days in a department store or on the streets can see for himself at every hand, foreign manufacturers have been making big inroads into our consumer-goods markets, usually by offering some combination of style, quality, and lower price. Italy and Spain have scored in shoes and other leather products; Britain and Japan in bicycles and motorcycles; and Japan, Hong Kong, and Taiwan in sporting goods. Japan accounts for fully 70 percent of the spectacular invasion of the American radio, TV, phonograph, and tape-recorder markets; imports of these products alone climbed from $96 million in 1960 to $368 million in 1967. Japanese cameras are everywhere.

Total imports of consumer goods grew to more than $4.2 billion in 1968, more than double the $1.9 billion of 1960. Not all of the increased imports of consumer products represent business that has been completely lost to the United States, for some of the goods involved are manufactured abroad by affiliates or licensees of American companies. Nevertheless, in simple balance-of-payments terms, United States exports of consumer goods—the most important being appliances and medicines and drugs—fall far short of imports. From 1960 through 1967, imports of consumer goods jumped by 120 percent, and in 1967 the dollar value of imports was double that of exports. Ten years ago United States exports of steel exceeded imports by a wide margin; recently, net imports exceeded exports by about $720 million a year, and are rising rapidly.

The unkindest cut of all for American industrial pride has been the ever-increasing rise in imports of foreign passenger cars. In 1968 we imported more than $1 billion worth of cars—far more than we export. Imports are now taking something more than 10 percent of the United States new-car market, and about 20 percent on the Pacific Coast. Volkswagen, with nearly 60 percent of the import market, sells twice as many cars in the United States as American Motors. Currently there has been an astonishing increase in car imports from Japan. To meet the competition, American automakers are trying to expand sales of their own "captive" makes produced abroad, such as the G.M. Opel and the Ford Cortina, but these now account for only about 12 percent of all imports.

148

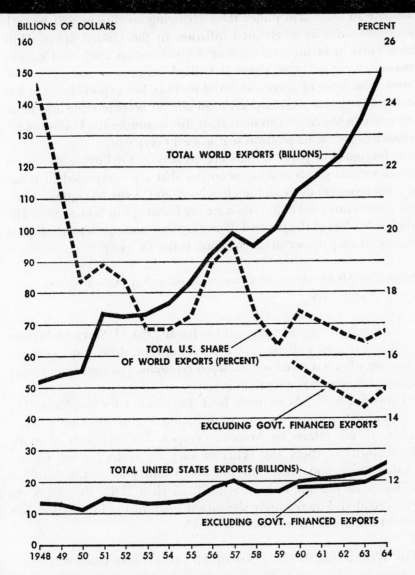

U.S. SHARE OF WORLD TRADE, 1948-1964

BILLIONS OF DOLLARS

PERCENT

TOTAL WORLD EXPORTS (BILLIONS)

TOTAL U.S. SHARE
OF WORLD EXPORTS (PERCENT)

EXCLUDING GOVT. FINANCED EXPORTS

TOTAL UNITED STATES EXPORTS (BILLIONS)

EXCLUDING GOVT. FINANCED EXPORTS

1948 49 50 51 52 53 54 55 56 57 58 59 60 61 62 63 64

SOURCE: U.S. Department of Commerce, *Balance of Payments Statistical Supplement,* (Rev. Ed.), 1963. *Survey of Current Business,* June 1965, and *International Financial Statistics,* Supplement to 1965-66 issues.

Overvalued U.S. Dollars Good Only for Overpriced U.S. Goods

In the near future, at least, the ability of United States industry to compete in the world under these changing conditions will be seriously impaired by accelerated inflation in the United States. Unit labor costs in manufacturing rose 5.3 percent in 1967, and greater increases have occurred since. If United States costs and prices rise faster than those of other industrial nations, her exports become less and less attractive, and imports from abroad become more and more attractive in the American market. If this continues the United States balance-of-payments position will worsen every year.

If foreign-held paper dollars are good only for buying American manufactured goods and commodities that are overpriced in terms of competing goods available elsewhere, and if the foreign-held dollars cannot buy gold either, then we are bankrupt in both senses. The foreign holders of the paper dollars may well undergo a psychological change. If they do, a run on the bank is not far away.

American Multinational Corporations as Salvation and Catastrophe

Although we should not say it too loudly, lest M. Servan-Schreiber overhear, it may well be that United States multinational corporations are what has saved our national economic position from deteriorating far more seriously than it has.

However, Servan-Schreiber's book exaggerates for emphasis. The international corporation—or multinational or transnational corporation—is not always an American corporation, although of course the majority of them are. Whether they are really "good" for the United States and "bad" for the host country as Servan-Schreiber indicates, or just the reverse, is far from clear. That they represent a powerful and increasingly significant force in the internationalization of the world economy is irrefutable.

The Worldwide Penetration of Multinational Corporations

Multinational corporations are hard to define and hard to measure. In the absence of more accurate data, it may be assumed that the scope of productive facilities established by world companies outside of their home countries is related to the magnitude and composition of direct investment in plant and equipment in foreign countries. For the United States, this totals about $65 billion at book values. Much less is known about direct foreign investments of other countries, but quite a few large firms of British and continental nationality rank as multinational companies, so foreign investments by non-American corporations are obviously important.

For 1966, for example, when United States direct foreign investments amounted to $55 billion, direct foreign investments of other industrial countries were estimated at $35 billion. The world total thus worked out to $90 billion at book values; at market rates these investments would probably be much higher. Since much of American foreign investment, especially in manufacturing in Canada and Europe, has been built up only since the late 1950's, while European investments date back to well before 1914, the market values of European foreign investments are probably larger relative to book values than United States investments.

Britain's direct investments abroad were recently valued at the equivalent of $18 billion. The Netherlands, Italy, Belgium, and Switzerland also have sizable investments abroad, France has expanded overseas investment in recent years, and Germany and Japan have begun to rebuild their foreign investments.

Of the estimated $90 billion world total of international direct investments in 1966, about two-thirds was located in developed countries. Foreign direct investments in the United States totaled some $9 billion, and by the end of 1968 had risen to about $11 billion. The remaining third was situated in the less-developed parts of the world. The greatest single component was manufacturing, with over $36 billion, of which three-quarters was in developed countries. Oil was next, with $26 billion, nearly half of which was in the less-developed countries.

U.S. ENTERPRISE ABROAD AS THE THIRD BIGGEST ECONOMY IN THE WORLD

How much the multinational corporations produce in their foreign-based facilities is nowhere recorded in official statistics. It has been estimated that $1 of direct international investment at book value generates $2 of foreign-based output each year. If so, the value of output associated with foreign-based facilities of American corporations would seem to be of the order of more than $110 billion a year.

Thus United States enterprise abroad is indeed, as Servan-Schreiber has charged, something like the third biggest economy in the world—comparable in size to the gross national product of Japan or Germany, the largest national economies after those of the United States and the Soviet Union.

It appears that sales of machinery by foreign manufacturing subsidiaries of United States corporations almost doubled during the first half of the 1960's, reaching $9.2 billion. During the same period, the exports of these categories of goods from the United States increased by only one-half to $6.7 billion. Sales of automobiles and other transportation equipment in 1960 by United States foreign subsidiaries were already almost three times as large as United States exports; but while the latter increased by two-fifths between 1960 and 1965, sales of United States subsidiaries expanded by three-fourths to $10.8 billion.

These two examples show that United States exports, while continuing to expand, have become relatively less important than the foreign-based output of American corporations. The average rate of expansion of United States exports as a whole over the past decade works out at about 7.5 percent a year; but the foreign-based output has increased at about 9 percent. The output has grown in the most strategic, the most profitable, and the most rapidly growing segments of foreign economies, particularly in Canada and in Europe.

American corporations establish foreign subsidiaries for many sound reasons, some obvious and some not so obvious. A corporation that has already expanded its exports is drawn into direct investment—at first in marketing facilities, and then, as necessary, in plants—to participate in growth and profit potentials abroad. Often the corporation has no choice but to establish manufacturing facilities abroad in order to overcome trade barriers (tariffs, quantitative restrictions, and so on) and, in particular, the discrimination arising from the establishment of integrated markets such as the European Economic Community.

Often, too, it must move into markets to which it may be unable to continue exporting from its home base—particularly if labor costs are also relatively attractive there. To secure economies of scale, the multinational corporation builds plants overseas big enough to

152

provide for market expansion; and, as a result, its involvement in international operations tends to grow by leaps and bounds.

Do Multinational Corporations Hurt the Balance of Payments?

Within the framework of the United States balance of payments as a whole, foreign subsidiaries of United States corporations are buyers of United States exports. While they may to some extent compete with their parent companies in export markets in third countries, they do not necessarily displace exports that would otherwise be made from the United States. Most importantly, what is referred to as the "foreign-based" output of United States corporations is a combination of foreign factors of production with American research-intensive engineering, management, and finance, although local financing has become increasingly important.

The United States balance of payments benefits from receipts of income, royalties, and fees of more than $6 billion a year, twice as large as the total of new funds flowing into direct investment abroad. In the meantime, the strain on the United States balance of payments is also relieved by the fact that a considerable part of the funds used by American corporations for direct investment abroad is now being raised in markets outside the United States.

Who Needs a Trade Surplus Anyway? Not the World's Banker

Looking back at the precedent which is always available in the experience of the former economic Atlas of the world, we note that during the century before World War I when Britain was the world's banker, she had a trade surplus in only three years during the entire period. Her large income from overseas investments offset her perennial merchandise trade deficits. American enterprise has now reached a stage of involvement abroad where earnings from foreign investments, issuance of equities in foreign capital markets, and borrowings abroad provide an entirely new source of offsetting favorable balances for her narrow margins in foreign merchandise trade.

Crossing Narrow Political Boundaries of Nation-States

Multinational corporations have created an economic world of their own. They make the most of their research facilities, technical

153

skills, patents, equipment, capital, and experience on a global basis. They play a vital role in raising world output and living standards. In host countries, multinational corporations are a growing source of economic progress: they create employment, pay good wages, provide tax revenues to the government, and help to build up exports. Shareholders of such corporations expect a reasonable return on their investment for the entrepreneurial risk involved, which is actually reduced by the process of geographical diversification. The home countries of multinational corporations anticipate that, in a world in which the political boundaries of nation-states are too narrow and constrictive to provide the best scope for modern business, their prosperity will be enhanced by the prosperity of others.

But national interests of host countries sometimes differ from the home countries of multinational corporations in such matters as taxation, antitrust questions, and balance-of-payments controls. Thus while the United States urges her corporations to step up repatriation of profits, their host countries favor smaller remittances and greater reinvestment of profits. In the process, governments like that of the United States shortsightedly overlook the fact that income from investments abroad is a significant aid in balancing the accounts of a nation that is prosperous enough to be able to export capital.

All governments are concerned about the goals and policies of multinational corporations and about their involvement in business and employment conditions in host countries. Not infrequently, host countries also fear that foreigners—even friendly and efficient foreigners—may acquire undue control over large segments of their basic industries. They want their own nationals to participate in the ownership, management, and technology of the multinational corporations that operate in their countries.

The AFL–CIO, contending that overseas installations are costing American union members jobs, wants a congressional investigation to establish the facts. Firms without overseas facilities are also complaining that competitors' components franchised and assembled overseas give unfair competition to purely domestic companies.

ARM'S-LENGTH TRANSACTIONS ACROSS NATIONAL BORDERS?

A considerable part of the international flow of money, goods, and services among national economies arising out of the activities of international private business and financial firms can no longer even be thought of as arm's-length transactions. Many of these transactions take place between the sister affiliates of multinational business entities. For instance, close to one-third of United States exports of nonmilitary manufactured goods, about $6 billion annually, is shipped to the overseas affiliates of American parent firms, while over $5 billion is returned annually to the United States by such affiliates in the form of dividends, interest, and royalties.

Apart from international transactions that take place under the mantle of a single multinational enterprise, there are also the transactions that take place among the members of more informal private international alliances. For example, the commercial banking and investment banking systems of the advanced countries are now so intimately intertwined that it would be distorting reality to think of many of their transactions as representing arm's-length exchanges.

When international transactions are effected between parties whose relationships are long-term and organic in character, the regulatory capabilities of intervening sovereign states inevitably decline. For brief periods of time, perhaps, regulatory controls may have a real impact; for longer periods the illusion of such impact may persist simply because the specific channel that has been blocked by a particular set of controls was responding in line with governmental expectations. But given the complexity of multinational institutions and the presence of so many alternative channels for the legitimate international movement of funds and other resources, the regulating sovereign is increasingly at a disadvantage.

THE THRUST OF AMERICAN ECONOMIC HEGEMONY—AT HOME NO LESS THAN ABROAD

Even such a temperate observer as Robert L. Heilbroner agrees that this may be a highly undesirable phenomenon. Commenting on Servan-Schreiber's book in an essay on "The Perils of American Economic Power," Mr. Heilbroner writes:

> Year by year the flow of American funds to foreign markets, and the accumulation and reinvestment of profits within foreign markets, increases, with all the consequences—unplanned as

well as planned, unwanted as well as wanted—that such an extension of American economic hegemony entails." *

This tremendous and perhaps unmanageable thrust toward an American corporate economic imperialism, both in Europe and in the underdeveloped world, as well as within the United States itself, is the real problem that emerges from Servan-Schreiber's stunning description of American economic drive. Expansion without design, growth without plan, the extension of power without an extension of responsibility are the consequences of the ferocious dynamism of the American corporate system that he so well describes. In the end the American challenge is that of a society caught in the grip of the dynamic momentum of large private corporations for which there exists no real social control other than the corporation's own for the most part admirable self-restraint and responsibility for the consequences of their activities. Whether such a control can be forged may determine whether, as Servan-Schreiber warns, America's economic leadership will someday prove to be dangerous for America and disastrous for the world.

The momentum of the American corporate system that Professor Heilbroner describes as American imperialism in Europe and the underdeveloped world is no different from the momentum with which it penetrates the United States herself. It is either a good thing, a bad thing, or the future of us all. Or all three at once.

MULTINATIONAL CONTROLS FOR MULTINATIONAL CORPORATIONS

Multinational corporations are vitally affected by and concerned with the world money system, and their activities in turn have a powerful impact on it, on national governments, and on every one of us forgotten men. A governmental devaluation by one country in the system can inflict ruinous losses on the multinational corporation there, or provide it with an opportunity to realize enhanced profits. The reaction of the corporation's management to such a devaluation in turn creates important repercussions and new conditions in the world economy.

To strengthen the world's economic interdependence and cohesion, much thought has been given to removing obstacles that ham-

* *The Saturday Review*, August 10, 1968.

per international direct investment, elaborating an agreed-upon code of good behavior for both home and host countries, and providing for uniform treatment of multinational corporations throughout the world. A multilateral convention on the settlement of international investment disputes has been sponsored by the World Bank. Tariff and nontariff trade barriers, exchange-rate problems, double taxation of corporate income, antitrust matters, and numerous other areas in which the multinational corporation affects the national and international money system remain unexplored and uncontrolled.

FACING UP TO THE MULTINATIONAL CORPORATION—"THE AMERICAN CHALLENGE" AS THE CHALLENGE TO THE WORLD, AND TO AMERICA AS WELL

If governments could coordinate their monetary, fiscal, and other economic policies on an intimate and continuous basis, they could presumably affect all business, whether oriented to one domestic market or to many international markets. Multinational enterprises would have an especially heavy stake in such a trend. In some respects the trend could increase the freedom of multinational enterprises.

But intergovernmental coordination might also reduce the number of situations in which the rights afforded by some governments to multinational corporations were thwarted by the regulations imposed by others, and where the regulations imposed by some governments were thwarted by the privileges granted by others. On the other hand, since there are some things that governments can do together that they cannot do separately, intergovernmental coordination would have the effect of increasing the effectiveness of regulations by the public sector in many fields, including taxation and monetary regulation.

In general, multinational enterprises as a group have exhibited no great enthusiasm for a coordinated approach to regulation of multinational business by sovereign states. It is obvious that no separate country's efforts to correct the problems in its own economy caused by the activities of multinational corporations will succeed if other countries affected take countermeasures to protect their own balance of payments and their own economies against the effects of the first country's measures. Obviously, it would be easier for the

United States, and for all other countries, to solve these problems within the context of the framework of an international monetary organization. Ideally, such an organization would be able to adjust economic policies toward multinational corporations among the member states in such a way that no one member state could gain advantages over others by national domestic policies, such as debasement of its currency, or other policies that might be good for itself but bad for all the others.

The sketch of such an organization for beneficial regulation of the multinational corporation now exists in the International Monetary Fund and its satellite organizations. From this sketch the major countries of the world should now begin to draw a blueprint for a worldwide structure to challenge on an arm's-length basis the powerful reach of multinational corporations. Mr. Servan-Schreiber can then write a sequel entitled *The World Challenge*.

10

EVERYBODY HATES INFLATION UNLESS
THEY LOVE IT: GERMANY, FRANCE,
URUGUAY, AND THE UNITED STATES,
AND SOME CURIOUS CURES

Not this August, nor this September; you
have this year to do in what you like. Not next
August, nor next September; that is still too
soon; they are still too prosperous from the
way things pick up when armament factories
start at near capacity; they never fight as long
as money can still be made without. But the
year after that or the year after that they
fight. . . .
The first panacea for a mismanaged nation
is inflation of the currency; the second is war.
Both bring a temporary prosperity; both
bring a permanent ruin. But both are the
refuge of political and economic opportunists.
ERNEST HEMINGWAY, "NOTES ON THE NEXT
WAR," ESQUIRE MAGAZINE, SEPTEMBER, 1935.

A BIGGER RAISE THAN WALTER REUTHER WON

The middle-age, middle-class Peruvian should have looked jubilant.
He had picked up his newspaper that mid-October morning and
found that overnight the government had decreed a 10 percent wage
increase for everybody. Starting the next month, he would get an
additional wage of 350 sols, a bigger percentage jump by far than
Walter Reuther had won for his automobile workers in the United
States the same month.

Yet he was not jubilant. He had done some figuring on the back
of an envelope and he had found that meat, milk, and flour were
up more than 150 sols in the last month. Allowing only for necessities such as rent and telephone and water, his monthly cost of living
had risen 428 sols, or almost 20 percent, in a month and a half. And

159

so, despite his whopping 10 percent wage increase, he was far behind the game.*

"ENHANCEMENT" AS DEBASEMENT—AND INFLATION AS NATURAL PHENOMENON

What is inflation and what causes it? Different people use the word in different semantic senses, each with a different temperature and shade of emotional coloration. Economists and standard dictionaries usually answer the question perkily: "Inflation is a disproportionate and relatively sharp and sudden increase in the quantity of money or credit or both, relative to the amount of goods available for purchase." This describes a common symptom of inflation but does not reach the heart of the matter. In the recent inflation in the United States, credit has been tight and often unavailable, goods available for purchase have been plentiful, but the price of both credit and goods has kept right on going up.

The economists' definition implies that inflation is a natural phenomenon, but includes nothing about the role of the government, the breakdown of the monetary unit, the change in peoples' expectations, the human misery, and the distortion of the social order that are what inflation means in real life. It tells us little about what happened in Germany in 1920–1923, is happening now in Uruguay, and has been well under way in the United States since shortly after large-scale escalation of the Vietnam war began. The economists' definition is only slightly true, and only sometimes true, just as light is the same thing you see in a lightning bug and a lightning bolt.

WHAT HAPPENS WHEN THERE ARE NO LINKS BETWEEN PAPER MONEY AND INTRINSIC VALUE?

What if the government that issues your money approaches the democratic ideal, and is truly responsive to the will of its people, and can continue in office only so long as it keeps the affirmative support of a majority, and must surrender the powers and perquisites of office when it no longer commands that majority?

Are economists right for all places and times when they assure us that people will go right on accepting and passing and accepting and

* Edwin L. Dale, Jr., *The New York Times.*

160

passing paper money whose value depends on nothing more than the strength and responsibility of the government which issues it, and not on its tie to gold or convertibility into another currency tied to gold?

What happens in a free society when the forgotten man finds out that all official links between money and gold, or some other commodity that has intrinsic value, and that all non-governmental restraints on the creation of money, are gone?

GOVERNMENTAL RESPONSIBILITY FOR INTEGRITY OF MONEY

In the Middle Ages, governmental responsibility for the integrity of the money was not clearly defined. The monetary system established by Charlemagne (742–814) on the basis of the denarius or silver penny, 240 of which were cut from a pound weight of silver, was subject to continual debasement in the weight and fineness of its silver content. The English penny, or sterling, suffered less from debasement, and it fulfilled most needs of trade in the 11th and 12th centuries. Because the authorities frequently tampered with monies by raising, or more often by debasing, the standard—that is, by reducing the silver or gold content of the basic coin on which the prevailing systems of accounts rested—the Middle Ages, like our own age, was a period of monetary instability. Monetary debasement would call for an upward adjustment of the rate in which all other coins were current. Otherwise such other coins would largely disappear from circulation, or circulate only at prices above the proclaimed rates.

In France and England, debasement consisted in reducing the silver content of the Denier Tournois, or the sterling, 12 of which were equal to a shilling and 240 to a pound. Gold coins, such as the franc or the rose noble, were not usually debased at the same time as the silver, so they would be "cried up"—that is, they would be rated up in terms of deniers or sterling. This is the reason people in medieval times used the expression "enhancement of the currency" when they meant what we mean when we say debasement.

The opposite of debasement was "crying down" the currency, and consisted in raising the standard by increasing the gold or silver content of the basic coin. Such a rise was deflationary and called for a downward adjustment of the price level. "Enhancement," or debasement, had inflationary effects. The idea of debasement of the currency, or the breakdown in the value of the monetary unit, seems closer to the essential meaning of inflation than the conventional definition supplied by the economists.

PRINTING-PRESS MONEY—FROM HARD LUCK TO HARD CURRENCY

Everyone has heard cautionary tales about the dangers of "galloping" inflation. In 1923, the German mark fell to 160,000 to the dollar on July 1; 242,000,000 to the dollar on October 1; and 4,200,000,000,000 to the dollar on November 20. The price of a single copy of a newspaper rose to 200 billion marks. Postage for a local letter cost 100 billion marks. Barter replaced other commercial dealings, and food riots broke out. The middle classes and pensioners saw their savings completely wiped out.

To conserve paper and printing-press time, notes were printed in billion and trillion mark denominations. At the peak of the inflation, one trillion paper marks had about the same purchasing power as one prewar German mark, or about 24 American cents. Paper money lost half or more of its value in an hour, and wages and salaries were paid daily, or more often, to facilitate quick spending. Entirely by the use of the printing press, the government increased the quantity of paper marks in circulation from about 2 billion in 1914 to about 500 quintillion (500 followed by eighteen zeros) at the end of 1923.

Today, after another world war, near total devastation, surrender, military occupation, partition, the Berlin blockade and the Berlin wall, and the European common market, the German deutsche mark is one of the hardest currencies in the world. It would be tempting to conclude that the people of one popular democracy learned a hard lesson well. However, there are so many other complex factors involved that it would be just as easy to ascribe the current solidity of the deutschemark to wise fiscal and monetary policies, hard work, or a loser's inevitable change of luck.

FRANCE CAPITALIZES THE ASSIGNAT BY CAPITAL PUNISHMENT

After the revolution, between 1789 and 1796, France went through a similar experience with her assignats. This was an emergency paper-money substitute for metallic currency, which in original concept

162

was a form of mortgage participation bond on the national lands. By 1790 the nominal value of the assignat note of 100 francs had sunk to less than twenty francs coin. It was decreed by law that anyone caught selling coin for a greater number of assignats, or commodities for a varying amount, depending on whether payment was to be made in specie or assignats, for the first offense would be sentenced to six years imprisonment, and for the second a minimum of twenty years and a maximum of death. Naturally none of these Draconian penalties worked, and by 1796 all the assignats were worthless.

URUGUAY—MODEL OF A MODERN WELFARE STATE

It is generally predicted that Latin American countries have a brighter future than they have had a past, which is a small prediction indeed. Our grandfathers made the same prediction. There seemed no reason why this should not be as true of Uruguay as any other. Yet Uruguay, where the cost of living has doubled almost every recent year, is a showcase of modern inflation at its worst. A striking contrast to most of the violent, unstable, feudal countries of Latin America, Uruguay always used to be an oasis of calm and stability. She has an even, temperate climate and no decidedly rainy, or dry seasons. Her sophisticated capital, Montevideo, is set in the middle of the country, and from it stretches a succession of beach resorts eastward to Punta del Este. Indigenous palm trees grow tall in the fertile soil, and flowering myrtle, rosemary, mimosa, and scarlet sasebo fill the hills and valleys with their fragrance.

FULL PAY AFTER RETIREMENT AT FIFTY-FIVE

Uruguay is governed by a democratically elected national council and a senate and chamber of deputies, with proportional representation for all political parties and an elected supreme court of five judges. She has the highest or second highest literacy rate in Latin America, and has produced some of South America's most notable writers, novelists, playwrights, and poets.

Less than twenty-five years ago, Uruguay boasted more gold bullion in her reserves than she had currency in circulation. She was one of the most prosperous nations in Latin America, and one of the model welfare states of the world. Her citizens were assured of

163

full pay after retirement at fifty-five. All that was before creeping inflation began. The creep turned into a trot, and the trot became a gallop.

Montevideo, where about half the people live, still has a prosperous look, especially when compared with other Latin American capitals such as Santiago and Lima. Well-dressed residents still bustle through attractive streets going to work on trolley buses, or stop to look in the windows of amply stocked shops. Factory chimneys pour out smoke, and the port has a thriving appearance, despite chronic waves of strikes. Theaters, concert halls, and art galleries are well attended, and food in restaurants is adequate. But for long recent periods, price tags disappeared from almost all goods in the shops. As inflation soared, Montevideo shopkeepers found that it was not worthwhile to change the price tags every day.

In November 1967 the peso had been valued at 100 to the dollar. At the beginning of 1968 its value was slashed in half, and in June it was devalued again from 200 to 250 to the dollar. It dropped to about 300 by the end of the year. In 1967 the cost of living rose 135.8 percent.

CREEPING INFLATION TURNS INTO A TROT, AND A TROT BECOMES A GALLOP

When a devaluation occurred in June 1968, 100,000 Uruguayan state workers went out on strike demanding higher pay to meet their family's needs, and another 250,000 had wage claims pending, all out of a population of about 2.6 million. They shut down the docks, railroads, schools, and government and municipal offices, openly defied government security measures, and brought the country to a virtual standstill.

The leadership of the national workers' convention and most of the other unions is almost entirely communist, so the leaders call strikes for political as well as economic reasons. They called them more and more frequently as the workers' wages failed to keep pace with the rising rate of inflation.

Montevideo's minor industries depend almost entirely on expensive raw materials imported from abroad because the country has almost no mineral resources. Uruguay basically depends on its exports of agricultural products, such as wool, wheat, and meat, but

164

agricultural productivity is getting lower instead of higher. In the United States, for example, one head of cattle can be brought to maturity on a scientifically planned diet in two and a half years, but in Uruguay it takes four. The $35 million a year in aid to agriculture that the United States supplies is not much help. Each year more and more Uruguayan farmers move from the productive farms and ranches to the cities where more than four-fifths of the people now live, and join the ranks of one of the largest and most irrelevant government bureaucracies in the world, or join the urban unemployed.

DEBASEMENT OF PUBLIC MORALS AND PRIVATE SOULS: INFLATIONARY VIVOISM

The swollen government payrolls, the high rate of unemployment, and the galloping inflation gnaws at the probity of the people. There are endless complaints from businessmen that they receive bad checks from customers, or simply no payments at all. In the time their lawsuit to collect the money takes to come to trial, the amount in suit will have been cut drastically by the continuing progress of inflation.

In the argot of Montevideo, a "vivo" is a sharp operator who is able to beat the system by shady operations. "Vivoism" becomes almost the only successful way of life. Cabinet ministers and top officials of the central bank have repeatedly leaked advance word of each devaluation of the peso to currency-exchange houses, and have made large profits from the information.

The condition of the country not only saps public and private morals but destroys individual souls. In his novel, *The Shipyard,* the Uruguayan author, Juan Carlos Onetti, one of Latin America's finest novelists, created a haunting symbol of this bureaucracy-ridden, inflation-wracked, former model welfare state and some of its typical people. Larson, a man of shady origins, takes charge of a shipyard somewhere on a river such as the Plata, where no ship has called for many, many years. Once there had been feverish activity there, but now a staff of only two men remains, and both of them belong to management; no workers are left for them to manage. Larson is appointed general manager by the bankrupt proprietor, and sits out the endless hours fingering his way through dusty, yellowing stacks of plans, surrounded by useless screws, bolts, jacks, and rusting cranes

165

that broke down long ago, working in offices where hardly any of the windows have panes to keep out the rain and wind. To combat the gloom, the shipyard administrators obstinately play out their ritual parts, sorting out and discussing ten-year-old files, elaborately pretending to believe in their relevance. But they are never really successful in making themselves believe that the game of business is more real than the spongy rotting planks, the wrecks, the spiders, and the rats.

Vivoism, Decay, Emigration, or Despair

People are overpowered by the feeling that there is no future for them or the country, only more decay; and that there is no way out. No way out, that is, but to emigrate, with all the uprooting of lives, friendships, careers, and jobs that emigrating necessarily involves. In 1967, when inflation was only at a trot, Uruguay issued passports at the rate of 300 a month, but in 1968, when inflation turned into a gallop, the passport rate quadrupled to 1200 a month. For those who remained and were lucky and had money or contacts, there was little left but vivoism; for others who were lucky and nothing else, there was decay in jobs such as Larson's; and for the rest, there were neither jobs nor even hope.

Yet in 1969 the government took tough, unpopular emergency measures: wage and price controls and curbs on strikes, and inflation slowed. But the inflation, and the stern repressive measures it had brought on, left terrible scars in their wake: an urban guerilla movement known as the Tupamaros, dedicated to urban guerilla warfare and eventual takeover of the government by force.

Robbing from the Rich and Giving to the Poor to Reverse the Effects of Inflation

Not long ago a machine-gun–carrying band of Tupamaros stole $220,000—the biggest heist in Uruguayan history—from Casino San Rafael, a plush resort hotel at the Punta del Este. Several days later the thieves discovered that some of their haul belonged to a pool for casino employees' tips. With much fanfare they publicly offered to return the tips to the workers.

By thus publicizing how they rob from the rich and give to the poor, the Tupamaros reversed the usual effects of inflation, which does the opposite. They also dramatized the economic squeeze and the repressive government measures that inflation had brought with it, won new recruits for themselves, undermined the existing social order, and helped pave the way for eventually destroying by force the freely elected popular government of this former model welfare state.

The progressive destruction of Uruguay's once successful social and political order when inflation accelerated from a creep to a trot and from a trot to a gallop is a dramatic case, but not an isolated one.

COASTING ALONG WITH CHRONIC INFLATION

In countries such as Chile and Brazil, chronic inflation goes on decade after decade at the rate of 20 percent to 50 percent per year. The people suffer, but they seem to learn to live with the condition, although none very well except the "vivos." They hoard goods, buy houses and real estate on borrowings, never lend money at ordinary interest rates, and invest their capital not in productive job-creating projects in their own countries, but send it abroad, often for investment in the securities of American business corporations through numbered Swiss bank accounts.

CHRONIC INFLATION IN EUROPE, AT A CREEP INSTEAD OF A GALLOP

Inflation is an old story for most European countries, too, except those such as Germany where the most traumatic memories of it still linger. After the June 1968 riots in France, prices shot up, and the rate of inflation exceeded 5 percent. Britain's cost of living has gone up at about a 6 percent rate since the pound sterling was devalued in November 1967, and in the Netherlands inflation is close to a 5 percent annual rate. Europeans do not use the word "vivoism," but many a forgotten man in Europe understands the idea. A leading British economists says, "Publicly it is fashionable to condemn inflation, but privately everyone likes it," and a French government adviser agreed, "Some of the bankers preach price stability, along with virtue and love for one's mother, but no one listens when it comes to inflation."

The middle class turns to unions for protection. Doctors, school-teachers, civil servants, professors begin to join unions to get their pay pushed up more frequently. Middle-class people become less and less inhibited about bargaining for more money. Some countries, such as Italy, rely on escalation plans based on the cost of living to pull up wages automatically as prices rise.

Hardest hit in an age of inflation are those who live on fixed incomes or on pensions. In Europe most government pensions are tied to the cost of living so that pensions rise with prices. Where escalators do not apply, governments periodically raise pensions to offset prices.

INVESTING FOR INFLATION HEDGES ACROSS MONEY BORDERS

As more and more people become aware of perpetual inflation, investment patterns change. More people purchase common stocks as an inflation hedge. In Britain, middle-class and working-class people buy unit trust shares—the equivalent of United States mutual funds. Some financial experts estimate that Italians invest as much as $800 million a year clandestinely outside Italy. One method is to carry money across the border into Switzerland and put it into stocks—both Italian- and American-company stocks—where the shares can be concealed and where taxes can be avoided. The chase by Europeans after stocks raises problems for companies and governments that want to sell long-term bonds. If a bond pays 6 percent interest and there is 4 or 5 percent annual rate of inflation, the bond-holder barely comes out ahead, not even allowing for taxes. Nine percent interest on bonds, after inflation, would leave such an investor with a return of 4 percent or so. Such steep interest rates retard the investment needed for real growth and prosperity.

Real estate investments as a way to protect savings are popular, whether in a cottage in Kent, a small cabin on the Swedish lakes, or merely ownership of a home or apartment. Typical Germans try to put at least one third of their savings into land. Europeans estimate that in the past few years the price of land has gone up about 10 percent a year.

Gold in bars and coins retains its attractions as distrust for paper money has grown. A Belgian office worker says : "Up to 90 percent of the savings of myself and many of my friends goes into gold. It's he only thing you can leave your kids that doesn't lose value. You can buy a one-kilo bar, about the size of a deck of playing cards, for the equivalent of about 1130 of your dollars. Gold is enduring." Germans also buy gold at a brisk rate, even though they must pay a stiff price and an 11 percent sales tax. Gold's attraction is strongest of all in France. Private gold hoards there are put as high as $6 billion. A typical Parisian explains that "this gold buying is not speculation on a higher gold price, for the most part. The little people are frightened. They see the value of paper money sliding downhill. They just want to protect what little they have. Gold during two world wars often meant the difference between being able to buy food and starving. People don't forget quickly that only gold is honored in times of war and revolution."

The typical Frenchman asks, "If your money had been cut in value time and again, what would you do?" He answers his own question his way: "The little man in France grumbles about inflation—and buys a gold Napoleon coin each Friday just to be on the safe side."

Europe's more sophisticated investors buy gold-mining shares rather than the gold itself. Such investors buy antiques, paintings, rare books, and jewelry, too—items, which, if properly selected, advance faster in value than the cost of living and gold as well. In all these countries inflation has eroded people's willingness to be frugal and saving. The inclination is to accept inflation—and to get rid of paper money before it loses value.

GOING INTO DEBT AS AN INFLATION HEDGE

Going into debt is more and more popular. Buying on credit, while not so widely done as in the United States, is catching on, as Europeans become more aware that borrowed money can be paid off in cheaper currency.

For many years the feeling was that inflation, once embraced as a way of life, would inevitably gain momentum and bring on a depression. That fear seems to be subsiding. Economists have said that creeping inflation—say 3 to 4 percent a year—inevitably would lead to galloping inflation, but in real life this has not happened, at least not yet. A number of Latin American and European countries have gone on for years with creeping price increases, but not galloping inflation.

169

CREEPING INFLATION, NOT RUNAWAY

As people have observed this, the fear of runaway inflation has eased. People and governments have become more willing to accept a degree of inflation, believing that it will not inevitably lead to runaway inflation. There are two reasons for this, and they seem applicable to the United States as well: First, there is a superabundance of goods, turned out by modern, efficient factories. In fact, there is excess capacity in important industries such as steel, chemicals, textiles, and many types of farm products. Such an abundance of goods assures competition, and assures that the increasing amounts of paper money will not chase after a limited supply of goods.

Second, the central banks of Europe—equivalent to the United States Federal Reserve System—clamp down on inflation when it threatens to get out of hand. Their weapons are powerful. The supply of money and credit in a country is squeezed, making loans costly and hard to get. Rising interest rates discourage borrowing and spending. This firm control exercised by the central bankers is an important reason European inflation has continued to be of the creeping variety, and stopped short of the galloping kind.

But prices of one nation's goods may rise to the point where sales of that country's products in world markets is undercut by other countries. When that happens, the country that has inflated too much finds that it no longer can earn its way in the world. Its reserves of gold and currencies dwindle. Soon the nation faces a financial crisis. Bankruptcy threatens. Britain once again provides a dramatic example of such a trend of events.

AN "OBSCURE FOREIGN CULT" SETTING IMPORT LIMITS

In 1967 Britain obtained a $1.4 billion credit from the International Monetary Fund upon her pledge to seek a $1.2 billion surplus in her balance of payments in 1969. But Britain's budget for the fiscal year ending March 31, 1970, substituted the lesser goal of $720 million for her balance-of-payments surplus. When Britain sought a further credit of $1 billion from the fund in May 1969, Roy Jenkins, the Chancellor of the Exchequer, made a pledge to the fund that Britain would hold public and private credit expansion down to below $960 million, a decrease of almost $2 billion from the $2.94 billion ex-

170

ansion of the preceding year. This obviously meant a drastic further elt-tightening and credit squeeze for Britons.

In the House of Commons, Ian McLeod, the Conservative Party's nance expert, charged Mr. Jenkins with "capitulation to the mone-ary policies of the IMF." Jenkins responded crisply that his pledge 'as consistent with his budget, and, for domestic consumption, he enied "my sudden conversion to some obscure foreign cult." But here could be no doubt that the fund was tightening the screws on ¡ritain.

Inflation such as that which led to Britain's 1967 devaluation car-ies with it a steep price: economic restraints on businesses and on eople, and lowering of people's living standards to restore stability. 'he inflation game as many Europeans see it is to hold down the rate f your country's own inflation so that it is less than that of others. 'ou will have an advantage in trade because your prices will not be oing up as fast. In an inflationary world, in short, nations consider hey are doing well if their inflation proceeds no faster than that of heir neighbors.

The rather surprising fact is that there is greater acceptance of imited inflation in all countries. People want their governments to uarantee good times and plenty of jobs. The full-employment com-nitment is a matter of law in most countries. People remember the ard times of the 1930's, and the disadvantages of rising prices are hought to be small by comparison.

N THE UNITED STATES—CREEPING INFLATION TURNED INTO A TROT

After each of her wars before World War II, the United States xperienced a decline in the general price level, but there was no omparable price decline after World War II, and no significant lecline at all following the Korean War. Whenever prices seemed ikely to begin to fall, the government or the Federal Reserve Board ras taken one action or another to prevent an anticipated recession. 'hus prices and wages have risen in good times, and scarcely fallen t all in bad times.

The years when there have been fractional price increases or ctual decreases have usually been years of relatively large-scale un-mployment. Neither the United States nor any other free world ountry has yet discovered how to have virtually stable prices with

171

full employment. It is very nearly an article of faith with economist that an inflationary rise in the price level is the inevitable concomitant of full employment.

In the eighteen years from 1947 to 1965 the official consumer price index went up from 81.2 to 102.5 or 26 percent. In the four years since then, with President Johnson's escalation of the Vietnam war, the revised index has risen from 110 to almost 130 or nearly 2 percent. At the present 5.5 percent a year rate, prices are climbing at a steeper rate than at any previous time in this country's economic history.

A rise in prices of only 2 percent a year means an erosion in the buying power of the dollar over a ten-year period from 100 cents to 82 cents. Many economists assert that income gains will generally outrun price increases if the price increases are held to a rate of only 2 percent a year. While economists regard a 2 percent rise as reasonable price stability, they generally regard a 3 percent yearly rise for any extended period of time as inflation. In 1967 and 1968 the rate of increase rose to 4 percent and then to 5 percent, and during part of 1969 prices were increasing at a 7 percent annual rate. The "creep" had turned into a crawl, the crawl into a walk, and the walk into a trot, if not quite a gallop.

A 3 percent yearly rise in prices means that the dollar that buys 100 cents of goods and services today will buy only 74.4 cents worth in ten years, and only 55.4 cents worth in twenty years. A loss such as this which approaches 50 percent in only two decades, obviously invites massive flight from paper dollars. A yearly rise of 4 percent slashes today's 100-cent dollar to buying power of only 67.6 cents in ten years, and to a buying power of only 45.6 cents in twenty.

The loss in the buying power of the United States dollar in four years of the Johnson Administration—January 1965 to January 1969 —was an ominous twelve cents.

This is a worse inflation record than the World War II administrations of Franklin Roosevelt and Harry Truman—during a period of global war. This is a much steeper erosion than the dollar suffered during the Korean War. In that four-year period—January 1949 to January 1953—the loss in the dollar's buying power was 9.8 cents.

The dollar that was worth 100 cents in the marketplace in 1939 was worth 39 cents in 1969; the 100-cent dollar of two decades ago was down to a mere 49 cents; the 100-cent dollar of only one decade go was down to 66 cents; and the 100-cent dollar in the month Lyndon B. Johnson was elected to office was an 88-cent dollar in the month he left.

THE HIGHEST PAID UNEMPLOYED STEEL WORKERS IN THE WORLD

In typical United States labor contract negotiations involving 100,000 aerospace workers and 500,000 steel workers, Roy A. Siemiller, president of the International Association of Machinists, boasted that his union had smashed the Administration's earlier anti-inflation guideposts of 3.2 percent increases per year. He warned that his union would accept no pact unless it carried increases of 6 to 7 percent a year, or double the guidepost rate. The United Steelworkers of America obtained annual increases of about 6.5 percent, which matched contracts that had been negotiated by the copper, aluminum, and can companies. Union labor won these demands despite import competition in steel that permits Japan to sell steel in the United States at less than American steel prices. One steel executive pointed out that the companies cannot meet these wage demands without raising steel prices and losing more markets to overseas competitors and added, "What we may wind up with is the highest paid unemployed steelworkers in the world."

INCREASES FOR BUILDING TRADES UNIONS SET THE NATIONAL PATTERN

It may well be that the seeds of all labor's wage demands are sown in the building trades unions, where workers demand and get substantially larger and earlier wage increases than production workers. Under some recent contracts plumbers, for example, will be earning $19,000 to $21,000 a year by 1971 or 1972. Drivers of concrete, sand, gravel, and asphalt trucks in New York City obtained hourly wages rising from $5.23 an hour to $6.67 an hour, or $266.80 a week for a forty-hour week by 1971. In addition, they are entitled to pensions of $400 a month after twenty years of service, regardless of age.

Skilled workers in the building trades and Teamster drivers are in short supply, and they have been able to enforce demands for wage rises of 10, 12, and as much as 15 percent. Wage rates of rank-and-file workers are then boosted proportionately. These rises create "inequities" for workers in industry, so a plumber or an electrical worke employed in an industrial plant demands that his wages be brough into line with those of a similar worker in the building trades. Thes demands usually win sharp rises for the skilled factory workers, an these in turn lead to larger increases for semiskilled and unskille factory workers. Finally, minimum wage rates under federal and stat laws are increased sharply, from $1.50 to $1.60 for example, an Social Security taxes and benefits go up. Realistically, how can wage ever go back down, even if unemployment should rise substantially

After entering into new collective-bargaining agreements wit steel workers, aluminum workers, and other large unions in 1968 in volving increases in wages and fringe benefits averaging more thai 6 percent per annum, most of the companies that granted the in creases raised the prices of their products by almost an equivalen amount. Later, after being sharply criticized by President Johnson some cut back some of the increases. No known formulas for the pre vention of inflation include a factor to take account of the effect o such a jawbone attack against part of one industry's price structure by a lame duck President who has said nothing about earlier, highe wage increases.

Organized and unorganized labor is not the only contributor tc inflationary pressure. Between 1960 and 1968 federal governmen spending rose 100 percent to about $190 billion while creating little in the way of new goods and services to take up all this new pape money spending power. During the 1960's consumer installment deb outstanding in the United States more than doubled and by the end of the decade had reached almost 1 trillion dollars.

The brutal pressure of the upward push of the wage, cost, deb profit, price and paper money spiral implicit in these facts and figures makes mincemeat out of fragile guidepost formulations of the economists, and the wishes of Presidents as well.

"Everything Went up More than We Dreamed Possible"

At times in 1969 the government's Consumer Price Index wa climbing at an annual rate of over 7 percent. In the words of one dis mayed government official, "Everything went up more than we dreamed possible. We had no idea it would hit like that."

Small Latin American countries such as Uruguay can limp along

174

year after year with this kind of erosion in their money by throwing up more tin shacks in the sprawling favelas that girdle their glittering capitals, demanding more United States aid and issuing more passports to emigrants, but a great power cannot. Who would be foolish enough to buy a twenty-year bond of a government that was inflating its currency at a rate of 5.5 percent per annum, or of a corporation repayable in such currency, except at an absurdly high rate of interest such as 10 percent? No one, except perhaps some of the "little people" whose innocence about the future of money lets them go on buying United States savings bonds in response to appeals to their patriotism. United States government savings bonds bought for $75 nine years ago recently paid off at about $100. But 100 of today's dollars have less purchasing power than 85 ten-year-old dollars. Less innocent though equally patriotic citizens might demand hard foreign currencies such as the 1969 German deutschemark, for example, or land, commodities, or gold. By demanding hundreds of millions of dollars' worth of gold each month, or about $3 billion worth in the months before the London gold pool was abandoned on the 1968 Ides of March in money, people who understood money were saying they no longer trusted the United States dollar.

Patriotic Patsies—Purchasers of U.S. Savings Bonds

U.S. savings bonds now bring maximum returns of 5 percent; so-called "freedom shares" maturing in less than seven years little more. Yet late in 1969 United States Treasury Notes maturing in less than two years yielded more than 8 percent and government-agency issues well above 8 percent. The savings-bond buyer who purchases his bonds through payroll deductions gets no interest on his savings until his payments are completed; if he wants to cash in his bonds at maturity, he must wait two months before he can tender them for cashing. The United States government pays its most patriotic citizens lower interest on their savings invested in this most desirable, noninflationary form of financing than does any other country in the world.

Not surprisingly, redemptions of United States savings bonds have lately exceeded new purchases. In the immediate future of money it will be an urgent matter for the Treasury to overhaul completely the United States savings bond system. Yields should be increased, and income tax features changed so that patriotic citizens who are simply unaware of the severe economic penalties that the government's economic policies impose on them will not have their pockets picked by inflation when they trustingly respond to their government's expensively advertised appeals to demonstrate their patriotism by purchasing its "savings" bonds. The recent high rate of redemption is the forgotten man's angry vote against his government's current economic policies, or lack of them.

Passing Unlegislated Tax Increases

One of the most significant, powerful, and little-noticed effects of inflation is that the rise in the level of prices, and the accompanying rise in wages and incomes, push taxpayers whose increases in income just keep even with the increases in the cost of living up into higher income tax brackets. Or at least they push a larger proportion of their income into their highest incremental tax bracket. The 1969 tax reform bill would change some of the details of the following example, but not this general principle.

Each tax bracket is expressed in fixed dollar terms, and the fixed percentage of the forgotten man's income within each bracket that the government takes is greater by sharply increasing percentages in each higher bracket. So as the whole price, wage, and cost level rises, he has less money left after taxes to pay for the other things he needs to live. He is poorer.

Individual income tax rates are now at their highest level in the history of the United States. When the personal exemption was fixed at $600 in 1948, it represented about $856 in purchasing power in today's terms, and might have represented a significant part of a year's support of a child. It means less and less as prices advance. For 1964 to 1968, as the general price level advanced 10½ percent, an individual who earned $10,000 in 1964 would have to earn $11,050 to maintain (in 1968) a constant real income. With a wife and two children—four personal exemptions—he would remain within the wide 19 percent incremental income tax bracket; but a much larger proportion of his income would be subject to the 19 percent rate of tax. So his tax would increase from $1114 to $1294, assuming that he had deductions of 10 percent of his gross income. While his 1968 tax would be paid in cheaper dollars (the 1968 dollar had 89.4 percent of the purchasing power of the 1964 dollar), he would have to pay the equivalent of $1172 versus $1114 in 1964, an advance of 5.2 percent. When one takes in state and city income and sales taxes and increases in all his tax brackets over the years, the effects of inflation as an increase in taxes is multiplied.

The impact of estate taxes and gift taxes is similar. A larger number of inflated dollars with less purchasing power pushes the decedent's estate into a higher estate tax bracket, more of the estate's capital is taken to pay the tax, and the remaining capital of the estate or gift is accordingly reduced. With Social Security taxes the same effect occurs, and, in addition, the rates themselves increase each year.

Thus at the same time the purchasing power of a country's currency erodes, the portion of it the people have left to spend after paying their taxes is reduced. If they do not take up some form of "vivoism" to preserve their status, the affluent are ground down closer to the subsistence level of the poor. No violent Marxist overthrow of a republican government is required, no change in graduated income tax rates is necessary to put into effect the basic dogma of the communist manifesto: "From each according to his ability, to each according to his needs."

In the long run, inflation at current rates, continuing without any change at all under a progressive tax rate structure, will accomplish the Marxist political objective without political violence. Unlike the strong arm methods by which Marxist governments seize their people's money, the free capitalist government's people help it seize theirs by assessing themselves on Form 1040, and mailing in what they owe.

ITEMS OF INFLATIONARY PRICE INCREASES

Inflation strikes different forgotten men in different ways. If you have not been hospitalized recently, you will not realize what it means that hospital room services charges rose 140 percent between 1958 and 1968.

We all eat and thus we all felt the 17.4 cents that rising food costs took out of each $1 of overall price increases between April 1968 and April 1969. The following table shows how many cents of each dollar in price increase between April 1968 and April 1969 was accounted for by each of the most important items that contributed to price inflation. (Reported by Sylvia Porter; prepared by Arnold Chase, Bureau of Labor Statistics):

Item	Share of Each $1 Rise, in Cents April 1968–April 1969
Food	17.4
Mortgage interest	13.9
Clothes, clothes care	11.8
Medical care	8.2
Furnishings and appliances	6.1
Home maintenance and repair	5.0
Reading and recreation	3.9
Property taxes, home insurance	3.4
Auto repairs, other services	3.2
Auto-purchase, new and used	2.4
Public transportation	1.8

REDISTRIBUTION FROM OLD TO YOUNG, WITHOUT DONATION OR DEATH

Some modern research suggests that the greatest redistribution of income resulting from inflation is from older people to younger people. The dollars that the older ones have put aside at twenty-five have shrunk in purchasing power by the time they have retired at seventy. If prices rise at an average rate of about 3 percent per year, the real purchasing power of a dollar put aside at twenty-five and held for forty-five years will halve, and then halve again.

On the face of it, a serious degree of inflation produces a violent redistribution of income and wealth, generally away from fixed to flexible income receivers and away from creditors to debtors. Bond holders and landlords may be affected adversely, while entrepreneurs in business may be gainers. But it is not clear whether overall inflation substantially alters the shares of national income going to the rich and the poor. Creditors and bond holders, who on the face of it should suffer from inflation while their debtors gain, seem to get along. Creditors are largely in higher income groups and have superior speculative opportunities and an understanding of economic forces. They can move their capital to other investments, or as a last resort to other countries, and so avoid discomfort.

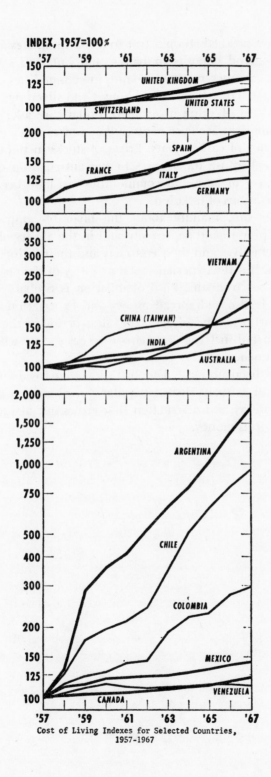

INDEX, 1957=100%

Cost of Living Indexes for Selected Countries,
1957-1967

As inflation proceeds from a trot to a gallop, money is withdrawn from cash-demand deposits in banks, and put into speculation in securities in the stock market, in land, in commodities, and in automobiles, manufactured goods, and houses and silver and gold.

All statements of value in terms of dollars are askew. Corporate financial statements are false because they represent values in dollars or other money of earlier years. Prices of stocks in the stock market are also false because they represent the anticipation of continued inflation. Prices of land and commodities are false because of continued expectations of inflation.

Economists talk blandly about the favorable impact of rising prices in helping to end depressions and in the ability of individuals to adjust themselves and their contracts and their actions to continuing inflation. But the experience of a majority of the people in countries that suffer from this kind of inflation is probably to the contrary; there is also widespread misery and expectations and fear of more. In short, the kind of decay and destruction of the social order that has occurred in Uruguay occurs in every society where inflation marches on unchecked.

There has been no clear demonstration that freedom as we have known it, and a freely elected popular government, can effectively prevent the decay and destruction that grows out of the unchecked debasement of its money.

11

LAYING HANDS ON INFLATION: THE INVISIBLE HAND AND THE VISIBLE

*I would attach more importance to the
belief to which reputable economists are ever
susceptible that God is a conservative
gentleman with a marked tendency toward
orthodoxy in economics. Accordingly, if you
are orthodox, and speak firmly about
"economic fundamentals," He will not let you
down.*

JOHN KENNETH GALBRAITH

UNDERPRODUCTION CAUSES INFLATION OR ELSE IT DOES NOT

Although no economist has produced a comprehensive theory to explain the causes and cures of inflation, many superficial ideas have been put forward.

Arthur Milton, in *Inflation: Everyone's Problem*, says that the cause is underproduction:

> The only lasting counterbalance to inflation is increased production. Drastic deflation is like a massive dose of an antibiotic drug, but just as antibiotic drugs will not do anything against a virus infection, only against bacteria, so drastic deflation does not get at the real cause of inflationary forces in the economy. It only deals with the symptoms.
>
> The root cause of inflation is more likely to be under-production and under-consumption. When the output of goods and services goes up faster than the supply of money, that has to bring prices down or put the brake on their advance.*

But John Kenneth Galbraith is not carried away by Milton's metaphorical tide. He disagrees. In *The Affluent Society* Professor Galbraith says:

* Citadel, 1968.

181

The almost inevitable temptation to regard increased production as a remedy for inflation is perhaps the commonest error in contemporary attitudes toward inflation.

If production is at capacity, increased output will actually require an increase in capacity. The increased investments that this implies will, in the form of wages, payment for materials, returns to capital and profits, add to purchasing power and the current demand for goods, before the added capacity resulting from the investment is in place to meet the demand. Thus the effort to increase the production adds to the pressure on current capacity—and to the prospect for inflationary price increases.

A cat chasing its own tail may, by an extraordinary act of feline dexterity, on occasion succeed in catching it. To overcome inflation by increasing production, while superficially similar, will not so often be successful.*

Increasing production is really just a rather glib panacea. Sooner or later economists and all the rest of us will have to face up to the fact that on a small finite planet production cannot keep on expanding indefinitely. Some other solution for economic problems must be found. The one that instantly suggests itself is decreased reproduction.

Conventional Wisdom: Inflation Occurs at Full Employment, at Under-Employment It Does Not

The conventional wisdom of economists is that serious inflation does not occur in a country until substantially full employment is reached. In some economists' definitions of inflation, price rises during periods of high unemployment are not even counted as inflation.

During the latter part of the Eisenhower administration, when prices rose at a rate of only about 2 percent per annum, the rate of unemployment stood at about 5½ percent of the work force. In 1960 John F. Kennedy defeated Richard M. Nixon largely through skillful exploitation of the ideas subsumed under his slogan "Let's get this country moving again." With the Kennedy-Johnson escalation of the Vietnam war, the rate of unemployment under a semiwartime economy fell to somewhere near or below 4½ percent of the labor force, and the rate of inflation rose to about 4½ percent. Economists have said that if Kennedy's slogan and his election meant anything,

* New American Library Edition, 1958.

182

they meant that the United States electorate will not tolerate an unemployment rate as high as 5½ percent, and that neither party could win a national election in this country today, or stay in power long, if it allowed the rate of unemployment again to rise to near this figure. More recently, the unemployment rate has been as low as 3½ percent.

This logically neat idea that the rate of inflation automatically rises when the rate of unemployment falls, and falls when the rate of unemployment rises, like a teeter-totter, seems almost as simplistic and remote from the conditions of real-life inflation as the earlier faith that Adam Smith's invisible hand would always bring the economy back into static equilibrium at the optimum level for the greatest good of all. Uruguay, for example, has suffered from serious unemployment at the same time it suffered from galloping inflation. Indeed, the economists' formulations that we have looked at so far do not come near describing or explaining any of the real-life inflation described in the previous chapter—galloping as in Latin America, creeping as in Western Europe, or trotting as in the United States under the Kennedy-Johnson and early Nixon administrations.

John Maynard Keynes himself led the attack on Adam Smith's theory that depressions were self-correcting. He pointed out the possibility, indeed the probability, that there was no reason the economy would not find its equilibrium at an unspecified and perhaps very high rate of unemployment. National governments and the people alike saw Keynes's point, and came to realize that it was the government's responsibility to take positive action to reduce unemployment.

The belief has persisted that peacetime inflation might somehow be automatically self-correcting without positive governmental action. As Professor Galbraith observes, "The notion that, in peacetime, prices might as a normal thing, rise continuously and persistently has had no Keynes."

M AND V: THE TOTAL VALUE OF MONEY AND THE VELOCITY OF CIRCULATION

To be fair to them, economists recognize two other factors as playing important roles in inflation and its cure: the amount of money in circulation, M, and the velocity of circulation of the money in a year, V. Economists include as money the coin and currency in circulation, checkable demand deposits, and time and savings deposits in banks. In the United States M is now more than six times as large as it was before World War II.

V is the rate at which the stock of money turns over each year to consummate income transactions. The size of V can change over time with changes in financial institutions, habits, savings, attitudes, expectations, and relative distributions of M among different kinds of people, institutions, and classes of income. With these letters economists construct formulas, such as the formula for the quantity equation of exchange: $MV = PQ$. In this equation P stands for the average price level and goes up and down with an index of the price level, while Q stands for real (as distinct from current) dollar national product and has to be computed statistically by the process of taking the net national product and applying a price index to the dollar values in it.

But all such formulas are meaningless if the M factor, money itself, loses its value as money. If M is so unlimited in amount that it becomes practically a free good, people will have so much of it to spend that they will bid all prices, prices of goods, wages, commodities and incomes sky high.

M is under the control of national governments and central banking agencies who can limit it, although with some difficulty. Or they can expand it without limit, and it is very much easier for them to do so.

GOVERNMENTAL POWER OVER CURRENCY AND CREDIT

The power to issue currency, to control, limit, or expand the amount and availability of credit, and the power to do all other important things that affect money and banking, has in the course of history been removed to an increasing extent from private hands and vested in national governments, even in the poorest of countries.

Today governments all over the world casually substitute copper or nickel or zinc or aluminum for gold and silver in their coins, and pass the coin. Governments print paper money to finance government spending in excess of tax revenues, and hire more employees than are necessary to perform make-work jobs that produce nothing, in order to reduce the rate of unemployment and social unrest and create economic security for their people.

Governmental fiscal authorities, such as the United States Federal Reserve System and the Bank of England, raise or lower requirements for bank monetary reserves, and thus make it possible for banks to lend more money, or less. This increases or reduces bank money by increasing or reducing the demand deposits in circulation. Production is maintained at the highest levels of output in order to provide sufficient jobs to prevent widespread unemployment.

If production does not increase as fast as the money supply increases, and individuals do not change their rate of spending, land, agricultural products, and manufactured goods will rise in price. The higher prices will require higher government expenditures. This will increase the government's deficit and increase the amount the government must raise by borrowing. The government's borrowing in turn will increase the money in circulation.

A national government can control the level of employment or unemployment simply by hiring more government employees—to deliver the mail, collect taxes, build roads, guard the President, carry rifles in Vietnam, or attend economic conferences. Governments can also control the rate of production in the private sector of the economy by raising or lowering rates of interest. This will decrease or increase the amount of capital available to an entrepreneur to increase production. By raising income tax rates, the government can increase the costs of production and reduce the possibility of producing goods at prices competitive with those of other countries.

By increasing the rates of estate and gift taxes, the government can decrease the amount of capital any one of its people can transmit to his descendants, thereby limiting the ownership of property and of capital to a single individual in a single generation. By limiting the personal exemption in the income tax to say $600 per person, the government can make it economically painful for married middle-class wage earners to have children. However, under current welfare systems in the United States, it is often profitable for a single woman who is on relief to have as many children as possible.

EFFECTIVE REMEDIES WOULD COLLIDE WITH THE URGENCIES OF PRODUCTION FOR ECONOMIC SECURITY

People are organized as workers to demand more pay. They are not organized as consumers to demand lower prices. The attitude, then, seems to be that if it means inflation, so what? Most of the population is protected from its bad effects. In modern economics, price inflation is becoming almost as normal as breathing. As Professor Galbraith observes, "The remedies that would be effective collide with the urgencies of production for purposes of economic security."

These problems that are so acute and seem so intractable in a free democratic capitalist society such as ours scarcely arise in totalitarian countries. In them, of course, the people are working their way toward a different political ideal: They are aiming to become the collective Marxist or socialist economic man, wholly responsive to the will and economic purposes of the monolithic state which, when it ultimately reaches its perfect form, will be a beehive or an anthill on a grand scale.

But in a free country the purpose of the state is to respond to the will of the people, including the forgotten man. The conventional wisdom, at least until very recently, is that there are not enough votes against inflation to elect an alderman, let alone a congressman or a President. So elective governmental policy in free countries usually does little about inflation. It justifies this on the ancient authority of Adam Smith that the "hands-off" policy will permit the "invisible hand" of the market to pull prices down and back into line. There is the feeling that however bad inflation is, its opposite, a depression, would be worse.

Both M and V in the formula for the quantity equation of exchange are allowed to increase with no upper limits in sight. But production or lack of it, full employment or high rates of unemployment do not prevent the upward spiral of inflation, nor slow it nor stop it nor, indeed, seem to have much necessary correlation of any kind with it. What real-life governments of real-life countries do and fail to do can and does.

LIKE A MOUSE ON A SELF-ACTIVATED TREADMILL

The people who cause the spiral are the ones who vote governments into power, and vote them out. As long as economists and politicians present the subjects of inflation and unemployment to the voters as natural phenomena like rain, and not as things caused and cured to a large extent by governmental and popular action, voters are not likely to vote a national government in or out of office for economic reasons except when a depression occurs. During inflaion, the forgotten man, like a mouse on a self-activated treadmill, eems to prefer to try to stay in the same place by running ever faster, ather than standing still and simply letting it stop.

Redefining inflation as a "breakdown in the value of the monetary init," or as a debasement in the value of money, places emphasis on he essence of the problem. Responsibility is assigned to the human nstitutions and other human factors, primarily but not exclusively iational governments and central banks, which are responsible for he value of the monetary unit and are in a position to do something bout it.

Debasement of the U.S. Dollar by Governmental Policy

Debasement—the breakdown in the value of a national currency rimarily as a result of the policies of the government that issues the urrency—is occurring in the United States. Prices of American steel iave gone up relative to those abroad, so Japanese steel is sold on the 'acific Coast and foreign-manufactured barbed wire is sold to our armers at prices lower than domestic manufacturers are willing to neet. Foreign cars are everywhere.

In a vacuum, as an isolated case, governmental debasement of the Jnited States dollar would not be serious. For the twenty-five years rom 1933 to 1958, American economic policy had no concern for he United States international balance of payments. The country vas not devastated by World War II, investors from abroad wanted o put their money in the United States, and the United States and ier foreign trade enjoyed the benefits of the favorable "dollar gap." But since 1958 the United States has had to consider the effects of ier foreign balance of payments on her economic policy.

For example, domestic interest rates cannot be lowered very much below interest rates in Britain or France. If they were, foreign investors here would withdraw their dollar holdings. If they demanded gold for them there would not be enough gold in the United States Treasury to honor their dollar claims against it.

Another form of debasement has occurred in the overgenerosity of the government in foreign military and aid programs, such as the decision to wage a war in Vietnam and carry on aid programs to other countries with dollars, which then become available in those countries to send back in exchange for our gold.

187

Partly through American aid, foreign countries became mor productive and competitive in their manufactures as the devastation of war were repaired and the level of technology rose. Multinationa American private firms spent paper dollars abroad in order to buil up their foreign branches and subsidiaries and participate in th rapidly expanding markets in the more developed countries, placin still more paper dollars in foreign hands. The Common Market re duced tariff barriers among its member countries, but erected highe barriers against outside countries. President de Gaulle criticize American penetration of French industry, and foreign countrie discriminated against American goods and companies.

The Shift in International Liquidity Preference

Debasement by the policy of the national government is not th only cause of the deterioration of the dollar in the world economy As paper dollar holdings abroad grew to more than three times th value of the gold available to redeem the paper dollars, and th national government did nothing to change its policies, the gol drain grew so great that on the Ides of March in money the Unite States was forced to limit, and indeed for all practical purposes t repudiate her pledge that the paper dollars held abroad could b converted to gold.

Thus foreign governments stopped trusting in the dollar and de manded gold from the United States instead. Economists blandl called this a shift in international liquidity preference. It left us ou on a long limb, with the chain saw in other hands.

The control that the national government exercises over the live of its people is vast, but not unlimited or exclusive. Not all possibl powers over money are vested in national governments, and not al powers inherently vested in them are exercised. Individual decision to buy or sell, to hold or redeem savings bonds, to pay or accept mor or less interest, to borrow or lend, to save or spend, still make up th vast majority of money transactions. There are also corporate an banking forces that are independent of both national government and individuals, that no one national government completely con trols. These cause movements of gold and trade from country t country.

International organizations like the International Monetary Fund and the communist bloc's Bank for International Economic Cooperation also have powers over money that override the powers of all other agencies, whether national governments, individual activities, or international movements of gold and commodities. The interaction of these independent forces, individual decisions, actions of national governments, private international transactions, and activities of official international organizations all play a part in crying up or crying down any one national currency. The once mighty dollar is no longer immune from such a crying jag.

"This Cannot Be Allowed to Continue"

Money is accepted because it is accepted. But if everyone who has it is rushing to get rid of it in exchange for land, agricultural products, manufactured goods, and travel and services, before very long there will be no acceptors. Unlimited amounts and denominations of money can be printed up by governments, as well as by counterfeiters.

Governments and individuals, by creating more demand deposits in banks, can create almost unlimited amounts of new money. The rate and velocity of spending increases. The inflationary spiral we have observed accelerates. Prices of manufactured goods rise and price themselves out of markets in foreign countries where the level of prices and wages is lower. Manufactured goods from foreign countries undersell local manufacturers in the domestic market. Foreign countries refuse to lend money to provide capital to increase local production, except at increasingly higher rates of interest because of the debasement of the local money in which they expect to be repaid. The upward spiral goes on unchecked. The forgotten man runs ever faster on his treadmill.

When the government's money is no longer a valuable commodity in itself, and no longer has gold or other commodity backing, and no absolute limitation on the total supply, there will be no acceptors. Then money is not accepted because it is not accepted, as was the case with the dollar at Orly and at Heathrow during March 1968.

The 1968 experience seems intolerable in the leading financial power of the world. The first words of Dr. Paul W. McCracken, after he was chosen chairman of the Council of Economic Advisers under President Nixon, were: "This cannot be allowed to continue."

Serious inflation feeds on itself. Its most important effect is the psychological switch it brings on in the forgotten man's mind which unlike that of the economists' everlasting economic man, can indeed change. When the forgotten man's dollar travelers' cheques are dishonored at Orly, he suffers a seismic mental shift. He begins to count on continuing inflation. This activates the price-wage-profit-expectation treadmill.

To the Forgotten Man, Inflation Is Simple but Confusing

The forgotten man sees the cause of inflation in fairly simple terms. He sees himself, the members of his union, the members of his profession, his friends in like businesses, all seeking and obtaining higher wages and salaries, and borrowing more money, and buying more goods on time. He raises the prices he charges for his goods or services. The corporation he works for must increase the prices of its products to cover the costs of his wage increases. Wages rise, salaries rise, prices rise, taxes rise, people's expectations of inflation rise, his expectations of further inflation rise, and the treadmill speeds up some more.

The Expectation of Inflation

Dr. James J. O'Leary, executive vice-president and economist for a Wall Street bank, has noted that "the expectation of inflation is the most powerful force affecting our economy today."

What do economists mean by "the expectation of inflation?" It is the conviction shared widely by investors, corporate planners, the labor unions, consumers, and the public at large that, for the forseeable future, the American economy is destined to grow strongly in physical-output terms at full employment, and that inherent in this process will be a chronically high rate of increase in the price level. The expectation has, of course, been nurtured by the sharp and steady rise in prices during the past few years. And as former Federal Reserve Board Chairman William McChesney Martin warned, unless the expectation of inflation is dampened down, it may ultimately

190

lead to serious dislocations and a dangerous blowup in the United States economy and in the international monetary system.

What are the consequences of continuing expectations of inflation? The rise of general interest rates to the highest levels in the history of the United States; an increase in the proportion of investment funds placed in equities—common stocks and real estate—and a decrease in funds invested in bonds and mortgages; a willingness to take greater investment risks in an economy of prices that seem to be a one-way upward street; greater incentives for corporate investment in new plant and equipment; higher sales of more automobiles and other durable goods more easily in the anticipation of higher prices later on; and rising wage and fringe-benefit demands from organized and unorganized labor.

THE OVERWHELMING IMPORTANCE OF MONEY

What is the chief end of man? To glorify God and enjoy Him forever, as the shorter catechism answers question number one? Is it the pursuit of happiness, as the Declaration of Independence suggests? Do individuals find a God, true freedom, and fulfillment for their lives in service to an economic regime—for example, by active service in the Red Guards?

What, indeed, is the chief end of man today?

Considering the overwhelming importance of money in the lives of all people everywhere today, not only in the Marxist world but in the free world as well, here at the open end of a 5000-year sweep of recorded history that began when King Menes went up from Abydos to Memphis, it is remarkable how comparatively modest a part money seems to have played in the lives of the vast majority of people, or in the speculations of their philosophers, in all the years prior to 1776, the year when Adam Smith published his *Inquiry into the Causes of the Wealth of Nations*. But after his inquiry the world was never the same again. The change in the attitudes of the world's people toward money in the 200 years since has been as fundamental as a reversal of the earth's magnetic poles.

In white clapboard frame houses on quarter-acre lots along elm-shaded streets of small Midwestern towns, where embroidered samplers hung over the kitchen door and etchings of Abraham Lincoln

191

on the parlor wall, it used to be considered the gravest breach of good manners even to mention money. This attitude probably disappeared sometime before exhaust fumes from the big new models out of Detroit killed off the elm trees' shade.

Now Dr. Buber has persuaded our free society that God is dead, and Dr. Freud has convinced us that love is only a reflex of the psyche and a physical twitch. The mysteries of the human personality and violent death that enthralled us in *Oedipus* and *Hamlet* seem to have lost some intangible part of their age-old magic now that images of the assassinations of Kennedys and Kings, and B-52's blowing up infantry rifle squads in the suburbs of Saigon, confront us all day and night between deodorant commercials on TV. The nifty new models from Detroit reached a peak of technical perfection in 1949 or so, and the subsequent models' annual rearrangement of chrome, tailfins, and grille hardly give us enough status to stun the neighbors any more. All that really is left to lift the ennui of our affluent lives is to assuage our few remaining commercial-inspired desires by getting and spending some more money.

"A Touch of Monomania Is Quite Palpable"

As Professor Robert Lekachman has remarked, "Like many another amateur student of economics, this one has found the key in money. Which is to say that a touch of monomania is quite palpable." Yet it would not be so surprising, either, as time goes by, to hear that the names of more and more economics courses in schools and colleges had been changed to include the word money, and had turned their focus directly upon the future of money instead of tactfully averting their eyes.

A touch of monomania about money is quite palpable in most forgotten men today, and it should not be too long before economics professors join them in discovering that M for money is the axis of their discipline.

Perhaps the time has come to admit that money, using the word broadly to include the pursuit and enjoyment of economic advantage that it brings, is almost the one remaining activity all of the overprivileged masses and underprivileged classes of the most highly developed countries in the free world now also regard as the chief end of man. Those who are not yet willing to agree with this proposition

SIGNIFICANT INTERNATIONAL TRENDS

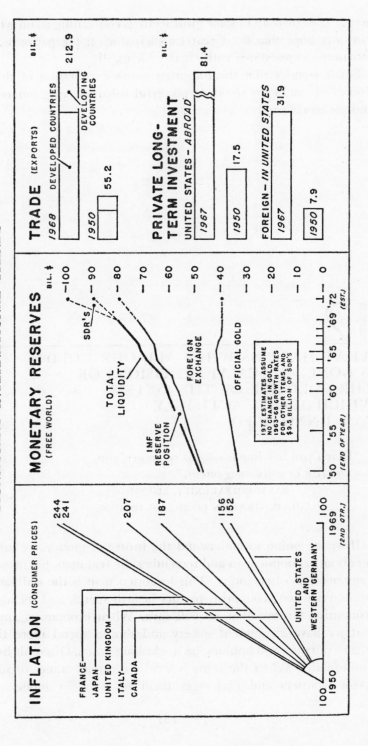

may at least own up to some guilt feelings concerning it, on which we can only hope that the Great Emancipator on the parlor wall will continue to gaze down with charity for us all.

Small wonder that the forgotten man's expectation of the inflation of his money is the most powerful force affecting our economy and the world's today.

12

WHAT HAPPENS WHEN ALL OUR GOLD IS GONE—APOCALYPTIC VISIONS OF THE COLLAPSE OF THE SYSTEM, WHICH MIGHT ACTUALLY PASS UNNOTICED

"When you live in a managed economy, you run the risk of mismanagement."
RAYMOND SAULNIER, EISENHOWER
ADMINISTRATION ECONOMIC ADVISER.

If we are going to understand the future of money, we must forget about economic man and remember the real man, the man whom economists so often forget. This forgotten man is the ordinary man who saves when economists predict he will spend, and spends when economists forecast that he will save. When economists announce that we have an affluent society and should spend more time in leisure pursuits and hobbies, he works long hours. Often his hobby is numismatics. When the franc is weak he carries francs in suitcases across frontiers and exchanges them for sounder money. When

194

economists tell him the money he has today is every bit as good as the money of olden times, he perversely thinks back not to gold-standard money but if he is German he thinks of what a billion marks would not buy during the runaway inflation of 1923, or if French of what his grandpère told him you could not do with the awful assignats on pain of a severed head. If he is American, he saves his silver quarters and pops them into a piggy bank on his bureau, or into his fast-growing coin collection, and happily passes the silvered bronze ones off on the taxi driver who still believes that "money is accepted because it is accepted."

THE FORGOTTEN MAN BOTH CONTRARY AND WISE

Economists' predictions about the future behavior of this forgotten man have been wrong so often, indeed so consistently, that such an economist's public prediction usually carries its own refutation within itself. The forgotten man has had the experience of hearing so many economists' predictions turn out wrong, that when he hears a new one he often goes and acts contrariwise and thus proves to be both contrary and wise.

There are two rather large, simple things in the future of money that influence the thinking and acting of the forgotten man more than anything else: the continuing rise in all prices and costs he must pay, which he thinks of as inflation; and the lingering fear of a catastrophic depression on the scale of the one of the 1930's. For the American forgotten man, there are two additional concerns of a lesser order of magnitude: the continuing loss of the United States gold reserve, and the continuing deficit in our foreign balance of payments. For an American these four things all interact upon each other. These concerns fester until the forgotten man finally decides he should act for his and his family's economic self-preservation. When he does, one and two of him, and then five and ten, and then all the rest spread fear through a whole population. Lesser governments in the world economic structure can weather economic storms by bending with them, or fail to weather them and fall, without sending shock waves through the structure itself. But if the United States, the economic Atlas that carries the whole world's economic system on its shoulders, should falter, the whole free world's economic structure would come tumbling down too.

If the whole structure of the world money system rests ultimately on the opinions and emotions of the American forgotten man, where does he get these important opinions? All kinds of economic opinions are in the air around him. They are in the writings of the great economists such as David Ricardo and Thomas Malthus and their descendants, whom Thomas Carlyle meant when he complained about "respectable professors of the dismal science." The forgotten man never forgets the possibility that out of such economic writings he may dig some useful economic insights, or some bona fide inside information that will help him make a private fortune of millions, as such insights did for Ricardo and Lord Keynes. A miasma of bone-chilling gloom permeates most writings on economics, but such literary depressions are easier to live through than real ones, and no pain at all if they tell of the way to a fortune.

A MIASMA OF BONE-CHILLING GLOOM

One of the most picturesque contemporary purveyors of gloomy economic insights is C. V. Myers, editor of the *Myers' Finance Review*, a private weekly economic letter published and distributed by C. V. Ranch Ltd. Like many of his colleagues, Myers is a pervicacious Pursides. He sees the monetary world from Suite 903, Lancaster Building, Calgary, Alberta, and lets American investors in on his apocalyptic visions by means of a folded typewritten sheet with sometimes a center page insert for $46 a year. His pronouncements are salted and peppered with the names of "hot" gold and silver mining stocks. He betrays no special reverence for the veracity of United States government officials. This annoys the United States Securities and Exchange Commission (SEC), which tends to suspect that the mines he mentions may be salted too, so it sought to enjoin him from sending his news letter to forgotten men in the United States because he had not registered with the commission as an investment adviser.

Myers contends that he does not have to register because Canada is a free country, and he can use its mails to send apocalyptic visions to anyone he likes, including Americans. But ever since the SEC got out an injunction against him, he writes the letter in the name of his incorporated ranch, not in his own name. Notwithstanding the vision of a Securities and Exchange commissioner poring over endless bags of general mail in the Calgary Post Office, Myers' letters are still arriving regularly in New York.

Typical was the June 1968 Special Edition of the letter, which Myers dictated by transatlantic and trans-Canada telephone from Switzerland to Calgary. He wrote that in two hours it would be at the printer's and would be mailed the following day, adding with rare humility that "since I have not had a chance to even read what I am writing, much less edit it, I hope you will understand if the wording is less smooth than usual, and perhaps even sometimes clumsy."

THE PAPER BLOC VERSUS GOLD

Myers went on:

> The battle lines are drawn. The struggle between the inflationary paper bloc and the solid gold bloc is nearly ready to be joined. Hostilities can erupt at any time. Already today this battle is being desperately fought, without fanfare—in the dark of the night.
>
> The entire monetary system is based on the dollar. Because of Bretton Woods, the dollar came to represent the foundation of world money, and a collapse of this foundation means worldwide collapse and chaos. Therefore, it is to the interest of every advanced country to prop up the structure as long as it can, in the hope that somehow, a NEW AND WORKABLE ARRANGEMENT may be devised.
>
> The very structure which the United States Treasury created and designed—in all its glory when it had the world's gold—is by the principles on which it rests, dedicated to the rights of South Africa to sell her gold if she so wishes at $35 an ounce, and to receive currencies of other nations, and no questions asked.
>
> So the battle, eyeball to eyeball—is on. The United States is trying to force other countries to break rules of the fund, so that South Africa will be forced to sell her gold on the open market, thereby depressing the price, resulting in the victory of paper over gold. If the fund does not rule in favor of South Africa, the fund is defunct, all its principles are shot, and it must throw its rule book away, and dissolve itself.*

* *Myers' Finance Review,* June 1968, Special Edition.

You will recall from chapter 8 South Africa's steady streak of winnings in the Great World Poker Game in Gold, but as this book went to press, the International Monetary Fund had not dissolved itself, and the system had not collapsed. Indeed, "special drawing rights," or "paper gold," had just been invented. Still, there is plenty of basis for genuine concern for the system, and visions such as Myers' encourage making a new start.

Myers rumbles on about the battle between the Pursides and the Midases:

> Unfortunately, the above is completely true. And it is known to be true by all the bankers of the world. Unfortunately, the world is caught in a dilemma and nobody—I repeat, nobody—knows what to do except to try going forward on the present path as as long as possible.
>
> Perhaps gold is not the ideal, but what else is there to vote for? United States paper and United States promises? French paper or promises? (We have already seen a surprising and ruinous strike.) Russian rubles?
>
> Reviewing the above, I think you can see now—despite the silence of the financial press—why McChesney Martin of the Federal Reserve Board has been twice moved to say, "We are in the midst of the worst monetary crisis in world history." Why King of the Bank of England said almost identical words and resigned his position. It is on, never fear. The crisis is on. And the public will not know about it until it explodes.

Please do not take the above quotations from Myers as investment advice from me to go long on gold stocks and put kaffirs in your coffers, particularly since I cannot hide in Calgary from the SEC. The quotation is intended both to show you one widely read assessment of the world money crisis and to show you how much pep is still left in the Pursides.

Lest the oracular tone of Myers' weekly apocalyptic visions be confused with omniscience, equal time for the Midases makes it necessary to disclose that in his March 22, 1968, letter, Myers also made the following predictions:

> End of the 2-tier gold system in 10 to 40 days, ending in big run by central banks—a plunging stock market from 830 to 780 next

30 to 40 days—then after short time, beginning of panic. —War—as the discredited Johnson Administration seeks the magic formula to silence opposition and retain power. War declaration would transform dissenters into traitors—justify controls, curfews, military suppression of rights—war if successfully declared would bring in China and Russia, and will culminate in nuclear conflict with Russia.

Two years and more later, the two-tier gold system was still in effect, there had been no run on central banks; instead of plunging to '80, the Dow Jones Industrial Average after some backing and filling had swung up toward its historic high of 1000 and down below 800 again, but nice profits were still being made in standard investment-grade stocks. The price of gold had crashed back to $35 an ounce and even dipped below $35, and silver and kaffirs had fallen far below the prices at which they had sold after the Ides of March in money. Instead of nuclear war, peace talks were plugging along and troops were being withdrawn from Vietnam.

Writers of gingery letters like Mr. Myers' tell readers sternly to throw away all back issues, but I keep mine anyway and leaf through them now and then for just such reassurances as this March 22, 1968, letter affords.

GLOOM AND DOOM FROM MIDASES TOO

One might be surprised that a leading Pursides like Mr. Myers should quote the grand panjandrum of the Midases, William McChesney Martin, in support of any thesis. Martin sometimes has visions almost as apocalyptic as Myers, and what is more unnerving, unlike Myers up there in Calgary, Martin, as chairman of the Federal Reserve Board until his retirement in January 1970, had his finger on the pressure points and his hand on the throttle, if anybody did. Sometimes he also sounded as if he was sitting on a red hot safety valve.

On April 19, 1968, after apologizing several times "for appearing to be emotional," Martin told an audience attending the annual meeting of the American Society of Newspaper Editors at the Shoreham Hotel in Washington, D.C.: "The nation is in the midst of the worst financial crisis since 1931."

This was just what Myers had been saying. Martin went on:

> We must have a tax increase, reduce the budgetary deficit and correct the adverse balance of payments to avoid disaster. The nation cannot tolerate price rises almost twice the gains in production, nor can it ignore the warnings of foreign friends. After all, the Europeans are depositors in this country, and a banker doesn't kick a depositor in the teeth. . . . During the recent gold crisis, we promised them [Europe] to put our affairs in order, and end domestic deficits as well.
>
> We all know that unless we correct the balance of payments, we will see a worldwide devaluation of currencies, from which it will take a long time to recover. I am convinced our nation's production gains of 3 percent this year, compared with wage rises in the order of 7 percent, and our poor balance of payments figures will lead us to uncontrollable inflation and eventual deflation or depression—unless checked as soon as possible. We saw what procrastination did to Britain. The devaluation of the pound last November led to a flight to the dollar—for the purpose of buying our gold. Now the French appear to think that the United States is following the British pattern, and because we stabilized the gold problem for a time, many in Congress think all our troubles are over. The measures taken last month to stem the outflow of gold were effected by promising the European central bankers that the United States would tackle its payments deficit and domestic and budgetary problems.

Martin's actions confirmed his words. He explained that the crisis had prompted "orderly increases in the Federal Reserve discount rate recently, the latest being the rise from 5 to 5½ percent announced yesterday, which brings the level within half a percentage point of its historic high—and that was 1929." A couple of years later the rate had risen to 6 percent and seemed to be headed still higher.

Martin then told us all, in the most emphatic way possible, what we had to do: "I hope I am not being too emotional about our situation, but we are faced with an intolerable budget deficit and also an intolerable deficit in our international budget balance of payments. Both have to be corrected over the next few years or the United

200

States is going to face either an uncontrollable recession or an uncontrollable inflation." Two years later, at the beginning of the 1970's, things had changed. Prominent economists were predicting that we were going to have the recession, and also the inflation, both at the same time.

The United States gold supply reached a peak of $24 billion in 1949, but by 1969 it had dropped back to $11 billion or so. On the Ides of March in money, when Congress removed the 25 percent limitation on the value of gold behind the paper dollars in circulation, and at the United States' bidding the remaining seven major free-world money nations adopted the so-called two-tier gold system, all but the most tenuous remaining ties between gold and the dollar were severed. Now no one, neither foreigners nor citizens, no one other than foreign central banks in certain limited circumstances, is allowed to obtain gold from the United States Treasury for their dollars.

WHAT COULD HAPPEN TO THE DOLLAR?

What could really happen to the dollar? A European banker quoted in *The Wall Street Journal* says: "The dam is weakening. With a lot of foreigners nervous about holding dollars, anti-inflationary moves extensive enough and swift enough to forestall devaluation might require plunging purposefully into a recession—which no one expects Washington to do."

Bankers envision a chain of events something like this: Some small central banks, perhaps in Latin America, might exercise the privilege of cashing in surplus dollars for Treasury gold in order to profit by selling it for paper dollars whenever the private market price rose above the $35 official price. That would give them more paper dollars with which to keep playing the same game. They would turn in the new paper for gold metal. Then central bankers in one or two European countries would come under intense domestic political pressure to avoid being left holding a bag of devalued paper dollars, so they too would cash them in for Treasury gold. With the Treasury stock of $11 billion falling ever lower, the Treasury unilaterally and formally would have to repudiate its pledge to redeem paper even for central banks' gold before we were left without an ounce. Disorder would begin. Exchange rates would fluctuate freely. Once again, no one would cash dollar travelers' cheques abroad.

If the Whole International Monetary System Collapsed, Would Anybody Here Notice the Catastrophe?

Initially, at least, a collapse of the world money system woul probably have less direct effect on the lives of people in the Unite States than it would have on the lives of people in any of the othe major countries of the free world. People would suffer from collaps of the system in direct proportion to the magnitude of their cour try's international trade in relation to its economy as a whole. In ports would cost more; for the Dutch, imports amount to about 3 percent of what they consume. The effect would probably be disas trous for Britain.

We speak of the dollar at home "losing its value" as prices rise fc solely domestic reasons; it is "devaluing" in that sense. But an inter national devaluation simply means a change in the exchange rat against other currencies. Except in so far as the price of importe goods rises, a devaluation is not "inflationary." Domestic prices nee not rise at all; only imports would rise in price.

In the United States, imports amount to only 3 percent of ou gross national product, and we are one of the most self-sufficient na tions in the world, like the Soviet Union. What, then, would be s bad about devaluing the dollar in terms of gold?

It probably would not be so bad for us, even if it was for every body else, because of the unique strength of the United State economy. In recent years the gross national product of the Unite States has been moving upward from $800 billion toward $100 billion. In relation to this, a deficit in United States international payments of $4 billion or so seems insignificant. The United State could be compared to a man who earns $9000 a year, has a rising in come, and owes $40 to a creditor in another city. He does not worr much about the creditor, and the creditor probably is not too worrie about eventually collecting his $40—so why should creditors of th United States be concerned?

Businessmen in free-world countries will still gravitate toward th dollar as a currency for commerce and exchange, since there is noth ing else safer. If a businessman in a foreign country accumulates hi own currency, is skeptical about his government, and does not wan to lose all interest on his money and pay the price of storing gold, h may well decide that the very best thing he can do with his money i

202

till to buy dollar assets; securities, for example, in United States corporations such as American Telephone & Telegraph Company, or other excellent investment values represented by most of the thirty companies whose stocks are included in the Dow Jones Industrial Average. If it does nothing else, any kind of money crisis will bring plenty of talk on the telephone.

In fact, this buying is what has been happening. The brightest spot in the United States balance-of-payments picture has been the enormous amounts of foreign funds pouring into the United States for investment in the securities of American companies. But this is still no reason to be particularly cheery in the face of all the warnings from leaders of both Pursides and Midases, keening in unaccustomed close harmony about the collapse and disappearance of the entire system.

Martin stated the basic problems as succinctly, authoritatively, and urgently as anyone could. They are all closely related to each other. They exist in all countries, and one country's attempts to deal with them alone are rendered ineffectual to a greater or lesser extent by her position in the international economy. Because of the position of the United States and her dollar as the Atlas of the free-world economic system, our domestic policies have more effect on the international economy than those of any other country. The United States' problems of inflation, of the obligations of the government to its people, of the balance of payments, of domestic budgetary deficits

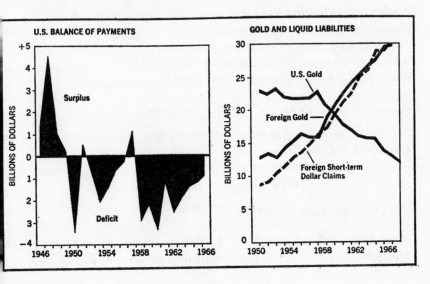

and losses of monetary reserve gold, are the whole world's problem and the everlasting problems that threaten the future of all money.

The dollar is not only the most important currency in the world, it is also the most vulnerable. It is at the same time the strongest, and the weakest.

13

FINE-TUNING OR UNNECESSARY STATIC: DIFFERENT GOVERNMENT ECONOMIC POWER CENTERS TWIDDLING DIFFERENT DIALS ON DIFFERENT SETS TO DIFFERENT TRANSMITTERS SIMULTANEOUSLY

Money is what the state says it is. The state claims the right not only to enforce the dictionary, but also to write the dictionary. The right is claimed by all modern states and has been so claimed for some 4000 years at least.

JOHN MAYNARD KEYNES, *Treatise on Money*

I am a man of principle and one of my first principles is flexibility.

FORMER SENATE MINORITY LEADER
EVERETT MCKINLEY DIRKSEN.

VERBAL INFLATION IN ACTION

Here is the official statement of the basic economic policy of the United States: ". . . It is the continuing policy and responsibility of

204

he Federal Government to use all practicable means consistent with
ts needs and obligations and other essential considerations of na-
ional policy . . . to coordinate and utilize all its plans, functions and
esources for the purpose of creating and maintaining, in a manner
:alculated to foster and promote free competitive enterprise and the
general welfare, conditions under which there will be offered useful
employment opportunities, including self-employment for those able,
willing, and seeking to work, and to promote maximum employment,
production and purchasing power." *

The United States Employment Act of 1946 establishes the "basic
guidelines" of United States economic policy. It is a horrible example
of verbal inflation in action.

To promote "maximum employment" may cause inflation and reduce purchasing power. Promoting "full competitive enterprise"
will not foster the "general welfare" where a public utility is concerned. Laws that fix high dollar levels for minimum wages deprive
the untrained and uneducated of "useful employment opportunities." Right there in the United States Code is express statutory authority for a United States government to do almost anything it
wishes to do, either for the good of the country as a whole or just to
keep getting itself reelected to office, short of installing a Marxist
communist regime, which, presumably, would not "promote free
competitive enterprise." The Employment Act of 1946 embraces so
many different and more or less conflicting economic philosophies
and policy goals that it cancels itself out.

In vote-catching politics it has usually been asserted and assumed
that the Employment Act of 1946 is a mandate for any governmental
policy that assures substantially full employment, regardless of side
effects, even though it may price production out of the market, or
reduce the purchasing power of the dollar through inflation. In the
United States most people regard an unemployment rate of 3½ percent as full employment, and as equivalent to unemployment rates
near zero which prevail in some other countries, as measured by different statistical standards used there.

Careful reading of the Act does not support this exclusive emphasis on "full employment." In the Act "employment," or rather
"maximum employment," is the label for a goal on a parity with

* Employment Act of 1946, effective Feb. 20, 1946, chapter 33, section 2, 60
U.S. Statutes.

205

"production" and "purchasing power." This is the case regardless of whether the adjective "maximum" is read as modifying solely the word "employment" or as modifying also the words "production" and "purchasing power" as well. It makes no difference: Employment, production, and purchasing power are coequals—"employment" does not overbalance the other two. Nor is "maximum employment" the same thing as "full employment," or even the same as "substantially full employment," or the "optimum level of employment." It means only the maximum level of employment consistent with achieving the other two economic objectives. You cannot say "giddap" to one horse in this economic troika and "whoa" to the other two. Indeed, if greater importance should be assigned to one of the three than to the other two, the position of the phrase "purchasing power" as the last in the sentence and paragraph, following "employment" and "production," qualifies it for such import.

Therefore, under a careful reading of the statute, the governmental agencies responsible for maintaining national production and the purchasing power of our money have no statutory mandate to feign helplessness when faced with the problem of taking antiinflationary action that might result in a higher rate of unemployment.

How Many Heads Has the Economic Government?

How does our government operate in the economic sphere under the grab-bag mandate of the Employment Act of 1946? With a government like ours it is not even possible to put one's finger on what the "government" is. Who, or what, is actually in charge of our money? Is it Congress, the President, the Treasury, or the Federal Reserve Board? Or is it the Bureau of the Budget? Or the Defense Department, the State Department, or the Department of Health, Education, and Welfare or of Housing and Urban Development? Whose requirements, and whose restraints ultimately determine the country's economic fate?

While there is no easy answer to this question, the agency which is most conspicuously in charge of what happens to our money, and most effectively isolated from anything that we, the President, Congress, or anyone else can do about it, is the Federal Reserve System.

While economists seem generally to agree that the primary objec-

206

ives of monetary policy are a stable price level, high employment, and a sustainable balance in international payments, there is wide disagreement about how these objectives should be pursued in the day-by-day operations of the central bank.

What's Wrong with the Federal Reserve? Purposes, Policies, or Personnel?

The Federal Reserve can buy and sell securities, raise or lower reserve requirements, set maximum rates that banks can pay on time deposits, and raise or lower the discount rate banks pay when borrowing from Federal Reserve banks. Through manipulation of these instruments, the system influences the rates of growth of bank credit and the money supply, various market interest rates, and the borrowings or free reserves of the member banks. There are wide differences of opinion regarding how well the central bank can control these measures, and even wider differences concerning how these in turn influence the ultimate goals.

The Federal Reserve seems to base its actions on a variety of factors, ranging from the "tone" of the money market and the growth of bank credit to the need to help the Treasury finance the national debt. Growth or contraction of the total money supply has seemed to be an almost accidental result of the actions it has taken.

Does the Federal Reserve really know what it is supposed to be doing? If so, does it know how to do it? If it does, should it not be able to do much better than it does? What is wrong with it, anyway? Purposes, policies, or personnel?

Leaning Against the Wind—When It Is Blowing in the Same Direction

For example, in early 1965, while economic activity was expanding and prices were rising, the Federal Reserve acted vigorously to increase the money supply instead of reducing it. This stimulated business even more. It caused a dramatic new round of price rises and increases in the cost of living.

In early 1966 economic activity declined. The Federal Reserve reduced the money supply sharply at the very time that money rates were getting tight on their own. The result was the 1966 money crunch, when bond interest rates soared to their highest point in generations, housing starts declined dramatically, and a recession threatened.

At the end of 1966, to some extent as a result of these spectacular mistakes, the economy had begun to cool off. The United States Treasury's money managers then suspended the investment tax credit that would have encouraged expansion of production and business by encouraging investment in new plants and equipment. To help out with the "fine tuning," throughout this entire period, the President first suggested, then withdrew the suggestion, and then finally pressed again the proposal for a 10 percent income tax surcharge.

At the time of the Ides of March in money, the inflationary thrust of our economy and the loss of so much of our remaining gold reserves had created an alarming situation. So the President began to press in earnest for passage of the 10 percent tax surcharge as an all-purpose elixir to cut the rate of inflation, reduce the domestic deficit and reverse the deficit in our balance of payments. Congress, on the other hand, insisted on the opposite prescription for the same ailments: a $6 billion cut in budgeted governmental expenditures.

While Congress and the President were wrestling with this double dose of deflation, the Treasury and the Federal Reserve Board were blithely injecting more inflationary adrenalin into the economy. They allowed the money supply to go up by $10 billion to a new high of nearly $187 billion in the two months after the Ides of March of money, an annual rate of increase of 5.6 percent. Later in the year the rate of increase in the money supply approached 10 percent and more, thus increasing the rate of inflation instead of curbing it, while the President and Congress were still trying to make each other swallow the tax surcharge and budget-cut pills. Finally Congress had to choke down the tax surcharge, and the President had to accept the mandated budget cuts in the hope of slowing down the accelerating pace of inflation that the Federal Reserve was fostering by increasing the supply of money so swiftly.

Within its own house at the same time the Federal Reserve was briskly moving in two other separate and mutually contradictory economic directions simultaneously. It raised the banks' rediscount rate, thus raising general interest rates so that there would be less demand by borrowers for loans, and at the same time reduced bank reserve requirements, thus making more money available for banks

208

to lend at the higher rates. The later reduction and still later in-creases in the discount rate to the highest levels seen in years, creating chaos in all bond markets in the Greater Credit Crunch of 1969, are still other striking examples of sour notes in the Federal Reserve's fine tuning.

The Federal Reserve's forecasts and its actions based on them have spectacularly failed in the last four years of the 1960's. The conclu-sion is inescapable that its own fiscal and monetary policies them-selves have been a major source of erratic movements in the economy. Prominent economists who are not connected with the Federal Reserve now ascribe some of the board's mistakes to its failure to appreciate the importance of changes in the money supply in eco-nomic management. Are the good gray gentlemen of the Federal Reserve really just well-meaning dunces?

Many eminent economists who are their peers seem to be saying just that. They are saying that the course of the economy, including the rate of inflation, is largely determined, though with varying time lags, by the rate of growth of the money supply, and that the Federal Reserve Board has demonstrated a failure to understand what the economics of the supply of money are all about.

To the layman who knows about Germany of 1923 and Uruguay of 1968, and has to pay 9 percent for a mortgage (if his bank will let him have one at all), this is as unsettling as if all the professors of physics had started saying that Albert Einstein did not understand the multiplication table.

But economists in a pack are currently crying down all who do not agree that a better understanding by our money managers of money-supply economics would lead to a cure for economic ills. The idea seems simple enough to the layman, who has the smug feeling that the professors have suddenly caught up to where the goldsmith's guild of London was a long time ago. With the change of adminis-trations, the professors of economics have all suddenly jumped off Lord Keynes's investment and spending gravy train and onto Profes-sor Milton Friedman's money-supply monorail.

"Keynes Is Now a Defunct Economist"

Lord Keynes said in effect that the quantity of money did not count, that what influenced economic activity and employment most

209

were private investment and consumer spending. Lord Keynes's complex view was founded on his belief that the Great Depression that began in 1929 occurred *despite* an easy-money policy. But the recent experience of our test-model economy—Britain's—has been otherwise. In spite of the 1967 pound devaluation, cuts in public expenditure, and the "toughest budgets in British history," consumer spending in Britain—the chief source of Britain's balance-of-payments difficulties—hardly declined at all.

The British retail sales index recently stood almost exactly where it had at the time of devaluation, and installment credit stood at almost as high a level. Industrial production was up and so was employment. And the retail price index—the cost of living—had risen more than 5.4 percent in a year. The money supply in Britain grew at an annual rate of about 6½ percent in the first part of 1968, not much lower than the 7¼ percent rate of the 1967 period before the government embarked on its tough tax and spending program; and in the worst recent period the rate of increase was 9.9 percent.

Britain's experience paralleled that of the United States where the tax surcharge and mandated spending cuts similarly failed to curb consumer spending and dampen the inflationary boom for more than a year. The failure of the Keynesian prescription boosted the reputation of the monetary doctors who hold that the outsized growth of the money supply assured continuance of the United States boom.

The British weekly, *The Economist,* recalled that at the end of *The General Theory of Employment, Interest and Money,* Keynes had observed: "Practical men, who believe themselves to be quite exempt from any intellectual influences, are usually the slaves of some defunct economist."

The august publication then concluded: "The piquant situation today is that Keynes himself is now a defunct economist."

To rub it in, the International Monetary Fund, which is Britain's biggest creditor, sought to teach Keynes's disciples the money-supply economics of the "Chicago School" founded by Professor Milton Friedman of the University of Chicago, which strikes at the heart of Keynesianism: The fund sent experts to London to conduct a "joint study" with the British Treasury and the Bank of England of the question of Britain's money supply.

THE SUPPLY OF MONEY IS THE INDEX TO SMOOTHER ECONOMIC MANAGEMENT

In the final chapter of Professor Milton Friedman's and Anna Schwartz's *Monetary History of the U. S.—1867–1960*,* the authors stress the importance of the money supply in determining the level of economic activity. They state that a large part of the 1929 market break and the ensuing Depression could have been averted by a proper monetary policy.

They cite three instances—in 1920, in 1931, and in 1937–1938—when restrictive actions by the Federal Reserve were followed by sharp declines in the indices of economic activity. They also discuss other periods when the evidence of cause and effect is somewhat less conclusive. Their researches showed that the money supply in the United States dropped one-third between 1929 and 1933, not because of unwilling borrowers but because the Federal Reserve had "failed to exercise the responsibilities assigned to it in the Federal Reserve Act to provide liquidity to the banking system."

Professor Friedman showed that the ratio of income to investment spending, the so-called Keynesian multiplier, was less stable and predictable than the turnover or velocity of the money supply, which is defined as demand deposits plus currency in circulation. Thus it was less useful as a short-term forecasting tool. On the other hand, he suggested, proper regulation of the growth of the supply of money, not government-induced employment or tight money, will smooth out the ups and downs of the economic roller coaster we have been riding during recent years.

Essentially, Friedman believes that successful economic growth, over the long pull, depends on a relatively modest, steady, month-by-month increase in the nation's money supply. The increase, according to Friedman, should be held within a yearly range of perhaps 2 or 3 percent, or in unusual circumstances up to 5 percent—just enough to permit healthy economic growth without inflationary strains. That would be a far cry from what has been happening in recent years. In some months of 1968 the nation's money supply increased at annual rates of 10 percent and more, while in some months of 1966, on the other hand, the money supply actually declined.

* Princeton University Press, 1963.

211

Friedman has said that fiscal action, such as the recent tax surcharge, merely "determines what fraction of the nation's income is spent through the government and what fraction is spent by individuals." He concedes that fiscal action can indeed affect interest rates. For example, government borrowing policies may change, but the state of the government budget has no significant effect on income, inflation, deflation, or on cyclical fluctuations of business in general. In short, his argument holds that, to an overwhelming degree, it is the supply of money contained within the total economy that really counts.

Professor Friedman has recently been reported as saying: "The American economy is depression proof, not because of the positive values of fine tuning" but because "we will not for the foreseeable future permit a monetary authority to make the kind of mistake that our monetary authorities made in the Thirties.

"I challenge anybody to go back over the monetary history of the United States and come out with any other conclusion than that the great bulk of the time, you would have been better off with the fixed rule of the steady monetary expansion. You would clearly have avoided all the major mistakes."

One of the best things about Friedman's ideas in contrast to those of Lord Keynes, is that they appeal to the common man's common sense. The forgotten man has always felt that inflation is caused by the government's printing, or permitting the creation of too much paper money. Professorial approval of a simple point like this should embolden us all to speak out more forcefully against the experts when we disagree with what they are doing to the future of our money.

PUNISHING FEDERAL RESERVE BOARD MEMBERS FOR THEIR PECCADILLOES

Some professional economists have charged that the Federal Reserve has not yet bothered to acquire adequate knowledge of how monetary policy affects economic activity. They have said that the Federal Reserve has been deceived lately into thinking it has been following a tight money policy when in fact policy, as measured by the money supply, was "aggressively expansionary."

Congress is also beginning to swing toward Professor Friedman's views. In the future there is likely to be legislation requiring a drastic shift in the way the Federal Reserve now operates, in order to require it to reorient its economic analyses, forecasting, and regulating activities in the direction of money-supply economics.

Some economists have even gone so far as to call for enactment of procedures for identifying and disciplining members of the Board of Governors or subsidiary staff members responsible for egregious and continued breaches of the proposed money-supply rules. Capital punishment did not make the assignats good capital. If economists are going to be put in jails for making inaccurate forecasts, the slump in the public contracting sector of the economy will soon be over.

The impression is abroad that the Federal Reserve tries to pilot us safely through heavy economic weather by the "seat of its pants" while many of the other variables that affect our economic lives are locked into carefully programmed, computer-controlled instrument flying systems, or should be. If the Federal Reserve is still flying blind through the holding patterns of other agencies which influence our economic lives it could be economically fatal for everyone. The "feel of the wind on Lindy's neck" is just not safe enough in the traffic around big airports any more.

TERMS OF THE INTEREST RATE—MONEY SUPPLY TRADE-OFF

Dr. Sherman J. Maisel, a member of the Federal Reserve Board, discussed the terms of the trade-off between controlling interest rates and controlling money supply at a recent University of Michigan seminar:

"An attempt to control growth in the money supply directly through controlling the amount of reserves created runs into the difficulty that in any quantity-price relationship if one controls the quantity tightly, the price must be allowed to move freely and through an extremely wide range. In addition to many other considerations, the problem would have to be faced of what costs and what structural changes the economy would experience if interest rates fluctuated widely as the result of an attempt to control directly a single use of monetary reserves."

The Federal Reserve's practice of moderating interest rate changes does not account for all of the variability in growth of bank credit and money supply. Nevertheless, one of the main arguments of the Federal Reserve authorities against trying to control money-supply growth more closely is that to do so might cause violent and damag-

ing fluctuations in interest rates. Large Treasury borrowing operations of recent years obviously contributed to the excessive growth
of bank credit and money supply. The Federal Reserve's concern
over interest rate effects of Treasury borrowing usually leads it to
follow policies which help stabilize interest rates when the Treasury
is in the market.

SMOOTHING OUT THE MONEY SUPPLY, AND LETTING INTEREST RATES JIGGLE

Using money-market conditions and interest rates as its guide for
open-market operations, the Federal Reserve emphasizes avoidance
of short-run interest rate fluctuations. Because fluctuations of bank
credit and money have been greater than is desirable, however, a
reversal of emphasis is needed. In other words, primary emphasis
should be placed on controlling monetary aggregates and less on
fixing interest rates.

A directive of the Federal Reserve's Open Market Committee
could instruct the manager of the Open Market Account to conduct
operations with a view to achieving a smooth, gradual change in
bank credit or money supply as Professor Friedman has suggested.
A proviso could call for modifying operations if short-run changes
in interest rates exceed some specified range. As experience with
this new strategy accumulated, the range of fluctuation permitted
in the monetary aggregates could be narrowed while the range of
fluctuation of interest rates could be broadened. Thus the public
would gain from a reduction in the real costs of excess variability of
bank credit and money supply, and at the same time it would be
protected against the costs of potentially excessive short-run fluctuations in interest rates.

DIFFERENT BRANCHES OF GOVERNMENT PURSUE CONFLICTING POLICIES SIMULTANEOUSLY—AND SOMETIMES THE SAME BRANCH DOES

From the perspective of the chronic economic crises of the 1960's,
it is possible to view the Federal Reserve's complete independence
as a mixed blessing. The system was useful as the mechanism of
monetary mobilization during total war, both in World War I and
World War II.

214

However, as Eliot Janeway pointed out in *The Economics of Crisis*,*

> In peacetime, on the other hand, the Board's record of monetary management goes a good distance toward sustaining Professor Milton Friedman's argument that no management at all is better than management that the Fed has actually provided. But Friedman's provocative "new laissez-faire" fails as prescription. No political authority can afford to foreswear the use of the monetary lever. Moreover, there is no *a priori* case for holding that any monetary authority must prove incapable of implementing responsible, even though limited, influence over the economy—even if the Federal Reserve has proved so all too often in the past.

THE ULTIMATE RESPONSIBILITY OF THE PRESIDENT AND CONGRESS FOR OUR ECONOMIC LIFE

In broadest terms, and to an increasing extent, our economic life is governed by the action or inaction of the President and Congress, not the Federal Reserve, in raising or lowering taxes and tariffs; adopting and funding health, welfare and poverty programs; and pursuing national security, war, and peace. The scope of and limits upon the things that we can do in any of these economic areas are determined largely by the amount of acceptable money we have with which to do them.

Our economic life is also governed by the action or inaction of the President and Congress in matters that affect other countries, such as changing the price of gold, restricting foreign travel and investment, giving foreign aid to poor nations, and encouraging or discouraging creation of special drawing rights and Eurodollars. The President and Congress are ultimately responsible to the electorate for the success or failure of their policies.

REDUCING THE BALANCE-OF-PAYMENTS DEFICIT

What, for example, can the United States government do to reduce or eliminate the deficit in its balance of international payments?

* Weybright & Talley, 1968.

215

Broadly speaking, it should avoid policies that debase the dollar as a domestic currency. This in turn means adopting some rather hard-headed, down-to-earth, undramatic and unpopular policies. These include somehow making workers and businesses increase domestic technical productivity; making American exporters improve their selling practices and salesmanship abroad; urging foreign governments to reduce discriminatory tariffs, foreign export subsidies, and other discriminations against the dollar; urging other developed nations to give more foreign aid to underdeveloped nations so as to replace the amount we must give, and to pay more of their own expenses for military aid and defense.

Economists also suggest that we could keep our economy depressed at home, eschewing low interest rates needed for expansion and growth, diminishing our demand for imports, and putting pressure on profit margins in export industries and making them hungry to drum up export business. This is the other side of the coin of some of the deliberately inflationary policies our government followed during most of the 1960's: a war carried on without imposition of wage and price controls, and vast public works and poverty programs without responsible provisions for financing the costs by increased taxes.

If the Federal Reserve should decide to operate from a different set of premises and without an awareness of what the government is trying to do, it could frustrate these policies by its own "easy-money" policies. There could also be a depreciation of the dollar relative to other currencies by a unilateral devaluation of the dollar in terms of gold. The Nixon administration finally faced up to the necessity of taking some of these economically important but politically painful decisions. By contrast, the embattled Labour Government of Prime Minister Harold Wilson in Britain had the political courage, born of economic necessity, to take many such tough economic measures, although in the end they may still prove to be unavailing.

The policy of restraint that is necessary for domestic reasons is also needed to protect the deteriorating United States trade balance. A slower-moving economy would ease the growth of imports at the same time as it improved price stability and so strengthened our overall competitive position.

If such a policy of strength is resolutely carried out and if a solu-

216

tion is found for Vietnam—two very big ifs—it is possible to foresee a substantial improvement in the United States balance of payments.

In spite of the basic problems that remain unsolved, and indeed may be worsening, the dollar has remained basically strong on world exchange markets. This was paradoxical at the time when the customary United States trade surplus had vanished. But the difficulties in France that led to the loss of 40 percent of her reserves in a few months reminded investors of the basic instability of Europe when compared with the United States, even with all our troubles. The Soviet move into Czechoslovakia raised additional fears. Serious as its problems were, the United States still looked attractive as a haven for money compared to any other.

Reversals of Psychological Attitudes Toward Preserving the System

A number of other reasons of varying importance explain why the world money system and the position of the dollar within it have survived. The effect of capital controls has been to reduce substantially the outflow of dollars, so dollars are scarcer than they otherwise would be, hence stronger. The final agreement on special drawing rights creates a world monetary reserve mechanism that can supply all the international liquidity that may be needed in years to come without the creation of more foreign-dollar holdings through United States deficits. There have been other striking examples of international monetary cooperation. Most important of all, there has been an improvement in psychological attitudes abroad toward the efforts of the United States to preserve the value of the dollar against inflation.

Fiscal Policy Versus Monetary Policy

In the course of the current debate over economic policy, there is frequent reference to the supposed conflict between fiscal policy, which essentially means the federal government's taxation, budget, and surplus or deficit spending, and monetary policy, which means the Federal Reserve System's expansion or contraction of the commercial banks' lending power. The idea of "conflict" is overstated, because one works through the other. If the government's deficit

217

spending is offset by borrowing from individuals, the inflationary effect is largely negated. If deficit spending is financed through an increase in the commercial banks' holdings of government bonds, the inflationary effect can be offset by Federal Reserve action; and so can a government surplus. In other words, the government's overall policy, including its fiscal policy, is the determinant factor.

The Federal Reserve's open-market operations and its control of reserve requirements should be exercised with a view toward accomplishing the same purposes. This is why the sharp swings in Federal Reserve policy from deflationary to expansionary and back again within short stretches of time have had such confusing and disruptive effects on the economy as a whole.

Fine-Tuning the Federal Reserve in on Everybody Else's Wavelength

The present complete and total independence of the Federal Reserve Board as an all-powerful center of countervailing power may be more of a luxury than we can afford in this new age when all governmental policies are increasingly dependent on sound economic policies and acceptable money.

If some of the Federal Reserve Board's independence is to be preserved, there should be an assurance that in its "fine-tuning" of the economy it is working from the same premises as to current economic conditions, and the same forecasts about future conditions and governmental policy, and changes in policy that will affect those conditions, that the President, the Treasury Department, and Congress are also using. Legislation to require the Federal Reserve Board to coordinate its activities with the Council of Economic Advisers' forecasts, and the economic blueprints made by other agencies, should receive more serious consideration in the future than ever before.

40 Percent Errors in Economic Forecasts Are "Fine-Tuning" to the Authors of the Errors

Statements issued by governmental economic agencies like the Treasury Department and the Federal Reserve Board lay ever greater stress upon how skillfully the agency issuing the statement is man-

218

aging the nation's economy, notwithstanding the inflationary pain the forgotten man may be feeling just then. The favorite phrase of the authors of such self-praise has been "fine-tuning," as used in the expression "fine-tuning the economy." Across the Atlantic, the Whitehall descendants of the ancient seafaring race use the phrase, "touches on the tiller." Despite all the talk of "fine-tuning" we have heard, inflation has proceeded at a faster rate and the dollar has faced more serious threats than ever before in our history.

Economic experts' errors in forecasting the gross national product in the ten years ending in 1964 averaged $10 billion, or approximately 40 percent of the average total annual change. A $10 billion or 40 percent annual error falls short of "fine-tuning" to anyone who is neither tone deaf nor addicted to reading self-composed self-praise. It does not inspire much confidence in government's ability to manage our economic lives.

President Franklin D. Roosevelt boasted that "we planned it that way," when things turned out well. When taking in such pronouncements by government officials throughout the future of money, it is just as well to keep in mind that all governmental economic manipulation, whatever the relationship between its intended effect and its actual effect, is self-applauded as "fine-tuning," and that governmental standards are so low that an annual error no worse than 40 percent is a better-than-average performance.

There is a lesson in this. While the dollar purports to be managed by experts with economic views, it is still in the broadest view managed by politicians for political purposes. Even the members of the Federal Reserve Board read the election returns. The object of politics is to win victories in elections, and keep the party in power in power. The chief attraction of the gold standard as a factor in regulating our money is that gold, although scarce in the ground, is not continually trying to elect itself to office.

Capitalism itself developed during the centuries when gold from the Spanish New World was raising prices, not because anyone planned it that way but simply because the monetary systems of the world used to consist of precious metals, and the New World Columbus accidentally discovered turned out to be rich in gold. If free national governments such as ours do such a bad job of preserving the integrity of their money, if indeed by their very nature and the nature of their voters they cannot do a good job, would it not be better to have some impersonal force, such as gold, the old international gold standard, help them with part of the job?

The elected and appointed managers of our national economic affairs have so far not done measurably better than the gold standard did, and their "mistakes" seem to be growing worse year by year. If for various reasons gold should no longer be counted on to do the whole regulatory job, there remains a strong argument for at least permitting central bankers and international public servants, instead of national politicians alone, to take a larger part in the regulation of our economic affairs with a view to the best interests of the world at large, not just our country alone. The whole world would suffer if Atlas collapsed, so it has an interest in Atlas' health. At least the International Monetary Fund managers do not have the same immediate, direct, personal interest that our Congressmen and Presidents and other national economic officials have in winning reappointments or running for election every two, four, or six years. For the first time in 4000 years, the modern sovereign state should consider sharing its right to write the dictionary of money with the international monetary managers. With the final ratification of special drawing rights, we will have taken a small but significant step in that direction.

14

SPECIAL DRAWING RIGHTS ARE LIKE ZEBRAS—THEY ARE A BLACK ANIMAL WITH WHITE STRIPES OR A WHITE ANIMAL WITH BLACK STRIPES

After Keynes' Treatise on Probability was published, Keynes was having dinner with Professor Max Planck, the mathematical genius responsible for the development of quantum mechanics, one of the more bewildering achievements of the human mind. Planck turned to Keynes and told him that he had once considered going into economics himself. But he had decided against it—it was too hard. Keynes repeated the story with relish to a friend back at Cambridge. "Why, that's odd," said the friend, "Bertrand Russell was telling me just the other day that he'd also thought about going into economics. But he decided it was too easy."

—ROBERT L. HEILBRONER

OVERDRAFTS? NEVER! BUT SPECIAL DRAWING RIGHTS? THE BIGGER THE BETTER!

During many years of peacetime international monetary conferences, various ways to salvage Lord Keynes's old Bretton Woods proposal for an International Clearing Union were eagerly explored, particularly by countries in deficit in their foreign trade balances, or low in gold reserves.

As it became a deficit country in its gold exchange and foreign trade obligations, the United States' pious disapproval of Keynes's Bretton Woods plan for international reserves based on "overdrafts" gave way to active support for the adoption of special drawing rights (SDR's) on the International Monetary Fund for all fund members, at the earliest possible date, and in the largest possible amounts.

221

An Honorary Degree in Monetary Architecture: SDR

In September 1967, the governors of the International Monetary Fund met in Rio de Janeiro with more fanfare than usual and voted for the creation of "special drawing rights," this mysterious something also called SDR's and "paper gold," and in September of 1969 the necessary amendments for the articles of agreement of the International Monetary Fund were formally ratified.

Special drawing rights will be a pool of monetary reserves in the International Monetary Fund that will become available to participating member governments as decided by the fund. But the units making up this pool, or quantum, will differ from units making up ordinary drawing rights in the fund, which are like loans or credits and must be repaid. "Special drawing rights" will have a continuing international life of their own, unless and until extinguished by fund decision. The decision-making process to create or extinguish units will be formal, with the safeguard against creating excessive SDR's resting in the requirement of approval by 85 percent of the fund's accredited voting power.

Members will be free to use these rights without conditions as to their own monetary and fiscal policies, but the expected use will be to meet balance-of-payments problems. Transfers of ownership must be effected through the fund's facilities.

The value of the SDR's will rest on the obligation of every participant to accept them when transferred through the fund, subject only to the qualification that no member will be required to hold rights in excess of 300 percent of her cumulative allocation. To provide continuity with present monetary arrangements, the SDR's are to have a unit value expressed in terms of a weight of gold.

Each participant country will be obligated to maintain holdings of SDR's equal on the average to at least 30 percent of her cumulative allocation. This will mean that if use of special drawing rights causes a member's holding to fall below 30 percent, the member will be obligated to reconstitute her holding to equal a moving average of 30 percent within a specified time span.

What this means is that Chile, for example, with a balance-of-payments deficit, would present her SDR's to another nation with a surplus, say Germany, and get deutsche marks. Chile could then use the deutschemarks to buy dollars for intervention in the foreign exchange markets to support the escudo. Chile would thus be preserving the exchange rate of her currency, and her foreign trade would go on—at least to the point where Chile had used up more than 70 percent of her SDR's and her other reserves as well and had to devalue the escudo.

SDR's Cannot Disappear into Swiss Accounts

. Thus, in effect, only 30 percent of the assets have to be repaid. SDR's really do look more like money than credits. They are strictly a bookkeeping entry at international banking levels and will not wind up in anyone's pocket. They will remain within the closed · international monetary system, and unlike gold they cannot disap-pear into any individual's private cave or cavity. The essential feature of SDR's is that each participant country is solemnly bound to accept the new asset when it is presented and to pledge convertible currency in return. Special drawing rights are thus backed by the world gold and currency reserve.

The process seems intricate, but the underlying point is simple: While they last, SDR's will be reserves like gold. Being deliberately created, they will reflect a collective decision by the nations on the amount of global growth that is needed, with each decision to create more reserves requiring an 85 percent "weighted" vote of the fund members, with the weights being based on existing fund quotas. By voting to increase special drawing rights, member nations can in effect, replace all the gold that they lost through the London gold pool in the last frantic weeks before the Ides of March of money. International trade and business thus need not decline for lack of gold reserves.

Remission of Past Balance-of-Payments Sins for a Present "Statements Equilibrium"

It seems significant for the future, however, that the way voting power has been allocated gives the Common Market countries, voting as a bloc, more than 15 percent of the voting power, and thus veto power over any increase in the amount of SDR's, and all other major decisions. The United States and Britain have retained a veto power over any decision to change the price of gold.

When she was still the dominant Common Market country before the strikes of May and June 1968, France was reluctant to join the other countries in approving special drawing rights. One reason was

223

that France felt the fundamental problems of the United States' equilibrium in balance of payments had not been solved.

The French objected that the United States had escaped the discipline of having to settle her foreign-trade deficit in gold, like other countries, because other countries were willing to hold United States dollars in place of gold. Although the activation of SDR's was not directly tied to elimination of the United States' payments deficit, one of the conditions for activating them was that the United States show "statements equilibrium" in her foreign trade—that is, an equilibrium in current foreign-trade statements, rather than any quantitative improvement of the United States' balance-of-payment deficit.

According to the agreement finally reached, the fund agreed to distribute a total of $9.5 billion in SDR's over a period of three years starting in 1970, $3.5 billion the first year, and $3 billion each succeeding year. The three-year total represents about one fourth of the world's monetary reserves of gold. The United States has the largest quota and will be allotted more than $800 million the first year and more than $2 billion over the whole three-year distribution period. The ten richest free world countries, or "Group of Ten," are allocated about 60 percent of the total and all the other members of the fund the remaining 40 percent. Of each $1 billion activated, the United States would receive about $246 million, and the Common Market countries as a group about $170 million.

Controversy remains over whether SDR's are really newly created money, as the United States argues, or merely credit, as France has insisted, although less vigorously as her own gold and dollar reserves have continued to fall.

Othmar Emminger, Vice Chairman of the West German Bundesbank, joked that the new assets are really zebras. "One can say they are a black animal with white stripes and another can say they are a white animal with black stripes."

A POULTICE FOR THE PAINFUL THOUGHT OF THE VALUE OF HIS MONEY BLEEDING AWAY

Our old friend C. V. Myers, in an apocalyptic vision expresses the most serious criticism of SDR's: The likelihood that their activation will lead to further expectations of inflation on the part of the forgotten man. According to Mr. Myers:

224

SDR's, if consummated on any usable scale, would bring on a WORLD-WIDE galloping cancer of inflation which could only end in total economic collapse for *all* the free world. WHY?

Because no government anywhere can *legislate* trust. When people see money depreciating at a fast rate they flee from money into something real—land, cars, boats, clothes, buildings—gold, silver. The last two in the end become preferred because they are easily exchangeable for any of the others at a moment's notice.

That's where we are now. That's why the whole situation is breaking down and that money jitters grips all of Europe.

So you pick it—What's going to happen?

(1) Increased gold price and deflation.
(2) Demonetized gold and financial ruin for the gold reserve countries.
(3) Two rival money blocs, one gold and one paper.
(4) SDR's and world-wide inflation and the eventual destruction of all world currencies.

But if the International Monetary Fund acquires and asserts the power to impose strictures on the domestic economies of member countries whose currency inflates excessively, or whose foreign-trade balance is in deficit, as it did with Britain in 1969, there may be at least some basis for arguing with the forgotten man that the creation of SDR's is not a one-way inflationary street.

The economic interests of countries with reserves of dollars in their banks who do not want to see them depreciated by domestically popular inflationary policies in the United States, may exercise their voting power in the fund to deny SDR's to countries which do not pursue deflationary domestic policies, as they denied further fund access to Britain. A realization of the existence of this power to impose sanctions may whip the forgotten American's latent xenophobia into a lather, but at the same time quietly put a poultice on his pained apprehension that all the value of his money is going to bleed away under the aegis of such a "foreign power."

FOREIGN VETO POWER OVER POPULAR DOMESTIC PROFLIGACY

As just noted, a veto power is given to the Common Market countries voting as a bloc, which they do not have under the present International Monetary Fund articles. At present, increases in IMF quotas require an 80 percent weighted vote, while the creation of more special drawing rights requires an 85 percent vote, giving the Common Market countries, which have just over 15 percent of the voting power, a power to veto creation of new rights. Any other relatively small bloc of votes adding up to 15 percent or more could also create a veto power in such a bloc. Some experts have compared the veto power granted to the Common Market countries in the creation of special drawing rights to the veto power that has paralyzed the functioning of the Security Council of the United Nations.

Another criticism involves the fact that there is little pressure on countries that run balance-of-payments surpluses to reduce the surpluses, in order to aid deficit countries in wiping out their deficits and bringing their payments into balance. However, when a country is designated a surplus country by the fund it must undertake to accept up to twice the amount of its own SDR allotment in SDR's from other countries.

The United States, as a deficit country, should be able to settle payments either by selling gold or by borrowing currencies of surplus nations from the International Monetary Fund. If the fund were short of the currencies the United States needs, the United States should be able to borrow them from the surplus countries concerned. And if a surplus country refused to lend, it should be made subject to "scarce-currency" provisions and forced to supply currencies or take other action to reduce its balance-of-payments surpluses.

"Current-Account" Convertibility Replacing full Gold
Convertibility

Closely related to adoption of special drawing rights would be adoption of "current-account" convertibility for the dollar. This would give the dollar the same status that all other major currencies have, but take away its present unique status. This means that the United States would defend the international value of the dollar in terms of other countries' currencies, instead of in terms of gold as is done now. Before putting such current-account convertibility into effect, the Treasury would have to acquire large amounts of foreign currencies so as to be able to provide a meaningful defense to the dollar against other currencies. The network of reciprocal lines of credit between the United States Federal Reserve Bank and foreign central

Assuming that the Board of Governors has, by the necessary 85 percent majority, taken the decision to activate the scheme and that for the first basic period an amount of SDRs equivalent to $1,000 million a year is to be allocated and assuming that all member countries join the scheme, the allocations of SDRs to the various major countries, on the basis of their existing IMF quotas, will be as follows:

Country	$ million
Australia	24
Belgium	20
Canada	35
France	47
Germany	57
India	36
Italy	30
Japan	35
Netherlands	25
Sweden	10
United Kingdom	116
United States	246
All other countries	319
	1,000

banks, which are known as the "swaps" arrangements, are an example of the type of arrangement that could be used to foster such current account convertibility for the dollar.

There would no doubt be a loss of prestige for the United States in this, because the United States would be abandoning even the myth of straight dollar convertibility into gold. There would also be a further shift of international financial power from the United States toward the International Monetary Fund. But this would tend to activate the fund to perform some of the functions now being carried out by the United States, at least in theory, as the one residual buyer and seller of gold. Gold at the present official price of $35 an ounce would remain an important international monetary medium because fund members could convert it on demand into currencies at the fund at parity for other currencies, and the fund could, if needed, likewise convert its gold into members' currencies on demand.

The crucial difference is that the International Monetary Fund under present rules cannot be compelled to sell gold if it does not wish to do so. The new plan proposed here would not materially change the two gold markets that exist now, in which the official price is the present $35 an ounce price, or a higher official price, and the private market price remains free to fluctuate.

If this plan were adopted there would really be no reason why the official price of gold should not be allowed to rise from its present official price of $35 an ounce. This would be a recognition of the increased costs of mining gold due to inflation, as well as the increased demand for gold in industrial, jewelry, dental, and other modern applications, entirely apart from its use in the monetary system. Within this new framework, the recognition of the demands of the Pursides that the price of gold be raised would, paradoxically, at the same time be removing the world money system one step further away from dependence on gold as the one basic reserve element in its purse.

15

EURODOLLARS ARE YOUR OLD DOLLARS ON THE GRAND TOUR—AND RETURNING AT INTERESTING RATES

*I know of no country, indeed, where the love
of money has taken stronger hold on the
affections of men.*

ALEXIS DE TOCQUEVILLE,
Democracy in America

The addition to the dollar amount of the world's monetary reserves which the mountainous labors of the world's leading economic architects over a quarter of a century have brought forth in the form of special drawing rights is modest, if not mouse sized, compared to the huge additions to world monetary liquidity which have "just growed" in the form of Eurodollars.

While economists and government officials have been struggling to create special drawing rights as a bookkeeping entry on the books of the International Monetary Fund, private businessmen and bankers, without governmental help, or much governmental hindrance or even notice, have been inventing and constantly expanding new uses of Eurodollars and Asiadollars and other forms of truly international money. In this way they have quietly solved many of the basic problems involved in creating new forms of international liquidity, and a single, universally acceptable world-wide currency as well.

WHEN THE DOLLAR DEPARTS THE INTEREST IS INTERESTING INDEED

Although historically there are many precedents for banks in one country accepting deposits denominated in terms of the currency of another country, the huge increase in Eurodollar deposits starting in 1957 was really something new under the sun.

Eurodollars are simple in their creation and can be adapted to an infinite variety of uses. Let us assume that a citizen or a business organization in a foreign country wants to invest some dollars at the

229

recent 9 percent or higher Eurodollar rate. He deposits dollars in a foreign bank, or the foreign branch of an American bank, which pays the going rate for them.

Thus Eurodollars start out simply as United States dollars deposited with banks outside the United States. They are deposits in the denomination of dollars in a country other than the United States. Technically, of course, the term is not strictly correct, because not all "Eurodollar" deposits are deposited in Europe. Many are in dollars in Japan, and many Eurodollar deposits have originated through deposits of dollars in Canada that have been reloaned to European banks. Similar markets exist in European countries; for example, sterling deposits in French banks are called Eurosterling deposits.

Eurodollar transactions usually consist of transactions between bankers, and business is in large amounts, the usual unit being $1 million, although items of $500,000 and $250,000 also frequently change hands.

$30 Billion Worth of Worldwide Money

Once the foreign bank has acquired the dollar deposit, the foreign bank uses it directly, or perhaps converts it into another currency, for lending to a nonbank customer, perhaps after one or more redeposits from one bank to another; or if the deposit was with a foreign branch of a United States bank, it may be sent back to the head office of the bank in New York.

Eurodollars are not a special category of dollars. They are just ordinary dollars interchangeable with other dollars in the United States. There is no separate exchange rate, as distinct from interest rate, for Eurodollars.

Eurodollar deposits began as the result of the prolonged American balance-of-payments deficit. Central banks, such as the Bank of England, would accumulate dollar balances and redeposit some of them in Europe instead of in the United States where interest rates were lower. The foreign holders of dollars did not want to get rid of the dollars, but they desired to obtain higher interest rates on their dollars than they could find in the United States. By 1962, European central banks, treasuries, and official international institutions such as the International Monetary Fund and the

Bank for International Settlements as well, had placed dollar deposits of their own funds amounting to some $2 billion in Europe. These official funds represented about two-thirds of the total Eurodollar deposits at that time.

Nobody knows the total of Eurodollars now available, but responsible estimates have recently placed the figure somewhere above $30 billion.

An International Money Beyond National Regulation

On the practical side, borrowers in Europe often find it more convenient to use Eurodollars than to borrow dollars from a New York bank. For a foreigner, negotiation of a large credit in New York is apt to be a slow and cumbersome process, in which the borrower may be required to state the purpose for the credit and the lender has to decide whether it is a sound purpose. On the Eurodollar market he can often raise the credit in a matter of minutes with no questions asked. The credit obtainable from New York might, for example, be for three months, possibly with one renewal; in the Eurodollar market, a deposit for six months is easily obtainable, and the borrower may safely rely on being able to renew the deposit or borrow a similar amount again and again.

American multinational corporations have floated large issues of bonds in the European market to finance their European subsidiaries and associated European companies. Purchases of these Eurobonds are financed to a great extent by the use of Eurodollars in Eurodollar accounts and lead to creation of more Eurodollars. An American company that raises $50 million on a fifteen-year Eurobond usually does not use all of the money it has raised immediately, and what it does not use it places in the Eurodollar market to earn interest at a higher rate than it could obtain in New York.

In some ways, Eurodollars are better than ordinary domestic United States dollars themselves. Money, like water, tends to seek its own level. United States banks have been turning increasingly to Eurodollars to finance their domestic needs in the United States. By borrowing from their branches abroad, sometimes at interest rates as high as 13 percent, the larger United States banks have been able to raise funds for use in the United States during times when money was tight or not available in the United States itself.

231

In so doing, they were avoiding—in completely legal fashion —United States regulations that prohibit payment of interest on demand deposits, that set the maximum interest rates that banks may pay depositors, that require banks to hold a fixed percentage of re serves against their deposits, and that require banks to pay premiums to the Federal Deposit Insurance Corporation.

All this they accomplished by the simple expedient of having their foreign branches, chiefly those in London, bid for the funds and then simply relend the funds back to their head offices in the United States. The foreign branches are largely exempt from American bank ing regulations, and their loans to their head offices do not fall within the definition (and hence the reserve regulation) of "deposits' in the United States.

Linking All Countries' Interest Rate Structures

Interest rates on Eurodollar deposits have been outside the control of United States authorities and of American banks. Consequently they have reached their own levels abroad, independent of the re spective policies pursued by the banks and the monetary authorities of the country (the United States) whose currency was used. This is the chief theoretical significance of the device.

The strong pull that the big American banks have been exerting on the Eurodollar market has been a major factor in shifting the United States balance of payments—as measured by transactions in official reserves—into "heavy surplus" during some recent periods, thus strengthening for a time at least, and in a sense quite artificially, the balance-of-payments position of the dollar. At the same time, the fact that American banks have been bidding aggressively for funds in Europe has tended to transmit the effects of tight money in the United States to money centers abroad and has forced the Federal Reserve authorities to judge the repercussions of their actions on a far wider tapestry than ever before.

Building Eurodollar Balances Through Worse and Better Payments Deficits

Some experts contend that the Eurodollar market will eventually shrink when the special reasons for its existence disappear. Such

easons include the contraction or disappearance of interest differen-
ials between London and New York to such an extent that the dif-
erence would not permit the Eurodollar market to work properly, or
emoval of British and American restrictions on foreign investment
nd trade, which now make it desirable to keep dollar funds in Eu-
ope to finance investment and trade there.

An improvement of the American balance of payments might re-
luce the volume of foreign-dollar deposits available. But such an im-
rovement would not seriously affect it, because if this happened,
he worldwide strengthening of confidence in the dollar would pre-
umably attract more funds into Eurodollars, ranging all the way
rom speculative "hot money" to official reserves. In any case, as we
ave noted many times before, foreign-held, short-term paper dollars
ow amount to about $41 billion, and only a portion of this sum is
ow employed in the Eurodollar market. So some reduction in the
otal of foreign-held dollars would not necessarily affect the amount
vailable as Eurodollars for a long time to come.

A further deterioration in the United States balance-of-payments
osition would not bring the Eurodollar market to an end either.
Higher rates would still attract deposits to Europe in spite of the
ncrease in the cost of covering the exchange risk. Borrowers who
eeded Eurodollars for commercial requirements could afford to pay
he higher rates, because they would have the benefit of a discount on
"forward" dollars, which they would buy as a hedge to protect them-
elves. Nothing short of a sweeping dollar scare that would induce
many holders of Eurodollars to sell them rather than lend out the
leposits would seriously affect the volume of Eurodollars available
o the Eurodollar market.

The most serious thing that could happen to the Eurodollar
market would be large-scale defaults. The Soviet government and
ther communist-bloc countries, it is reported, have made large,
ong-term borrowings in Eurodollar funds through intermediaries in
ountries such as Switzerland. It is also understood that the communist bloc countries lend in the Eurodollar market, but usually
or short terms, shorter than their long-term borrowings. If a communist country should collect its short-term lendings and default on
ts long-term borrowings, for whatever reason, there would of course
be a serious crisis in the Eurodollar market.

233

A Green Thumb on the Invisible Hand

So Eurodollars have come full circle. Their existence and availa
bility has increased the total of international reserves available tc
finance world trade. Their development has taken much of the pres
sure off gold as a medium for settling foreign trade accounts, and
lessened the urgency of creating special drawing rights as well. Their
widespread use and acceptability have made the dollar a de factc
world currency. They have linked the economies of the United States
and the other developed countries more tightly together than even
before.

They furnish a textbook example of the historic tendency of the
world money system to work out ingenious practical solutions tc
practical problems in a pragmatic way, long before the economists
and monetary officials have accurately identified the problems on
produced a theoretical model of the system after the fact.

Laying a Regulatory Hand on the Worldollar

Much as the International Monetary Fund represents the institu
tional or organizational approach to arranging monetary practice
among the nations of the free world, the Eurodollar market rep
resents something that "just growed" out of the ingenuity of business
men and bankers in various countries. In its way it is as remarkable
an international institution as is the International Monetary Fund. It
represents an important step toward overcoming the national barriers
that divide the international financial system into separate compart
ments.

Adam Smith himself would have enjoyed the free play of the
market forces involved in the fixing of international interest rates in
an international money market in Eurodollar funds. Flexible na
tional interest rates tend to ensure the balancing of credit supply and
demand in national economies. Flexible international interest rates
perform the same task in the international economy through the in
ternational medium of Eurodollar deposits and Eurodollar bonds.

When a European country supplies dollars to the Eurodollar
market, she loses the dollars, which become a debit so far as her
balance of payments is concerned. When such a capital movement
occurs, the nation losing the dollars also loses a basis for home credit.

The central bank of that country faces the choice of placing new money into the domestic market or letting her money market tighten and forcing her businessmen and foreign traders to pay higher interest rates. Imported deflation resulting from dollar losses replaces the imported inflation previously created by dollar gains. After all, dollars are freely convertible into home currencies, and in many countries home currencies are freely convertible into dollars. In the process the central bank gains or loses reserves.

Many foreign central bankers have been calling for restrictive Federal action to stem these dollar drains. At the same time the Federal Reserve itself has begun to regard the nonregulated pool of Eurodollar funds that domestic banks were able to obtain as frustrating the purposes of tight money policies in the domestic economy.

Since "borrowings" of Eurodollars from foreign branches is a way banks with foreign branches can cushion themselves, for a time, from the effects of restrictive Federal Reserve policy, the easy way out would be for the Federal Reserve to restrict such borrowings. But, after all, the Eurodollars that are brought back are foreign dollar deposits in the United States of foreign banks, or American banks' foreign branches. As dollar deposits originating in the United States they will have already been made subject to United States reserve requirements once. To put additional reserve requirements on Eurodollars brought back to the United States would, in a sense, be subjecting the same dollars to reserve requirements twice.

From another point of view, the problem is one solely for the foreign central banks, not the Federal Reserve. The foreign central banks may either offset the drains or prevent their nationals from having access to the Eurodollar market; and, indeed, some have done so.

Notwithstanding these arguments, Andrew F. Brimmer, a member of the Federal Reserve Board, offered a sweeping proposal that would have applied reserve requirements directly to Eurodollars borrowed by United States banks.

Apparently this was just a trial balloon that the Federal Reserve shot down a little later by offering a much more limited proposal. Specifically, the board adopted regulations that would prevent a member commercial bank from deducting from demand deposits—for the purpose of computing required reserves—any "cash items in process of collection" or "balances due from other banks" when these involve any account with or in a foreign branch of the member bank

International Monetary Fund Worldollar Regulation: Taking the Fun out of Fundollars

In Eurodollars we have an international money market with structure of international interest rates that has been created without the conscious intervention of any particular national or international governmental body, legislature or official. The conflict concerning Eurodollars and their uses and regulation, which has now arisen between the United States Federal Reserve on the one hand and the European central bankers on the other, makes it clear that international monetary authorities should now undertake to supervise the Eurodollar market. This is an evolutionary process roughly comparable to the way national monetary authorities have come to regulate national money markets—as the Federal Reserve Board regulates the money market in the United States. The International Monetary Fund is the obvious authority for this purpose, although in some ways the Bank for International Settlements might be a more suitable agency because it has had direct experience in dealing in Eurocurrencies, and, in Basel, it is geographically closer to their markets than is the International Monetary Fund in Washington.

Whatever the agency is, it should intervene to regulate trends in the Eurodollar market in the broad interests of all members of the fund. Such an arrangement would be the rudimentary beginning of a worldwide monetary policy that might be far more flexible and comprehensive than the laborious efforts to create modest additions to official world monetary reserves through special drawing rights. A comprehensible system for regulating the international money market in Eurodollars would also be one more long step toward making the United States dollar a true one-world money, or Fundollar or Worldollar.

16

RETURNING TO GOLD AND TAKING LEAVE OF IT AGAIN, WITHOUT GETTING NAILED TO THE CROSS OF GOLD

You shall not press down upon the brow of labor this crown of thorn. You shall not crucify mankind upon a cross of gold.
WILLIAM JENNINGS BRYAN,
DEMOCRATIC NATIONAL CONVENTION, 1896.

On the same day the President seeks to raise the price of gold without congressional approval, I will initiate impeachment proceedings.
DEMOCRATIC CONGRESSMAN
HENRY REUSS OF WISCONSIN

MONEY AS THE FORMER INDEX TO A NATION'S FATE

Money tells much about a nation's character because it is woven so tightly into national history, psychology, and destiny. Ever since stone Age men began bartering with furs, and the ancient Lydians introduced metal money, dominant nations have risen to power through their ability to create and maintain a stable, widely accepted currency.

Ancient Athens owed much of her glory to her money. After Solon drastically devalued the drachma in 594 B.C., it became the standard medium of trade throughout the Mediterranean, and helped carry Greek commerce and culture deep into Asia. Constantinople was able to dominate much of the world for centuries, not through military, intellectual, moral, or religious superiority, but because she had a solid, incorruptible currency. In the 16th and 17th centuries, as her explorers brought back gold and silver from colonies in the New World, Spain enjoyed her "Golden Age," and produced Cervantes, El Greco, and Velázquez.

With almost no natural resources, countries such as ancient Phoenicia and modern Switzerland have prospered because their people

mastered the mysteries of trading, banking, and handling money
Britain rose to power by making the most of what money and com
merce she had and using a shrewd combination of prudence and
daring. With her stockholder's share of Sir Francis Drake's voyage of
the *Golden Hind,* Queen Elizabeth paid off all of England's foreign
debts, balanced the national budget, and invested abroad a sum large
enough, at compound interest, to account for Britain's entire over
seas wealth in 1930.

But paying for two world wars forced Britain to sell off most of
those foreign investments, and meeting her obligations to other
countries and to international monetary agencies ever since has
wrung out of Britain most of what remained, leaving foreign-held
claims on her reserves of $10 billion or so.

In today's world nations are still politically sovereign but their
currencies and economies are not. They are tightly linked by fixed
exchange rates and by international interest rates established by flow
of Eurodollar and Eurosterling deposits. Today these persuasive his
torical precedents for national monetary hegemony are no longer ap
plicable, but their persuasive power makes them a serious obstacle to
the creation of one stable, universally acceptable worldwide money

Devaluation: A Painless Panacea for Monetary Ills, but Better than a Bloodletting

Throughout history, national rulers and sovereign government
unable to solve their money problems any other way have resorted
to devaluation. Economically speaking, ancient Rome was founded
on the exploitation of colonial areas and the plunder of enemies. As
an empire, Rome lacked the manufacturing, agriculture, and com
merce to pay for her costly imports, so she began to debase the denar
ius under Nero, A.D. 54–68. Rome had developed but failed to recog
nize balance-of-payments problems. Trajan added copper to the once
99 percent pure silver denarius, and the coin eventually became
wholly base metal. A hundred years before Alaric sacked Rome in
410 A.D., Roman money had lost its purchasing power and Rome her
self had lost the wherewithal to resist the barbarians at her borders.

Only 8 of the world's 120 currencies have survived the period since
the end of World War II without a formal devaluation: the United
States, Cuba, Ethiopia, Haiti, Honduras, Liberia, Panama, and E

Salvador. Since the beginning of 1949, Chile has devalued more than forty-six times, Brazil thirty-six, Uruguay twenty, South Korea seventeen. The Soviet Union has lowered the value of her ruble three times since World War II, not so much because of external pressures but to reduce domestic purchasing power.

The persistence of the idea that unilateral national devaluation of the currency is a painless panacea for a nation's economic ills is a second outdated precedent that remains a serious obstacle to the creation of a stable, worldwide money system.

In 190-plus years of history the United States has formally devalued the dollar in terms of gold only once. President Roosevelt closed the banks in March 1933, declared a gold embargo, and two months later Congress authorized him to devalue the dollar by as much as 50 percent. On January 31, 1934, the official price of gold was increased from $20.67 to $35 an ounce, a devaluation of the dollar of 40.94 percent. Concurrently, domestic gold ownership was forbidden to citizens. The principal reason advanced for the devaluation was to increase domestic farm prices during the middle of the Depression. This objective failed spectacularly, and farm prices kept right on going down. Dollar devaluation did cause a chain reaction of competing devaluations in other countries, more worldwide trade restrictions, and increased tariffs aimed at preserving local jobs and favorable balances of payments. It contributed materially to the devastation of worldwide trade, which fell 57 percent between 1929 and 1936. The worldwide economic depression continued throughout almost the whole decade of the 1930's. Devaluing the dollar in terms of gold brought no relief from the Depression; if anything it made it worse and prolonged it.

Not only has that devaluation come to be regarded as a failure because it did not accomplish any significant national economic purposes, but it has also come to be regarded in Congress with moral opprobrium as the greatest capitalist nation's dishonorable repudiation of a solemn immutable pledge to the other countries of the world in an important business matter. The idea that a reduction in the value of a currency in terms of gold may be all right for other countries, but unthinkable for the United States—indeed, as something unworthy of our honor—is a third serious obstacle to useful changes in the worldwide money system, and establishment of a worldwide money.

The "Gentleman's Agreement" Not to Change the Gold Value of the Dollar

Presidents Kennedy, Johnson, and Nixon, Secretaries of the Treasury Fowler, Barr, and Kennedy, and William McChesney Martin as well, have issued innumerable public assurances that the United States would not alter the gold value of the dollar.

The willingness of foreign central banks and private individuals to hold paper-dollar balances in excess of normal requirements to the point where they now hold about $41 billion or so in paper-dollar balances, or more than three times the United States' supply of gold at the present price, has rested mostly on this "gentleman's agreement" that the dollar would not be devalued. Such an unwritten agreement is probably the most difficult kind for a nation such as ours to repudiate.

It is perfectly arguable that if the United States should devalue the dollar in terms of gold by, say, doubling the official price of gold to $70 an ounce, she should pay to the foreign governments and central banks that had continued to hold paper dollars instead of exchanging them for gold, the difference between $35 and $70 in paper-dollar currency. This would compensate them for holding the paper instead of obtaining the gold in reliance upon these assurances, when otherwise they would have turned in the paper for the gold. In rebuttal, it may be argued that no compensation of this kind would be legally or morally required at all because in terms of purchasing power, of what the paper dollars they held would buy in the United States market (other than gold itself), the value of the foreign paper-dollar holdings would not be changed at all by raising the dollar price of gold.

The Dollar Is Stronger than Gold, but People Doubt That We Can Handle Our Own Affairs

Alfred Hayes, President of the Federal Reserve Bank of New York and Vice Chairman of the Federal Reserve's Open Market Committee, the top policymaking group of the Federal Reserve System, has, like his colleagues, firmly opposed increasing the dollar price of gold. During a meeting of international bankers at the Bank for International Settlements, commenting on various plans for a single sizable ncrease in the price of gold, for small annual changes in the gold price, or for an embargo on gold sales by the United States Treasury, ıe said: "In my judgment, any of these moves would have disastrous esults in and of themselves. None of them would provide a solution o the crying need for the elimination of the United States payments leficit. The answer for the United States lies rather in getting back o the serious task of balance-of-payments adjustment."

He pointed out that the dollar had acquired its role as "the major eserve currency" through "the free choice of monetary authorities." This element of free choice," he went on, "cannot and should not ɔe forgotten, for a currency can continue to serve as an international eserve asset only so long as the holders have confidence in the policy ɔf the country whose currency it is."

William McChesney Martin has said, "The dollar is stronger than ʒold, but like it or not, the world no longer has the confidence in he dollar that it once had. People doubt that we can handle our own ıffairs. I think it's barbarous to think that we haven't got the intelligence to manage our economy so that we have to depend on a netal—this barbarous metal. This country cannot just go on inlefinitely relying on gold."

Henry H. Fowler, former Secretary of the Treasury, who had gone ɔut of his way to give the British pound a rousing vote of confidence ust a few days before it had been devalued in November 1967, ıverred that the two-tier gold system that had been adopted on the ollowing Ides of March "will endure for decades." His Undersecreary, Frederick L. Deming, warming to the same theme, outstripped ıis boss, predicting that it would last " 'til Hell freezes over."

The Midases such as Hayes at the levers of our national economic ʒstablishment are ahead of the Pursides on points, but a few of the ranking brass sometimes flash gold epaulets. In guarded terms Dr. Arthur Burns, who headed the Council of Economic Advisors during the first four years of the Eisenhower Administration and now serves ıs Chairman of the Federal Reserve Board, and Professor Paul A. Samuelson, a distinguished economist and an adviser to President Kennedy, have both publicly thought about the unthinkable: an increase in the dollar price of gold. Dr. Burns once suggested a dollar levaluation because of his doubts about a national return to fiscal ınd monetary responsibility, and felt that it might at least head off more stultifying controls. Professor Samuelson once seemed to favor

the same thing for the opposite reason: it would buy time for estab
lishment of SDR's or "paper gold."

CONGRESS WILL NEVER INCREASE THE PRICE OF GOLD AND THUS REWARD THE SPECULATORS FOR ATTACKING THE DOLLAR

In June 1968 *The Wall Street Journal* quoted a "high" Unite
States government financial authority traveling in an airplane ove
the Atlantic to or from an economic conference as saying, "There i
no more chance of us raising the official price of gold than there is o
me jumping out of this window and landing on the White Hous
lawn." The *Journal* did not make clear in which of three possibl
senses it used the word "high."

Henry S. Reuss, a Democratic Congressman from Wisconsin and
leading member of the House Banking and Currency Committee
replied to the question of how Congress would react if a Presiden
tried to raise the price of gold without Congressional approval: "O
the same day," he said, "I would initiate impeachment proceedings.

But what if a President did seek Congressional approval for it?

According to the *Congressional Record,* Representative Reuss tol
his House colleagues that "this Congress is never going to increas
the price of gold and thus reward the speculators for their attack o
the dollar."

FURLED UMBRELLAS, PIN-STRIPED SUITS, PEARL STICK PINS, AND DAMP PALMS—A MAJOR TURNING POINT IN THE HISTORY OF THE WORLD?

At the time of the Ides of March in money, advertisements for th
Dines Letter, a popular investment advisory service which compare
with C. V. Myers' is only semi-oracular, carried the following teasers
"WHAT DOES THE GOLD CRISIS MEAN TO YOU? Gold sum
moned ministers across the world wringing damp palms, gold close
banks. Imagine what higher interest rates could mean, not only i
terms of a further collapse in bond prices, but also business slowdow
and layoffs, unemployment, and so on. Will we eventually follo
England when they announced in March that one of their new sti
taxes would actually exceed 100 percent? Why is it that Russi
stopped selling gold a few years ago and now China is gobbling it u
as fast as she can get it—why if gold is so useless? And—are Arab

242

planning to raise international oil royalties if the dollar is devalued—what would that do to the leading oil companies? Find out if the 'two-tier system' is any good, and why the Dines Letter says that recent events represent a major turning point in the history of the world."

Leading economists, bankers, and goldmining executives from Switzerland, Belgium, France, South Africa, Britain, and the United States had met in Geneva and signed a resolution demanding that the official world price of gold be approximately doubled in order to prevent the world's international currency system from breaking down. It was a remarkably calm, well-tailored, well-fed group, and Dines to the contrary notwithstanding, no damp palms were seen or heard wringing.

As they saw the issues, there were just four choices open to the United States and the other major countries of the world:

1. Try to continue the present International Monetary Fund system, which links gold to the dollar at $35 an ounce for gold

2. Allow all currencies to go on a paper basis and allow them to fluctuate daily on the foreign-exchange markets against each other

3. Continue to try to refine and improve the present gold-exchange standard at a higher price for gold

4. Restore a full gold standard at a higher price for gold

Their principal objection to the first choice was that the $35 price could be maintained for only a short time and merely as a fiction, or formal shell, by an increasing network of prohibitions, controls, restrictions on owning gold, on travel, on investing and buying abroad, and on buying and selling foreign currencies. At the $35-an-ounce price not enough gold could be economically mined.

The second course, to go on a pure paper basis, would be restrictive and disruptive, because importers, exporters, investors, and foreign-exchange dealers, forced to gamble on the gyrations in the cross-values of a hundred different currencies, would find it almost impossible to carry on international economic and financial transactions, even though a "futures market" might be developed that would permit hedging in currencies, much as the present commodity markets permit futures "hedging" by users of such products as wheat, silver, soybeans, barley, and frozen pork bellies. Furthermore, on a pure paper basis, there would be nothing to prevent each nation from debasing its own currency without limit, by following popular domestic policies such as hiring all of the unemployed off the farms to come to the city to work for the government and printing enough paper money to pay them, as Uruguay and many other countries have been doing for a long time.

The third course, continuing the present International Monetary Fund or gold-exchange standard but increasing the official price of gold, would be regarded by the international money men as setting off another round of international inflation. It would eventually fail because the expansion of paper money and credit would be too easy.

The international bankers concluded that the right answer was the fourth alternative, the restoration of a full gold standard at a higher price for gold.

BARBAROUS RELIC? GOLD HAS NEVER BEEN IN GREATER DEMAND

Barron's Weekly headlined a 1968 article, "Barbarous Relic? Gold Has Never Been in Greater Demand."

That same week gold quotations surged to new highs, well over $40 an ounce. Barron's went on to report: "Meanwhile, demand for the precious metal is mounting apace. As an underpriced commodity, it is sought with growing avidity by industry and the arts. As a source of value, it commands mounting respect in a world which is fast losing confidence in paper money. 'Sound as a dollar' now has a hollow ring indeed; in the free world's financial centers, nothing is as good as gold. Last week officials disclosed the outflow of another quarter billion dollars worth through mid-May."

Sir Roy Harrod, the biographer of Keynes, has written:

> Gold is a glorious substance, both for its beauty and its physical properties. If one has imagination, it surely brings some satisfaction to think that the most beautiful substance in the world is also quietly working away to perform the most utilitarian function in the world, namely to actuate that international division of labor, without which all our lives would be nasty, brutish and short.*

He turns aside for a passing glance at the other royal monetary metal:

> Silver is also a beautiful metal. When I was young I was a bi-metallist. It is true that the issue was dead at that time, but

* *Reforming the World's Money*, St. Martin's Press, 1965.

echoes of the great controversy were still audible, and it was natural to take sides. Before long, the United States silver coins—dimes, half-dollars, etc.—will all be melted down. That is a very sad thing, but no one seems to sigh about it. Has all romance and sense of history gone out of the world? It might be argued that there is no place for romance or sense of history these days, since we are practical people and every ounce of energy and attention is needed to raise up the hundreds of millions of people in the less developed countries out of their unhappy poverty. But it does not seem that this great purpose makes much appeal either. So, lacking romance and lacking a sense of purpose, we are all to be reduced to a life of complete boredom, just stepping in and out of automobiles.

Is the man who just stepped out of that automobile an economic man or a forgotten man? A Midas or a Pursides?

The Dollar Does Not Enjoy Unreserved Acceptance as a Reserve Asset—And Neither Does Gold

Why does this age-old debate between the Pursides and the Midases produce so much heat and so little light? Mostly because the debaters are using entirely different frames of reference for what seem to be basically similar fundamental objectives. Mostly they are treating the question of decreasing the gold value of the dollar as a purely domestic political matter for one country within the world system, not as a matter of worldwide concern for all countries within the system.

They are not looking at it from the point of view of what would be soundest and wisest for the world money system as a whole. Leaving aside for a moment the serious United States political obstacles with which Congressman Reuss is naturally concerned, and the whole question of how the matter should be handled, the argument for lowering the value of the dollar in terms of gold or increasing the gold value of the dollar for the good of the system as a whole is a persuasive one.

At present, because of the persistence of so many Pursides in the world, the dollar does not enjoy unreserved acceptance as a reserve asset. But because of the arguments of the Midases, and because of its intrinsic scarcity, gold metal does not enjoy unreserved acceptance

245

as a reserve asset either. Its scarcity is of course exactly why the Pursides prefer it.

THE ROLE OF GOLD IN THE MONETARY SYSTEM IN THE VERY LONG RUN .

As the decade of the 1950's was drawing to a close, the vast gold reserves behind the dollar were gradually seeping out of Fort Knox and reappearing on the shining sands of various foreign Patoclus rivers. During the decade of the 1960's, Presidents and Treasury officials turned Midases' ears to the rising warnings of the Pursides that as the gold disappeared we could no longer make the rest of the world of money dance to the clink of our dollars. As we enter the 1970's, even Midases agree that our government can no longer call the world's money tune and expect all other countries to get in step. In this sense the dollar's glory days are over for a long time to come and probably forever.

The Anglo-American Corporation of South Africa controls many of the gold mines of Africa. Because of its vast gold stake, Chairman H. F. Oppenheimer's statement to the company's 51st Annual General Meeting held in Johannesburg in 1968 are worth a careful hearing in this debate:

> The world monetary system is faced today with two distinct though interrelated problems. On the one hand, the level of new gold production is inadequate to support gold's monetary role, and on the other hand, there is a persistent deficit in the United States' balance of payments. The fact that the level of new gold production is inadequate is not due to the recent speculation in gold (which is really speculation directed against the dollar), but to the rapidly increasing use of gold in industry, the arts, and the substantial quantities that are absorbed annually for long-term hoarding as distinct from short-term speculation.

THE STRONG PREFERENCE IN MOST COUNTRIES FOR GOLD OVER OTHER RESERVE ASSETS

Chairman Oppenheimer continued:

> What has certainly become clear, as the result of the recent monetary disturbances, is that central banks outside of the

246

United States cannot be persuaded or forced to acquire and hold indefinitely whatever quantity of dollars may be necessary to finance the American balance-of-payments deficit. In other words, the dollar does not enjoy unreserved acceptance as a reserve asset. In these circumstances, there are certainly good arguments to be advanced for a higher official gold price, but perhaps they do not come best from the chairman of a large gold-mining group. However, I think it is pardonable for me to say that whatever the role of gold in the monetary system may prove to be in the very long run, a higher official gold price now would help to resolve the short- and medium-term problems of the monetary system, would give time for the American and British balance of payments to be put onto a sound basis, and would tend to reduce the strong preference felt in most countries for gold over other reserve assets.

Good sense on international monetary matters, however, is in shorter supply than gold itself, and may be pardoned, even from "the chairman of a large gold-mining group." The most remarkable part of Oppenheimer's statement, considering its source, is his reservation as to the role of gold in the monetary system "in the very long run."

Thus even the chairman of a large gold-mining group seems to envisage for the "very long run" some form of international monetary order, special drawing rights, Eurodollars, or some other comprehensive plan that will relieve both the dollar and the inadequate supply of gold from their present crushing monetary roles.

Hopefully, in the "very long run" the welfare of the world's people and the usefulness of their money will be relieved from the vagaries, naïveté, wishful thinking, self-serving statements, and tendency to vote-buying of recent United States government fiscal and monetary policymakers. Economists love to cite John Maynard Keynes' throwaway line, "In the long run we are all dead," as an example of profound economic wisdom. Wit it is, but as wisdom it is patently contrary to the experience of at least the young among us, and our concern for our issue, of which Keynes had none.

In any event, the acknowledgment by the chairman of the large gold-mining group that in the "very long run," contrary to the interests of his company's vast stake in the free-world's gold reserves, gold might no longer be the one universally acceptable monetary reserve, could scarcely be more convincing evidence that the long-run future of money for better or worse will belong to the officials of an international monetary order, whom Sir Roy Harrod has called a "gaggle of governesses."

THE U.S. AND BRITAIN CAN ACHIEVE BALANCE-OF-PAYMENT SURPLUSES ONLY BY DRIVING OTHER COUNTRIES INTO DEFICITS—UNLESS THE MONEY VALUE OF NEW GOLD MONETARY RESERVES RISES

The tonnage of gold mined is not closely connected with the price. The fact that the output of gold is naturally limited by geology and does not respond easily to a rise in price is precisely what renders gold universally acceptable as an "ultimate" form of international money. The very characteristic that makes central bankers want to use gold also tends to fix the real cost of using it.

In considering the impact of a rise in the gold price, one must remember that both South Africa and other countries have some mines that are unprofitable at the present price and are being subsidized to continue in production. If the price rose, these subsidies would probably be cut, and to that extent the price increase would not provide an additional incentive to gold producers. Much of the incentive given by a higher price would also be absorbed by higher wages to gold miners and higher taxes on the mining companies.

Because gold is a commodity, foreign sales of newly mined gold by producer countries are treated as a merchandise export like any other. So long as producers keep their own reserves constant and export only the current output of gold, they are not running a deficit.

Countries that buy gold to add to their reserves, however, are obviously running surpluses. Hence, combined surpluses of all countries can exceed combined deficits only by the increase in world monetary gold reserves. Conversely, if world monetary gold reserves are falling as they did from 1966 to 1968, combined deficits are bound to exceed combined surpluses. In reality, the increase in world gold reserves has been insufficient by itself to allow equilibrium of the whole system for the past twenty years.

The situation was tenable for a long time because the United States, which began the period holding two-thirds of the world's monetary gold stock (over $20 billion worth) against very limited external liabilities, was able to supply other countries with a steady stream of both dollars and gold by running external deficits. The surplus countries are unhappy now because they do not regard their surpluses as excessive, yet they are having great difficulty in financing them. They would prefer to take in at least some gold, but are under pressure from United States authorities not to do so.

REFORM OF THE SYSTEM IS A PRECONDITION FOR CURING THE U.S. DEFICIT, NOT THE REVERSE

The United States deficit is bound up with the condition of the world monetary system as a whole. At the start of 1968 President Johnson declared that an improvement of $3 billion was needed in the United States balance of payments. At the same time Britain was supposed to be improving her balance by something like $2 billion from the 1967 level in order to get into surplus and start repaying her short-term debts. Yet even if some special arrangements were concluded with South Africa, it is unlikely that world monetary gold reserves would increase by more than $500 million a year, at most.

Hence, if the United States and the United Kingdom are to achieve and maintain their balance-of-payments objectives, other countries would have to accept a deterioration of $4.5 billion or so in their external accounts for some years. A deterioration of this order would be unacceptable, even if it were distributed among the other countries in the most favorable way—that is, falling mostly on major surplus countries such as Germany. The fact that such a favorable outcome is unlikely only strengthens the point. Reform of the whole system is therefore a precondition for the correction of the United States' and Britain's past deficits—not the other way around.

HOW A RISE IN THE VALUE OF THE ANNUAL GOLD OUTPUT WOULD SOLVE THE U.S. DEFICIT

It is not the rise in the value of existing gold reserves that is crucial, but the rise in the value of the annual gold output. Suppose the official price of gold were doubled. The value of the quantity of gold mined each year would then rise from $1.4 billion to $2.8

249

billion. In addition, there might be a modest increase in the tonnage mined, as well as a resumption of Russian gold sales, raising total annual supplies to perhaps $3.25 billion.

Private demand in recent years—excluding the wave of speculation triggered by the devaluation of sterling—has been running at about $1.5 billion a year. The elasticity of this demand with respect to a large increase is likely to be somewhat greater than unity. That is, the elasticity of savings demand is unity, while that of industrial demand is substantially greater. Private demand would then fall somewhat, to perhaps $1.25 billion or $1.3 billion.

It is sometimes argued that the normal elasticity factors would be overridden by the expectations of a further increase in the price, so that private demand would on balance be stimulated. This is plausible for a small increase, but hardly for a large one. Indeed, some short-term selling of hoardings by speculators who were only waiting for the rise seems far more likely. On these assumptions therefore (and ignoring any short-term "dishoarding") the net outcome would be to make something like $2 billion of new gold available each year to go into official reserves.

This would transform the international payments situation. If the United States moved into current balance, other countries would still be improving their reserve position by $2 billion a year. This would first of all make the elimination of the United States deficit a feasible proposition. It would give United States policy measures in this direction a fair chance of success. But it would also do more than this. It would make a major active contribution, directly or indirectly, to getting rid of the deficit.

One way to see this is to imagine the position of the surplus countries if, initially, the United States deficit remained unchanged at about $3 billion a year. With new gold coming into monetary reserves at the rate of $2 billion a year, total surpluses (mainly, no doubt, of the continental European countries) would be running at about $5 billion a year. This would mean excessive reserves gains and stronger inflationary tendencies somewhere in the surplus group. The countries concerned would be under pressure either to allow a faster rise in costs and prices or to cut down their external surpluses by policy measures. Either course would benefit the American (and British) balance of payments. If, on the other hand, one starts with the alternative assumption that continental surpluses initially

remain constant, the benefit to the United States and British balance
of payments is more direct: They will immediately improve by $2
billion. The reality would be likely to fall somewhere between these
two extreme assumptions.

ARGUMENTS AGAINST INCREASING THE GOLD PRICE, WITH SOME BUILT-IN REBUTTALS

It is said that if we were able to provide a system of paper money
adequate to the world's needs, we could then release all the gold-
mining labor, except such as might still be needed to produce gold
for industry or ornamentation, and set it to more productive tasks.
We do not have to set thousands of men to work digging gold out
of the ground only to rebury it again in the vaults of central banks.

Raising the price of gold would be giving a present to the Soviet
Union, and this we do not wish to do. But the gold stocks and production of the noncommunist world are larger than those of Russia.
There are those who do not wish to give a "present" to South Africa,
whose racial political philosophy we deplore. However, it does not
show a good sense of proportion to injure the interests of the whole
world by seeking to deprive one rather small country of the benefit
of its natural resources. The South African mine operators would
no doubt pass on a portion of the net gain from an increase in the
gold price as additional wages to the Bantu mine workers. Their
improved economic status would lead to more self-help, and more
demands by the Bantus themselves, and would be likely to do more
for improving their status than outside agitation has done.

ALLOWING U.S. PRIVATE CITIZENS TO OWN GOLD "IN THE NATIONAL INTEREST"

Would a doubling of the gold price increase or decrease the
amount of gold that went into private hoards? Pessimists hold that
the seepage might be increased on the ground that dollar devaluation
might further undermine confidence in currencies, and one revaluation having been undertaken, others would come along later. This
is the opposite of what happened after President Roosevelt devalued
the dollar in 1934. At that time there was a very large release of gold
from hoards and no substantial evidence of hoarding of gold for
many years afterward.

Since 1934 the United States has limited the possession of gold by United States citizens to licensed industrial and artistic users, permitting individuals to own pre-1934 gold coins only as collectors' items. Under the 1934 Act, however, the Secretary of the Treasury has broader discretionary power than is generally believed, and he could issue licenses for other purposes that he may find "in the national interest." Before 1960 private citizens were permitted to hold gold outside of the United States. Indeed, it can be forcefully argued that nothing in the law forbids the Secretary of the Treasury from granting private American citizens authority, by administrative action entirely without Congressional approval, to hold all the gold they like. If the price of gold were raised to a higher level, there would be no national interest in continuing the present arbitrary, anachronistic, and discriminatory prohibition.

A "devaluation" of the dollar in terms of its value in gold would not, of necessity, involve any "depreciation" of the dollar, or lowering of the parity of the dollar vis-à-vis other currencies, all of whose values are fixed in terms of the dollar. In fact, unilateral devaluation of the United States dollar in terms of gold would probably hardly be noticed in our domestic economy, and might have surprisingly small long-term adverse effects on the international economy.

If SDR's Replace Gold as the Primary International Medium of Exchange, Who Cares About the Gold Price?

In reality, we cannot manufacture gold out of paper. While we can supplement real gold as an international reserve asset, we cannot *supplant* it. The structure of the present international monetary system is built upon gold: Gold is mentioned explicitly in ten of the twenty IMF Articles of Agreement, and in three of the five appended schedules to that agreement. The par value of currencies is defined in terms of gold or in terms of the dollar at a fixed gold content. The proposed special drawing rights themselves carry a constant gold-value guarantee, although not a guarantee of gold convertibility. Thus, trying to destroy the international monetary role of gold would really amount to revolution, not orderly reform. Eliminating it from the articles of the fund would simply be a political impossibility. It just will not go away.

Special drawing rights in the fund will have a continuing international life of their own, unless and until extinguished by fund decision. The decision-making process to create or extinguish units will be formal, and a safeguard against excessive action rests in the requirement of approval by 85 percent of the fund's accredited voting power. Members will be free to use these rights without conditions as to their own monetary and fiscal policies, but the expected use will be to meet balance-of-payments problems. When transfers of ownership occur, they must be effected through the fund's facilities. All other uses are, of course, conditional upon fund approval.

Will SDR's really take the place of gold as a medium of exchange? The final, perhaps most important, and in a sense the subtlest and most emotional argument in favor of increasing the price of gold involves the conditions the International Monetary Fund sets on the use of SDR's and ordinary rights to draw upon it as well. Certainly special drawing rights would create additional reserves for foreign trade, but there would always be a sense in which a country's power over even unconditional drawing rights would not be absolutely unconditional, at least not in the same way that the power of a country to use its own gold and foreign-exchange reserves really is absolutely unconditional.

The Gaggle of Governesses Muscling in on Marx, or He on Them

The free world's economic system will, we expect, someday broaden into a worldwide economic system that will include the Soviet Union and most of the other communist countries. We have already seen them reaching toward a fully transferable gold-backed ruble. As time goes on, Russia and other communist countries will gradually work out closer relationships with the free world through the International Monetary Fund. In the early stages, at least, it is logical to assume that with its substantial gold reserves and production, the Soviet Union will insist on a gold-backed ruble as an impersonal basis for international settlements, at least as between International Monetary Fund countries and Russian-bloc countries. Settlements through the fund itself involve an element of approval, surveillance, and assurances by central bankers. From this point of view it is desirable to maintain gold in existence as an impersonal method of international settlement for use by all countries, including

253

Russia, her satellites, and other communist countries. At least in the early stages, it is not to be anticipated that the Russians would welcome into Marxian economic management Harrod's "gaggle of governesses."

If the official price of gold should be raised, SDR's would to some extent be superfluous. Some surplus countries would feel that their political interests were best served by preventing or minimizing any growth of officially created reserves, and would exercise their voting or veto power accordingly. If, on the other hand, the official gold price is abolished, SDR's might have to replace gold rather than supplement it as the basic reserve medium of the system. Gold would in effect have been demonetized. The evidence of recent years, however, not to speak of earlier periods, is that neither national central banks nor all the forgotten men of the world who are still of the Pursides persuasion are interested in demonetizing gold. And countries cannot always be counted on to get together to agree to provide for a satisfactory expansion of reserves by means of collective agreements

DOUBLING THE VALUE OF EXISTING GOLD RESERVES WOULD BE MORE BELIEVABLE THAN MORE SDR's— AND A WHOLE LOT BETTER LOOKING

The establishment of a gold price of $70 or $100 an ounce would secure the regular but limited increase in world reserves that the Group-of-Ten countries have been arguing about for years. Doubling the value of existing gold reserves (about $40 billion at the present price) would be of particular benefit to the United States, since it would greatly improve the ratio of her gold reserves to her liquid liabilities.

But how do we break the political logjams in the United States? The prohibition against devaluing the dollar, and against repudiating our supposedly sacred pledge to buy and sell gold at $35 an ounce?

The political debate draws on the precedents of those independent sovereign nations of long ago whose strong currencies gave them dominant positions in a comparatively unpopulated, unintegrated world; and upon the ineffectiveness and opprobrium which surround the memory of the United States' only devaluation of the dollar in terms of gold. The debate rumbles on, mostly in terms familiar to the world of thirty-five years ago, mostly oblivious to the real issues of today.

No country, not even the United States, can act unilaterally any more in such an economic matter. If it did, the supposed advantages would prove just as illusory as the last time, and the consequences for the world economy even more disastrous. Whatever the United States does must be done within the framework of the world economic order and the free-world money system, which pivots on the International Monetary Fund.

THE GOLD-EXCHANGE SYSTEM CAUGHT IN THE CROSS FIRE

As we have seen, the 19th-century gold-standard system required each separate nation to set the value of her currency by weight of gold, and required her to guarantee to convert paper money to gold bullion on demand. Automatically honoring that arbitrary commitment forced many countries into ruthless deflations, panics, and recessions.

Whether we call the system we have now the gold-exchange standard or something else, under it gold crises, pound sterling crises, lira crises, and franc and deutsche mark crises have been occurring more frequently all the time. Britain has had to undertake a program of ruthless domestic deflation, and so has France. The United States is suffering from the tightest money, the highest taxes, and the severest rates of inflation in her history. Britain staggers under foreign claims of $10 billion against her $2 billion of reserves, and the United States hopes the strength of her domestic economy will make everyone forget the $41 billion of foreign-held claims against her $11 billion or so of gold reserves.

Are all the sovereign nations of the free world and all their peoples being crucified on a cross of gold? Of thirty-five American dollars for one ounce of gold?

"Yes," cry the Pursides, "for their economic sins! The system depends on gold alone, and gold is enforcing economic discipline as only it can do."

"Certainly not," retort the Midases. "These deficits do not matter! The system is based on the dollar alone, and the world is being crucified on a cross of gold for no good reason."

Purside and Midas enter the world money arena and square off against each other. The referee says a few words.

Here is the bell.

Nonsense, say the Pursides, it is not a dollar system at all. Despite appearances, the system is really based on gold alone. Though gold makes up only some 50 percent of total reserve holdings, the nongold portion largely consists of "bogus" reserves such as dollars and pounds, currencies whose true worth is constantly diminishing because of inflation. The purchasing power of the dollar fell at an annual rate of more than 7 percent during most of 1969.

In contrast gold has brought well over $40 per ounce in real, private transactions in London and elsewhere.

The dollar and the pound qualify as international monetary reserves in name only. Governments continue to hold these "eroding" currencies as reserves instead of gold only because they fear that to cash them in for gold at $35 per ounce would wipe out America's official gold reserve and the international monetary system would collapse forthwith.

Without gold, there would be no way to fix the international exchange rates of currencies—and without such fixed rates, in the hour-by-hour uncertainty of wildly changing currency values, international business, which has been expanding in recent years, would have shrunk. "Obviously, the entire system depends on gold," the Pursides conclude.

"Not at all," retort the Midases, "The Pursides are completely wrong about the system. It is really based solely on the dollar. Gold has only a figure-head role. It is just bright window dressing. Gold is worth only what the dollar says it is."

The dollar is used for payment in roughly 70 percent of international business transactions and its use has been increasing all the time.

Professor Milton Friedman of the University of Chicago says that "the dollar is the key currency in the world" and there "just isn't anything else."

While commentators and politicians have been slow to recognize the emergence of a "dollar standard," the Midases argue, the fact became unmistakable when the United States' gold supply, which had been declining for many years, began to increase in early 1968. Between the second quarter of 1968 and the first quarter of 1969, records show, U.S. gold holdings climbed $155 million.

Obviously, the Midases conclude, dollars are more useful and a better investment than gold. As for other currencies, the Russian ruble, like the dollar, is backed by H-bombs and a well-established political system. But Russia's xenophobic attitude towards international currency transactions prevents widespread use of the ruble, so the dollar is all there is left.

Whatever its ultimate reality may be, whether it is a system based ultimately on gold alone or whether it is based ultimately on the dollar alone, the only thing that is absolutely clear is that the system itself is caught in an economic no-man's land between the cross fire of the Pursides and Midases.

To the Pursides, the dollar is not acceptable as a reserve asset, and special drawing rights are no better. The dollar must be devalued and the dollar price of gold must be raised. Nonsense, say the Midases, gold is unimportant and unnecessary as a reserve asset, and the Pursides must simply learn to accept paper dollars instead of gold, and swallow special drawing rights as well. Between two such powerful polarities, the everlasting conflict between the Pursides and the Midases, world money crises flare up fitfully again and again.

The Unannnounced and Unmourned Death of the Gold-Exchange System

On the 1968 March weekend when you could not cash your American travelers' checques at Orly, the central bankers of the United States, Britain, and five other leading governments were "looking down the barrel of a shotgun." They had to act fast to stop the gold-buying panic. They did. They closed the gold pool, and they adopted the "two-tier" gold system. As widely reported and understood at the time, this meant that the private market price for gold would be allowed to fluctuate freely, or "fend for itself," and there would be gold transactions between central banks only at the official price of $35 an ounce.

But there was really much more to it than that. The action these important central bankers took that fateful mid-March weekend went far beyond mere technical consideration of what might happen to the market price of gold. In their published communiqué the bankers stated:

> The Governors believe that henceforth officially held gold should be used only to effect transfers among monetary authorities, and, therefore, they decided no longer to supply gold to

257

the London gold market or any other gold market. Moreover as the existing stock of monetary gold is sufficient in view of the prospective establishment of the facility for Special Drawing Rights, they no longer feel it necessary to buy gold from the market. Finally, they agreed that henceforth they will not sell gold to monetary authorities to replace gold sold in private markets.

This was a decision of far-reaching portent. *It meant that monetary demand for gold might be permanently withdrawn from the market. It further suggested a potential severance of national monetary systems from any further dependence on an ever-expanding supply of new gold. And it also hinted that the central bankers might be willing to accept the proposed new international money unit as a displacement of future available gold in monetary-reserve usage* Dethronement of gold was already an accomplished fact.

Of course. The solutions we have been groping for have been with us all along! In fact, the United States has already repudiated its supposedly sacred commitment to redeem paper dollars for gold metal at the rate of $35 an ounce. It has hedged on its commitment to buy gold metal at that price as well.

As the One Universal God of Money, Gold Is Dead

The dissertations by politicians and economists about the impossible political processes involved in changing the gold price are academic. The Secretary of the Treasury has said that we will no longer buy gold at $35 an ounce except from central banks, and he has privately told the central banks we will no longer buy from them, either, except on our own terms. No court, sheriff, or army exists in the free world to enforce the United States' self-imposed obligation to buy or sell gold at $35 an ounce. The President need not fear impeachment proceedings.

Does this mean that the dollar is valued in terms of gold? Or is gold valued in terms of the dollar? It means that gold is valued in terms of the dollar, and any other national currency that is freely convertible into the dollar. Such "tinkering" by the United States and other countries with the money price of gold and the convertibility of paper money into gold has done much to banish the popular

258

belief that the value of money is determined independently of the action of monetary authorities, and that gold provides an unchanging, immutable standard for all paper money values. Gold is just as dependent on manipulation by monetary authorities as paper currencies are. The Midases have finally crushed the Pursides once and for all, although by no means all of the Pursides have yet conceded the fact. But as the one universal God of money, gold is dead.

THE GOLD BOOM AND THE CRASH

For eighteen months, from the Ides of March in money of 1968 to October of 1969, the free market price of gold fluctuated between $40 and $45 an ounce. This represented a de facto devaluation of the dollar in terms of gold by as much as 20 percent. In the great poker game in gold, South Africa played her strong hand cautiously, by discreetly feeding small amounts of her ever-growing reserves into the free market through a consortium of large Swiss banks. But in October and November of 1969 rumors spread that Russia, as well as South Africa, was trying to sell some of her vast gold stock into a market that was proving to be surprisingly thin. Ever higher worldwide interest rates made it costlier than ever for speculators to carry purchases of gold metal with borrowed money. The free market price of gold fell back to around $35 an ounce.

In Johannesburg and Zurich fortunes were wiped out by the crash. In Washington United States Treasury officials were pleased that the two-tier gold system had successfully survived the 18-month period of testing. They professed unconcern about what the consequences might be if the price of gold should fall below $35 an ounce, as, indeed, it did. The dollar's victory over gold seemed to be complete.

Some monetary experts have estimated that if monetary demand for gold, that is, demand from governments and central banks for gold to add to their official reserves, were eliminated, the price would fall as low as $10 an ounce. If the free market price should fall to $10 it would mean that the United States' gold reserve which is now worth about $11 billion, would be worth only a little more than $3 billion, while the same $41 billion of paper dollars would still remain outstanding in foreign hands. If this happened would it mean that the dollar's victory over gold was no more than a Pyhrric victory? Or, indeed, a self-inflicted debacle?

Knowing that the United States paper dollar had been officially demonetized in terms of gold, and that the gold reserves of central banks were of dubious value in themselves, would worldwide holders of paper dollars continue to accept and hold them "because they are accepted" as readily as before? Expectations of inflation would, of course, not have been dispelled to any extent, so a negative answer seems inescapable. Holders of paper dollars would seek to pass them for land and goods and services at an ever faster rate, and owners and suppliers of land, goods and labor would demand ever greater sums of paper dollars in exchange for them.

What can be done to protect the United States and its $11 billion gold reserve from the potentially disastrous consequences of the dollar's total victory over gold?

As described more fully in Chapter 19, the United States could simply allow its Treasury gold to be surrendered to the International Monetary Fund in exchange for hard foreign currencies that would be used to cover deficits in our foreign-trade balances. As our gold reserve worked lower, Congress and the President would no doubt be forced to recognize the new realities of the United States' economic position in the world.

When the International Monetary Fund had acquired a reserve of the world's gold larger than that of any individual country, it would decree by vote of an appropriate number of countries an increase in the official price at which it would buy and sell reserve gold. The United States' Congress and the President would have had no public part in repudiating their innumerable public assurances nor the "gentleman's agreement" to hold the price of gold at $35 an ounce. As we know, every such reassurance carries less assurance.

The official upward revaluation of gold in terms of the dollar and of other currencies would be made by the fund. At the same time any necessary adjustments could be made in exchange rates of currencies, including the dollar. Restrictions of various kinds on international payments and trade controls might also be needed. But a general proliferation of controls among the industrial countries for purely balance-of-payments reasons would be harmful both economically and politically.

A rise in the official gold price is not inevitable. But a refusal to raise it (in the proper manner) seems likely to lead to disorderly and restrictive arrangements in world payments and to consequent economic loss for many countries. The likely extent of such loss is difficult to estimate, because of the wide variety of possible actions and outcomes. To assert categorically, however, that an increase in the gold price would be a defeat for economic management and would set back the cause of "rational" monetary reform for a generation shows a serious failure on the part of our economic officials to come to grips with the realities of the situation. They are simply reminding us that King Midas has ass's ears.

What these events would really mean is an armistice in the long war between the Pursides and the Midases. The faith of all the followers of both would be placed squarely behind the International Monetary Fund. The tottering American monetary Atlas would have passed the weight of the world money system onto the fund's broad back.

Persistent, pathological Pursides would have been given a one-shot profit of 100 percent or so on all the gold they had been hoarding all those years since 1934, a period during which all the believers in paper had been multiplying their paper money many times over through dividends and interest and long-term capital gains. In the reserves of the International Monetary Fund, somewhere back of all those special drawing rights, behind all those paper dollars, behind all those Russian rubles, there would be a reserve of real gold of substantial value. All the world's paper money would be backed by the fund's gold under an international treaty.

When all this has been done, parents who take their school-age children to Washington, D.C., during spring vacation to see the Smithsonian Institution and the Japanese cherry trees in blossom will add a stop at the headquarters of the International Monetary Fund, where armed guards will solemnly show them the stacks of gold bars that are the basic reserve standing behind the whole world's paper money.

AN END TO EXPECTATIONS OF INFLATION?

Will the forgotten man's continued expectations of inflation end? The announcement of the two-tier gold system on the Ides of March of money in 1968 undoubtedly contributed significantly to his intensified expectations of inflation and helped bring on the accelerated pace of inflation during the years which followed. By the same token, the reestablishment of a rational link between gold metal and the paper dollar and all other paper currencies would help to curb such expectations of inflation, in a way that no United States tax surcharge, nor budgetary stringency, nor the tightest money in United States history came close to doing. And from the forgotten man's point of view the entire process would be far less painful than any of these measures. In fact, it would not be painful at all.

Surviving by Monetary Management in a Poverty-Wracked, Dangerous, and Envious World

As the economic position of the United States in the international economy changed from creditor to debtor, and finally, by the standards which she originally imposed upon herself when she had control of gold, to "bankrupt," her power of economic control, and that of Britain as well, slipped away to the gold-surplus countries of the European Common Market and Switzerland. Congress and the President could dominate the Pursides and Midases of the world when they controlled most of its gold, but not when they did not.

If the world money system as a whole and the welfare of all the world's peoples is your frame of reference, this loss of control is probably a good thing. If the interest of the United States alone is your frame of reference, it is not necessarily a good thing at all. On a planet with limited resources and expanding populations in envious and aggressive countries that are political enemies of the United States, our future and the future of our money will depend more and more upon the skill—or lack of it—exercised by our government in managing our affairs in this fundamentally new and dangerous, poverty-stricken and envious world environment.

We Shall All Be Subject, in Fine, to a Gaggle of Governesses

Even if the dollar price of gold were raised and gold were retained as a basis for all other reserves in the International Monetary Fund, and as a basic form of national reserves as well, its importance in world money affairs will nevertheless diminish. The mystic intrinsic appeal of gold has historically permitted it to enjoy much freedom from governmental controls, and in this sense, it has served as a bul-mark of human freedom and as a sheet anchor of liberty for many hundreds of years of civilization. Gold has the virtue of being, in economist Sir Ralph Hawtrey's words, an "anonymous asset."

Although gold will no longer be the sole or even the most important medium for settlement of international payments, it should remain one important medium, and one on which a country or an individual who happens to be temporarily out of line with the latest fashion in economics and international thinking can fall back. If all else fails there are still satisfactions to be derived from giving a gold bracelet to one's girl.

In the future all countries will depend to a lesser extent on the gold and foreign currency reserves they own and have earned, and to a progressively greater extent on "by-your-leave" accommodations for dealing with their money troubles through the International Monetary Fund. The quantum of separate nationally owned and earned foreign-exchange reserves will not increase very much; as a component of total reserves they will diminish proportionately. Eventually, almost all reserves will be of the "by-your-leave" variety through the International Monetary Fund. In the end even sovereign national governments will be subject to the gaggle of governesses.

17

MEANWHILE, BACK AT THE MARKETPLACE...

*"Well, in our country," said Alice, still
panting a little, "You'd generally get to
somewhere else—if you ran very fast for a
long time, as we've been doing."*

"A slow sort of country!" said the Queen.

*"Now, here, you see, it takes all the running
you can do, to keep in the same place. If you
want to get somewhere else, you must run at
least twice as fast as that!"*

Lewis Carroll
Through the Looking Glass

TRADING OFF HIGH-RATE INFLATION FOR LOW-RATE UNEMPLOYMENT

Following World War II, the goal of government policy was to pro
mote economic stability and full employment. Memories of the De
pression of the 1930s and the recurring sharp slumps in the business
cycle were vivid. More sharp slumps occurred in the 1950s, but their
short duration was attributed to improvements in the ability of gov
ernment policy to smooth out big bumps in the business cycle. In the
recession years of 1958 and 1961, unemployment averaged close to
7 percent, but throughout most of the 1960s there was continuous
economic expansion, and the rate of unemployment reached what
seemed to be an almost irreducible minimum of 3½ percent of the
working force.

This minimum rate of unemployment also seemed to be the prin
cipal cause of the price inflation that accelerated as the 1960's wore
on. In the early part of the 1960's, prices rose only about 2 percent
per year, a rate of increase most economists would regard as not
abnormal and indeed "healthy." In 1964 the average annual gain in
prices was only 1½ percent. But from this low point the rate of in

rease began accelerating, and by 1968 the gain was an unhealthy 4½ percent. Gross national product, the most comprehensive and significant indicator of overall economic activity, grew at the rate of about 7.8 percent during the 1963–1968 period.

The Nixon Administration during its early months sought to reduce the "unacceptable" rate of erosion in value of the dollar. The Secretary of the Treasury said several times that wage, price, and credit controls were a possibility as administration policy, although the President rebutted these suggestions. The Administration urged extension of the 10 percent income tax surcharge, and elimination of the 7 percent corporate investment credit. It kept taxes at high levels and made efforts to cut planned expenditures on the Vietnam war and even on space projects.

Because of the adverse balance in United States' foreign-trade payments, because of the excessive accumulation of paper dollars in the hands of foreign central banks and individuals, because of the insistence of foreign creditor countries on "responsible" action to maintain current balance in our foreign trade so that the value of foreign-dollar holdings would not be depleted or diluted, because of the International Monetary Fund's insistence on our putting our foreign-trade accounts into current balance, because of the rising public clamor of older people who are holders of United States Savings Bonds and of other forgotten men for whom inflation has disastrous consequences, the Nixon Administration and its successors will continue making efforts to bring inflation in the domestic economy under control.

But when the unemployment rate rises, and when serious signs of slowdowns show up in some sectors of the economy, one or another of the branches of government responsible for inflation control will soften the hard line they were following during most of 1969. Sooner or later the Federal Reserve will intervene to support government bond prices at lower interest rates through open-market buying operations, or reduce stringent bank deposit reserve requirements, or raise the ceiling on permissible rates of interest which banks may pay on certificates of deposit, or take other action leading to monetary ease and flexibility. It would take a long spell of tight money to dispel the forgotten man's continuing expectations of monetary ease, and a real bust to break his morbid expectations of more inflation.

The above observations and those which follow about future

events in the United States economy claim no source of authority other than personal judgment. It is hoped that an attentive reader of earlier chapters of this book who was in general agreement with their contents would be able to project them toward the future, and arrive at more or less the same conclusions indicated here.

THE OUTLOOK FOR BUSINESS TO THE MID-1970's

Consumer prices have been rising recently at an annual rate approaching 6 percent. Important wage contracts are now being settled with 10 percent or better annual increases. New York public school teachers in 1969 secured a contract that specifies a 13 percent yearly decrease in the teaching time content of each educational payroll dollar. Construction workers' annual raises are more than teachers'. In July 1969 there was a $2.6 billion increase in the Federal payroll. This decreasing labor productivity in each dollar is not being controlled by any governmental agency, and none is trying to control it. No power group is in favor of wage, price, and credit controls.

Since the rate of wage increases will not be slowed, and will if anything accelerate, the rate of price increases will not be slowed to any great extent in the next year or two. Current interest rates of 9 and 10 percent on bonds offer real returns of only about 3 or 4 percent when the annual rate of price increases is subtracted. Borrowers are willing to pay 9 and 10 percent interest rates because they foresee being able to pay back in depreciated dollars.

The high rate of wage increases in the early 1970's will mean that consumers will have more money in their pockets, payrolls will be higher, retail store sales will increase, and sales of other items to consumers will increase. When the income tax surcharge is reduced or ends in 1970, and other Federal tax reductions are enacted, consumer purchasing power will jump even more. Government spending will continue to rise. The gross national product will pass $935 billion. In 1970 the gross national product is likely to pass the $1 trillion mark and by the end of the 1970's the $2 trillion mark.

DETERIORATION OF THE U.S. BUSINESS CLIMATE

Between 1962 and 1965 improvement took place in the United States' business climate when the government granted liberalized de reciation allowances and added an investment tax credit of 7 per-cent. In 1964 and 1965 two reductions in corporate income taxes were approved, and at the same time personal income taxes were reduced. But the last years of the 1960's saw a basic deterioration in the business climate. Rising taxes at local, state, and national levels, higher interest rates and tighter credit, increasing demands from labor for higher wages and more fringe benefits, and the threat that wage, price, and credit controls might be imposed by the government brought on the inflation that obscured this worsening of the business climate. Prices and profits have risen for many companies, but keen competition has prevented others from raising prices sufficiently to offset higher taxes and wage costs. In addition, because of inflation, earnings increases stated in dollar terms often concealed actual declines in earnings stated in terms of real purchasing power. While wage rises were averaging about 7 percent, labor productivity increases since 1965 were below the normal level of about 3.2 percent a year.

Late in 1969, as the decade ended, it became clear that a down-turn in economic activity was beginning from the slowdown in housing starts, a drop in the stock market, a lower rate of business investment in plant and equipment and in construction, tight controls on the money supply and high interest rates. From 1966 onward there had been relatively little growth in the earnings of basic industry, and this was reflected in the beginnings of the business recession, and the severe drop in stock prices. In 1970 we will probably be going through a recession more severe than anything we have had since World War II, but one entirely different from the 1929 Depression. Businesses will not shut down and people will not be selling apples on the street corners. Prices and Wages will not fall very much, and unemployment will rise but not very much.

CROUCHING DOWN ON THE STARTING BLOCKS FOR A
NEW UPWARD BOUND

After the recession period, government will stimulate business to get it back on the upward track, and there will be a renewed burst of inflation in which during some periods prices will rise about as fast as they had been rising before.

Over the period of the next five years the major measures of

United States business activity will advance about 7 percent per annum in dollar terms. After the recession period, gross national product, the most comprehensive indicator of overall activity, will grow at an average rate of about 6.7 percent per year. This rate would be somewhat lower than the 7.8 percent average annual growth in gross national product shown by the economy during the 1963–1968 period. The growth in gross national product referred to here is in dollar terms, not in physical or real terms of value.

The price inflation that has been proceeding at a rate of about 4–5 percent per annum for the general price level will be checked slightly from time to time by the recession and by governmental pressure such as the Nixon Administration, Congress, and the Federal Reserve System all applied during 1969. But the rate of inflation will not remain below 3 percent per annum for any long period of time. For the five-year period the average rate of price increases will be well above this rate. This will further accentuate the difference between past and future rates of growth in gross national product, when gross national product is stated in physical or real terms instead of in dollar terms.

The principal reason for the slowdown in overall growth during the next five years is that unemployment is and will remain near its lowest possible level. Whenever we are at or near the full-employment ceiling, growth in employment and employable people is limited to growth in the total labor force, because the labor force can no longer be increased by hiring the unemployed. Thus a major source of growth in production has been eliminated.

The projected increase in gross national product over the next five years is high by comparison with practically all earlier periods except the immediately preceding years. This continued high level of growth will be possible because more of the present "hard-core" unemployed will be drawn into the labor force through more effective and comprehensive training programs. Each labor hour will also become more productive because the economy will be deriving the benefits of the major investments in plant and equipment that have been made by businesses during the past five or six years.

The amount of money that consumers will have to spend will grow at a slower rate than during the 1963–1968 period, slowing from 7.8 percent per year during that period of growth of gross national product to about 6.2 percent. Future growth in consumer disposable in come will not keep pace with the projected growth in gross national product because tax payments by consumers will be even higher than they are now, primarily because of more sales taxes and local income taxes. Even though federal income tax rates do not increase, inflation will push taxpayers' incomes into higher brackets where taxes will take higher taxable percentages of their income.

Since the rate of inflation will continue at only a little below present rates, interest rates will not fall back to the low levels of the 1950's, and so will attract savings of perhaps as much as 6 percent of disposable income.

During the past five years, corporate profits grew at an annual rate of about 9 percent per year, but during the next five years such growth will come nowhere near matching this rate and will be closer to a rate of about 6 percent or so per annum. The reasons for this include the lower rate of growth in gross national product, the likelihood of higher overall tax rates, higher depreciation charges resulting from the high rate of capital investment during the previous five years, higher wages and the lower rate of growth in disposable income in the hands of consumers. Dividends of corporations may expand a little faster than corporate earnings and rise from $26.2 billion in 1969 to $33 billion or so in the period of the next five years.

People will not want paper dollars; they will want tangible property, land, natural resources, timber, minerals in the ground, and the stocks of companies holding these properties. They will want investments in companies that can increase their profits faster than the value of the dollar declines. Stocks of such companies should have demonstrated a long-term growth in earnings at a rate faster than the general rise in the price level. Dividend payments on such stocks as well as their market values will tend to increase as profits grow. One fairly reliable indicator of such a growth stock is a past record in which earnings and dividends have doubled about every ten years.

"It Takes All the Running You Can Do to Keep in the Same Place"

By volume, the average adult human body contains 65 percent oxygen, 18 percent carbon, 10 percent hydrogen, 3 percent nitrogen, and traces of silver and gold. These chemical elements were worth about 98 cents in 1936. By 1969 the value of your chemical elements was $3.50, not counting the value of the DDT, dieldrin, and stron tium 90 which were not present in any human bodies then but are it all today.

Congress has repeatedly boosted the minimum wage. It was onc $1.50 an hour, then $1.60 an hour, and now appeals are heard t(raise it to $2 an hour. This pushes up labor costs and keeps man) young people and unskilled workers out of jobs, thereby placing up ward pressures on all prices.

Today the highest interest rates in the last hundred years are a sur(indicator of everybody's expectations of more inflation. The erosio of the purchasing power of the dollar, and of all paper money, i probably the most important financial fact of all in the future of you money.

What practical investment options do you have to protect yoursel and your family against the risks of inflation? Undeveloped and im proved real estate, precious metals, precious stones, jewelry, antiques and art objects and other kinds of tangible property, of course. Bu the most widely used inflation hedge there is, common stocks and re lated securities, over long periods of time provide by far the best in vestment protection for most people.

Of course, not all common stocks can be counted on to stay aheac of or even with inflation. You must look for stocks that are able t(overcome inflation. Many companies are simply unable to improv(efficiency and productivity to cover 6 percent to 7 percent annual ad vances in hourly wages and 3 percent to 4 percent in nonlabor costs plus the surtax and increases in other tax costs and commodity costs To stay even, companies must usually increase their annual sale: volume by at least 5 percent or better. There are five important things an investor must look for in seeking protection against infla tion through investment in stocks.

1. *Low labor costs.* Wages, salaries, and related benefits represen about one-third of cost in most manufacturing operations, and in service industries they represent an even larger percentage of cost. Companies with relatively low payroll costs are in a better position t(deal with higher wage demands than those with higher payroll cos ratios. For example, company A's labor costs are 40 percent of sales company B's, 20 percent. Both show pretax earnings of 10 percent o sales. If hourly wages go up 10 percent, A's profits drop by 40 percent those of B drop by only 20 percent. If both raise prices equally at the

270

time of the wage increases, B's gain in earnings will be double that of A's. Industries with a low labor-cost factor include oil, personal care products, beverages, food processing, retailing, and electric and gas utilities.

2. *Low capital requirements.* In building construction the annual rate of pay increases has been high, amounting to 15 or 20 percent or more, while gains in productivity have been small. High interest costs go with rapid inflation. Industries with low capital requirements are not as hard hit by inflation as the ones with high capital needs. Plant construction can be even more inflationary than acquiring equipment. The company with low labor costs but high capital requirements and heavy investments in equipment may simply be substituting some other firm's labor cost for its own. Industries with low capital requirements include drugs, personal-care products, beverages, textbooks, photographic equipment, and service businesses such as banks and life insurance companies. However, low capital requirements often mean low profit margins because of the competition that arises from ease of entry into the business.

3. *High return.* The higher a company's return on its investments, the less vulnerable it is apt to be to inflation. Some manufacturers with high capital requirements earn a high return, but these are an exception to the general rule that companies with low capital requirements are better investments. The companies with low capital requirements usually have a high rate of return on their investments. Industries with high capital investment that enjoy a high rate of return are automobiles, synthetic fibers, computers, office equipment, industrial machinery, gypsum, and plywood.

4. *Flexible pricing structure.* A company that is able to raise its prices sufficiently to keep pace with inflation prevents its profits from shrinking. Obviously, companies in regulated industries such as utilities and transportation, including air transport, are seriously handicapped. Some large-scale industries that are not subject to direct regulation are nevertheless in markets that are rigid in pricing and in which prices are difficult to change. Typical of these are steel, aluminum, and automobiles. Companies with more flexible pricing structures fall into several groups. There are those that place emphasis on new products that can be priced more flexibly than products with a price history, such as ethical drugs, chemicals, electronics, plastics, and auto equipment. Products that emphasize quality per-

formance permit price flexibility: medical equipment, measuring and testing equipment, computers, office copiers, and business services. In nonessentials such as soft drinks, proprietary drugs, snack foods, candy, TV advertising, and personal-care products there is also considerable flexibility.

5. *Producer of raw materials.* A company that produces a raw material whose supply is limited by nature or national policy, such as timber, oil, uranium and precious minerals, is also likely to be a sound hedge against inflation.

Only a few companies will score high in all categories. Along with these factors, long-standing characteristics of a growth company include a strong demand for its products, heavy emphasis by the company on research and development, continued technological development, and a high rate of plowing back earnings.

GROWING HEDGES AGAINST INFLATION

A growth stock may be described as stock of a company whose management retains income that would otherwise be paid out in the form of dividends and reinvests the money in the business. Thus the cash dividend often seems small. But the retained earnings of the company should eventually be reflected in an increase in the market value of the stock, and in an increase of the multiple by which the market capitalizes the annual earnings of the stock.

In general, stock prices tend to reflect the prospects for future earnings of a company, rather than its invested capital. But invested or reinvested capital helps create future earnings, and evaluations of the stock in the marketplace reflect this. Thus, if you and your wife have joint taxable income of $44,000, and your additional income is thus in the 50 percent income tax bracket, you will pay one-half of every $100 you receive in dividends to the government and keep only $50 for yourself.

However, if you invest in a stock that grows in capital value by reinvestment of its earnings instead of paying out earnings in dividends, and the stock grows as you anticipated, when you sell the stock for a $100 long-term capital gain, the $100 will be taxed at only about 25 percent, leaving you with $75 after taxes instead of the $50 you would have had left if you had received the $100 as dividends. The trick here, of course, is to pick the "growth" stock successfully.

Looking for stocks of companies whose earnings are resistant to

272

inflation is not the same thing as looking for growth characteristics in a stock. The stock market makes the final judgment on whether a stock is a growth stock or not by setting the price. Once you have decided that a stock investment is fundamentally sound and reasonably well-protected against inflation, it is useful to test your conclusions against the following analysis made from a somewhat different angle of vision—how the market itself might appraise your selection in terms of its growth characteristics.

By current market standards, many of the stocks that will be sound investments for holding for five or ten years longer will probably be found in four major areas. The first is companies in electric data processing, business and office equipment, automatic merchandising, and the field of electronics and automation. These companies can help all other companies reduce labor costs. They can be small or large. IBM, Xerox, and General Electric are the large ones, and they will continue to grow over the years.

Another area is companies in the cosmetics and toiletries business, and services, and in fields that benefit from people's increased leisure time and the spurt in education and welfare activities. Avon Products, Revlon, Walt Disney Productions, Eastman Kodak, Polaroid, and Pinkerton are examples of stocks in this category.

A third area for investing includes stocks of the many new small companies engaged in science and technology and in applications of the scientific research done in recent years.

The fourth area is natural-resource companies that own land, minerals, gold, silver, uranium, timber, oil, gas, and other basic commodities. In five or ten years, raw land owned by such companies may be worth many times its present value. Such companies include General Development Corporation, Arvida, Castle & Cooke, Alexander & Baldwin, and other companies with extensive land investments in California, Arizona, and New Mexico. Promising timber-resource companies are Union Camp Paper, Weyerhaeuser, Georgia Pacific Plywood, and Boise, Cascade. Other natural-resource companies are, of course, Standard Oil Company of New Jersey, Mobil Oil, McCulloch Oil, Newmont Mining, Utah Construction, and American Metal Climax.

A wide range of consumer-oriented companies, such as medical equipment manufacturers, fish food producers, and auto rental agencies are active in areas where the economy will be growing fast.

On the other hand, not much growth can be expected from the

automobile industry, nor the railroad industry as such, although some railroads own substantial natural resources and their stocks may be growth investments for this reason. Utility stocks appear to be low in price but are adversely affected by high interest rates and the impact of regulation. When an American Telephone & Telegraph Bell System company, for example, must borrow capital at rates of 9 percent and more, and regulatory agencies allow it a rate of return no better than that, you cannot expect much from it in the way of dynamic growth.

An investor should never invest all his cash reserves. It is always wise to have about 10 percent of your reserves available for investment in cash or cash equivalents such as savings bank accounts or U.S. Treasury bills. If you have $10,000 to invest you should keep $1,000 available as your cash reserve, and if you have $1 million to invest you should keep $100,000 in reserve in cash equivalents. It is a fundamentally sound practice to follow "dollar averaging." No one can outguess consistently all of the ups and downs of the stock market or the economy, but if a regular sum of money is invested in the stock market at regular periodic intervals, if past history is a guide, over a long period of time they will show impressive gains.

To be arbitrary, a woman in her seventies probably should be "conservative" (in investment jargon) and keep her portfolio perhaps 50 percent in short-term or medium-term bonds and 50 percent in stocks. Young men in their thirties and forties should probably keep nearly all of their funds in growth common stocks, or convertible bonds, or preferreds with growth characteristics, except for an emergency reserve. A man in his fifties should probably keep about one-third of his funds in reserves of cash or short-term government securities, with the other two-thirds in stocks with growth characteristics.

An elderly widow who had only $100,000 in insurance money with which to support herself should put perhaps one-third of this in mutual funds, another third in high-yielding bonds, and the rest in savings bank accounts so that she receives a combination of high income from the bonds and low income but possible growth income from the mutual fund's stocks, and also has cash reserves in the bank from which to draw in case of need. By and large most typical investors are better off with good-quality growth stock than with bonds, because in one sense bonds are more of a speculation. If the

274

dollar is going to be worth less and less over the years, the money you get back when you sell your bonds is not going to buy as much.

Price-earning ratios (the market price of the stock in relation to its actual earnings) of many of the most volatile and popular growth stocks are high, and the yields are low. In the uncertain investment climate of the next few years, an investor should look for issues with above-average growth potentials, to be sure, but also above-average yields, and below-average price times earnings ratios. Above-average growth means greater growth in earnings during the past five years than the 9 percent mean annual growth rate of the Standard & Poor's average of industrial stocks. Another important clue is a bigger advance in estimated earnings in 1969 and 1970 and over the projected average gains of all industrial stocks for the same period. Another is a lower price-earnings ratio than the current combined average of sixteen times or so shown by the industrial averages. Still another clue is a yield of better than the 2.8 percent recent average of the industrials. An example of such a stock would be M. Lowenstein and Sons, with a five-year growth rate of 28 percent, $2.50 in 1968 earnings, a 38 percent increase over the prior year, a price times earnings ratio of 10.4, and a yield of 3.1 percent.

Averages of stock prices are, of course, not the same thing as the price of a single stock. When a company can maintain a rate of growth higher than 10 percent per annum, the market will place a higher value on the stock than the ratio of 12 to 13 times earnings which is typical of many of the investment grade stocks which go to make up the Dow Jones Industrial Average, its price will rise in the market. However, no stock is immune from the action of other stocks in the market. If high quality blue chip stocks such as General Motors and DuPont, and the other stocks which are components of the Dow Jones Industrial averages, sell at lower multiples of earnings, nearly all stocks will to some degree be affected, even though their multiples of earnings remain above the average.

In the summer of 1969 it became apparent that growth in corporate earnings and dividends in general was slowing. Interest costs of 8½ percent and more, and higher wages, higher prices of raw materials and higher taxes were also cutting into profits. It appeared to the market that the average stock should not sell at multiples of earnings of more than twelve to thirteen times, and almost all stocks declined sharply.

275

Your mother, your son, yourself, and every other investor can be assured of an annual return of 6 percent or more on your money if you invest a large enough sum in short term government bonds; in 1969 some United States Treasury Bills reached historically high yields of around 8 percent. But as a general rule, in longer term bonds you will have no protection from the attrition of inflation, no special tax benefits, and little or no possibility of capital appreciation. If you want to do better, you will have to accept more risk and face more possibility of loss.

Bond prices have been declining most of the time since 1948, and there have been recent periods when almost everyone who ever owned a bond owned it at a loss. They may go still lower in price, but in 1969 bond yields—that is, coupon interest rates plus the difference between the market price and the par value which would be paid at maturity—were at the highest levels that they have ever been in the history of the United States. If history is any use at all as a guide, bond yields can hardly go much higher than they are today and may well work their way somewhat lower. By the same token, bond capital values can hardly go much lower and may work somewhat higher. If you buy a bond selling at a deep discount from its maturity value only a few years away from maturity, you can be assured of a capital gain when the bond reaches maturity and is redeemed at face value.

If, indeed, the efforts of our government officials, the Federal Reserve System, and the International Monetary Fund to force the United States to reduce its domestic rate of inflation succeed, and the forgotten man's inflationary expectations subside, bond investments you make at current high-yield levels will prove to have been excellent investments. If the capital growth of common-stock values should be no more than 6 percent per year, and the dividend yield of such common stocks is no more than 3 percent, and bonds selling below par yield 9 percent, bonds offer a comparable yield overall, with much less risk (leaving aside tax and other considerations). If the particular stock you pick fails to share the average rate of gain, you will be well ahead with your bond. At current yields over the short and medium term, investments in properly selected bonds are likely to prove more re-

276

warding than many investments in stocks, and provide considerably greater security.

Over the longer term, however, bond investments will probably prove to be disappointing. For example, the manager of a large teachers' retirement investment fund pointed out that an 8½ percent current interest yield on the bonds in his portfolio versus an 8 percent return (5 percent annual capital appreciation plus 3 percent annual dividend yield) on the stocks might make it appear that prudent investors should put money into the bond market at current rates. But when he compared the results of the portfolio's stock investments and bond investments made fourteen years earlier, on the basis of cost of the stocks alone, the current dividend yield was 7¾ percent per annum on the investment. And when the capital appreciation on the stocks was added, the overall return on stocks was 13 percent or more. Over the same period the return on the bond investments was a loss. Taxable bonds may be fine for your mother, but not for you.

Pension-fund managers who have studied all the statistics over the long run find that the overall return from well-selected stocks, from price appreciation plus dividend income, is almost 10 percent per annum.

On the other hand, a tax-exempt bond paying 6 percent per year in tax-exempt income that could be worth at least 12 percent per annum to you in spendable income after taxes is a better overall annual return than you can make from all but the best selected stock investments.

NEW CONVERTS TO CONVERTIBLE PREFERREDS
STOCKS AND BONDS

Convertible bonds and convertible preferred stocks are an increasingly important investment medium that combines the relative security of bond investments and fixed yields with the possibility of capital appreciation of common stocks. In all such investments it is prudent to determine whether too great a premium is being paid for the convertible feature.

Convertible preferred stocks have an edge over their common-stock counterparts because they usually carry a higher yield. If the company's common stock drops, the higher yielding convertible preferred is usually protected from a portion of the decline because at a certain level it begins to sell on the basis of its value as a straight preferred stock on the basis of its fixed dividend rate. On the other hand, if the company's common stock advances, the conversion feature of the convertible preferred stock enables it to participate in the gain much as if it were actually the common stock into which it is convertible. In many cases the odds in favor of good performance in both directions are with the preferred. It is sometimes a complex matter to determine whether the price being asked for the conversion feature is too high, so the real values in convertible stocks and bonds are often overlooked by investors because they require an additional degree of investment sophistication.

An example of this recently given by a well-known investment service shows that if a certain company's convertible preferred stocks or bonds were purchased, and if the common stock were to rise 25 percent, the preferred would advance 20 percent. But if the common were to decline 25 percent, the preferred would decline only 10 percent. Here the preferred would seem to be a better investment than the common. But in some convertible preferreds, the leverage is unfavorable; such would be the case, for example, if the common were to rise 25 percent and the preferred would advance only 10 percent, while if the common declined 25 percent the preferred would decline 20 percent.

Convertible bonds and convertible preferred have many similar investment characteristics. Large numbers of convertible bonds are available in the markets all the time. For example, Gulf & Western 5½ percent convertible debentures due July 1, 1993, recently sold at around $77 ($772.50 per $1,000 par). This issue was convertible into 17.17 shares of Gulf & Western common stock ($1,000 par divided by the conversion price of $58.24 per share). Without the conversion privilege, this low-quality bond, which pays $55 annually in interest and is redeemable at par in July 1993, is estimated to have an investment value of $700 based on a recent level of interest rates. Thus the convertible bond was selling at a 10 percent premium over its straight bond value, and at 28 percent over its conversion value. With an investment value of $70 and a conversion value of $60, it sold at $77. The only reason for this was that it offered lower downside risk than the common, in this case less than 10 percent above the estimated "floor" at $70. It has a higher yield since at current prices it pays over 7 percent, while the yield on the common is only about 1 percent. On the other hand, it does have a lower upside potential, and may not advance as rapidly as the common.

GAMBITS FOR THE IMPOVERISHED RICH

If you are in a sufficiently high tax bracket, it might pay you to borrow money, even at today's historically high rates of 8 or 9 percent, to invest in properly selected investments, if the interest would be deductible on your income tax return. For example, when you are in the 50 percent income tax bracket (at $44,000 of taxable income on your joint return), the cost to you after taxes of 8 percent interest you would have to pay is only 4.01 percent; if you were to take the money you borrow at this net interest cost of 4.01 percent and buy a 6 percent tax-free bond with it, you would be gaining almost 2 percent by the use of the borrowed money. The higher your income tax bracket the greater your advantage. Although the tax-exempt bond you purchase will decline in capital value as a result of inflation, so will the money you use to repay the loan. There are limitations on your deducting interest from borrowings incurred to carry tax-exempt securities, so before embarking on a transaction of this kind you should check the applicable law.

Mutual fund shares and variable annuities are an increasingly popular method of protecting retirement income from inflation. The premiums you pay on a variable annuity contract are invested in equity securities, and the annuity contract provides for payments over the lifetime of the annuitant with the dollar amount varying in accordance with the performance of the investments. The underlying assumption is that stock prices and cost of living will tend to keep pace with each other. This is obviously subject to exceptions. The stock market is much more volatile than cost-of-living indexes and will sometimes decline while the cost of living continues to climb, as in 1962, 1966, and 1969. Ordinarily, however, there is sufficient correlation between the two to justify the basic selling point that these vehicles provide good long-term protection against inflation.

As we have seen, the price of gold officially has remained unchanged for many years. During the year after the Ides of March in money, when gold traded on the free market, its rise to over $40 an ounce about equaled the general rise in domestic prices during the decade in percentage terms. Thus if you had made a long-term investment in gold, you would have done no better than remain even with inflation during the ten-year period and would have had no interest on your money.

The United States government exerts a strong influence over gold and will continue to do so. There is the possibility of some official rise in the price of gold, such as a doubling, in the future. But gold is not recommended as an investment here because it is too risky and too slow, and besides it is illegal for United States citizens. Ownership of gold involves serious downside risks that outweigh the possible gains.

Silver is somewhat the same. The current price is far above what it was ten years ago. An investment in silver at the beginning of the past decade would have yielded a 6 percent to 7 percent return compounded annually (including insurance cost). This return would have been greater than the average rate of inflation of about 25 percent during the period, or 2 percent annually, and greater than the return on bonds, but lower than an average return on stocks, considering divided income of about 3 percent plus capital appreciation of about 5 percent, or a total of 8 percent. In a year or two the price of silver may well be twice what it is today. Currently, however, the metal has seemed to be in oversupply, leaving aside speculative demand. Domestic consumption exceeds production in domestic mines, but secondary sources of recovery and foreign sources of supply, unmelted coins, speculators' holdings, and so forth, would contribute to keeping the price increase at reasonable levels if there should be a rise.

Indirect ownership of gold and silver through purchase of stocks in mining companies does not appear to be a very promising prospect. South African gold-mining corporations pay high dividends, currently on the order of 9 percent or more. But South Africa has a progressive tax-rate structure for corporations somewhat like our progressive tax-rate structure for individuals and unlike our flat-rate structure that applies to corporate earnings. The richest South African gold mine, Free State Geduld, paid 66 percent of its profits to the government in various taxes in 1968. It has been estimated that if the price of gold were doubled, 63 percent to 74 percent of the increase in profits that would accrue to the mining companies would be taxed away by the South African government.

An examination of the price-earnings multiples and prospects and reserves of Homestake Mining, the only American gold-mining company of consequence, is not encouraging. The stocks of silver companies also lack quality and do not have great promise. Standard investment-grade stocks, convertible preferreds, and convertible bonds in the stock markets can serve your purposes better.

REAL ESTATE AS AN INVESTMENT

A recent study by the United States Chamber of Commerce projects a population of 325,000,000 people in the United States by the year 2000, or about two-thirds more than the current 200 million or so. The same study projects an almost five-fold increase in gross national product by the year 2000, based on current prices. The supply of real estate is finite and the demand for it will thus be backed by cash, so real estate values seem to have no upper limit. The growth in the economy that goes with a big increase in the gross national product, the demands of industry for land to anticipate the industrial explosion, the rising expectations of our increasingly affluent society for better homes, better schools, better shopping centers, better community planning, more recreation areas, and better transportation all combine to make real estate an irresistible prospect for long-term investment.

There is no other form of investment in which financing is available on as favorable terms. There are many situations in which you can put up as little as 10 percent and have the rest of the value of the property financed at prevailing interest rates. In effect, many real estate transactions are nothing more than options, with the promoters assuming the risk only to the extent of their investment of 10 percent or so, but being entitled to the benefits flowing from the entire transaction if it is successful.

Real estate also enjoys unique tax advantages: depreciation deductions while the property may actually be increasing in market value, capital-gains treatment for profits, delayed realization of capital gains, and favorable treatment of carrying costs such as mortgage interest and taxes.

Here is an example of the financial consequences of one of the innumerable types of real estate investment.

Assume you are single and that when you retire you will have a

281

taxable income of $6000 a year and $25,000 to invest. If you put it in stocks you will receive perhaps a 6 percent pretax return, or $1500. Out of this you will keep only about $1150 after taxes (less if surtax and local, state, and city taxes are included).

In tax-exempt municipal bonds you may earn 5½ percent to 6 percent if you play it safe, so you will earn about the same $1500, which will all be tax-exempt (unless the law is changed).

Suppose you put the same $25,000 into buying a piece of real estate that costs $125,000, and you give a mortgage for the $100,000 balance at 7 percent interest. Of the purchase price, $100,000 is allocated to the building and $25,000 to the land. You rent the building out for $20,000 a year. It has a useful life of twenty-five years and no salvage value.

The first year your mortgage interest will be $7000 and your real estate taxes and other expenses will be $4000, making your total operating expenses $11,000. Your $20,000 of rent less $11,000 of operating expenses leaves you a net income of $9000. But your annual depreciation allowance using straight-line depreciation is $4000; deducting this leaves only $5000 subject to tax. On your overall income of $6000 plus this taxable $5000, the tax is $2510 of which the portion attributable to the real estate income is $1380. The net return from the real estate after taxes to you is $7620. You can make a mortgage amortization payment of $2000 the first year and still be well ahead of the yield you would have derived from your stock or bond investment.

Raw land, land that is not presently in use and for which no specific use has yet been determined, is potentially the most profitable kind of real estate investment. Land patterns change slowly, and if a change is already apparent it will be reflected in the present asking price. Therefore any investment in raw land if it is to be highly profitable must also be highly speculative. But purely as an inflation hedge, for a long-term holding, the risks of a real estate holding in raw land are not likely to be great.

In terms of land needs, the next thirty-five years should see at least a doubling of land needed for urban development. Thus, carefully selected tracts of farmland on the outskirts of cities are not only a hedge against inflation but may have great profit potential as well.

But as in any kind of investing, there are lemons. It may be many

282

years before you will be able to get back what you paid for a plot of land in a central Florida development which an enthusiastic promoter who told you things were about to boom sold you the day after you arrived in the sunshine from Boston last January.

A LESSON IN ART APPRECIATION

Not long ago the *Times* of London and Sotheby's Gallery made a study of prices paid during the period 1951–1967 at public auctions at Sotheby's, Christie's, and the Parke-Bernet galleries in New York for paintings by six leading impressionist painters: Renoir, Monet, Fantin-Latour, Sisley, Boudin, and Pissaro. Prices of impressionist paintings increased almost ten times, while stock market averages rose only about 3½ times during the same period. Sisleys gained 1150 percent and Monets gained 1100 percent, while Renoirs showed the slowest rate of increase, gaining only 405 percent over the period.

There is increasing interest in the works of American artists. Paintings by Andrew Wyeth bring prices ranging up from $100,000. The works of Gilbert Stuart, Charles Wilson Peale, Thomas Sully, James McNeill Whistler, John Singer Sargent, Albert Pinkham Ryder, Frederic Remington, Charles M. Russell, Charles K. Bingham, George Catlin, Alfred Jacobs, John James Audubon, Thomas Eakins, Peter Hurd, Grant Wood, Edward Hopper, Childe Hassam, and Winslow Homer are in great demand. One of Charles Russell's finest works, "The Surround," which sold for $6000 in 1942, was being offered for sale a year or two ago at $125,000.

Rising living standards bring rising museum attendance and rising interest in art in general. More and more people are aware of the value of art not only for its beauty but as an investment and inflation hedge.

Richard H. Rush, author of *Art as an Investment* * suggests that of the sixteen major schools of painting, the following are the best prospects for investment: baroque and 18th-century Italian, 17th-century Dutch, modern expressionists, lesser impressionists and major French painters of the period, American 18th-century, contemporary British artists, and carefully selected American contemporary artists.

But some schools do not seem to offer good prospects because they have already attained such high prices and thin markets that not

* Englewood Cliffs, N.J.: Prentice-Hall, 1961.

much further appreciation can be expected: Italian schools earlier than baroque, German 16th-century art, the important classical Spanish artists, French artists of the 17th and 18th centuries, preimpressionists and postimpressionists, the greatest moderns, and 19th-century British painters.

Investments and Taxes

You will hear about many tax-saving opportunities which you should ask your lawyer to explain to you. But remember that the tax law is undergoing sweeping changes. Some of the possible opportunities are enumerated here in generalized form. These include (1) investments on which the losses are fully deductible from ordinary income but from which the income is received at capital-gains rates, such as breeding cattle, sales of timber, and capital-gains distribution from mutual funds. (2) Income that can be taken or reported currently or can be postponed, such as interest on United States Government E bonds. (3) Investments in securities that have special tax protection, such as tax-exempt bonds, and certain stocks of utilities and other companies whose dividends are nontaxable or partially nontaxable as representing a return of capital. (4) There are particular types of business investments, particularly in small companies with capitalizations of less than $1 million on which the gains are capital gains and the losses are fully deductible if the business fails. Some of these are known as Section 1244 stocks. (5) By paying premiums on an insurance policy there is an assured buildup in value that can be realized tax-free by the beneficiary through the life-insurance proceeds. (6) Certain types of investments produce an assured buildup in value that can either be realized at capital-gains rates or used to produce income. For example, natural growth or propagation enhances the value of a citrus grove or a timber tract or a cattle herd in such a way that the higher values cannot be taxed until the property is sold.

Basic Tax Strategies for Investing

A few basic rules for investing within the framework of present tax laws are worth repeating.

Invest in vehicles in which you can keep the capital loss small, within the limit that can be deducted against ordinary income, and in which the prospect of capital gain is high in relation to the impact

284

of possible loss. Speculative common stocks are the best example of this kind of investment.

Stabilize your income over a period of years and smooth out the peaks and valleys in order to keep the peaks out of the highest income tax brackets. If possible, make contractual arrangements to spread ordinary income over longer periods of time in order to avoid peak rates in one period and to defer the tax liability as much as possible.

Accelerate or postpone income and expenses to fit the tax rates prospectively applicable. If a 10 percent income tax surcharge applicable to 1969 income is reduced or terminated in 1970, it obviously would be sound planning to defer as much income as possible to 1970 or 1971 where it will be subject to a lower surcharge or none at all, and bunch as many deductions as possible in 1969 where they would offset income that otherwise would be taxed at the higher rates.

If possible, spread income among all of the members of a family group, each of whose tax brackets start from zero and each of whom would thus be in lower brackets than you. Gifts of income-producing securities to your children or parents is an obvious way to accomplish this.

If you have a business, build up capital values in it by expenditures that are deductible from its income; for example, for research, development, and promotion.

If you are a businessman, you can select a form of business appropriate to your personal plans for drawing down income. For example, during the early period of a business venture when you anticipate losses in getting started, use the form of a limited partnership, a proprietorship, or a "subchapter S corporation" (ask your lawyer what this is) so that the losses can be charged against your own individual income, which is taxed at higher rates. When the corporation begins to show a profit, incorporate the business so that the income will then be taxed to the corporation at the flat corporate rates (22 percent or 48 percent), which may be lower than your own graduated individual rates. The corporate income then brought under the corporate umbrella may later be converted to capital gain by liquidating the corporation or by sale of the stock of the corporation.

These investments with built-in tax benefits but which involve great risks are fine for taxpayers in high brackets but of no importance to taxpayers in low tax brackets. It is impossible to do more here than give a bird's eye view of the innumerable investment vehicles that are available and how they relate to the general scheme of the tax law environment.

Besides stocks and bonds or standard portfolio investments, there are many more esoteric types of investments such as wash sales, short sales, puts and calls, straddles, spreads, strips and straps, and options and warrants.

Trading in commodities markets in such things as silver, platinum, and palladium, frozen orange juice, cocoa and pork bellies, soybeans, and hides can be carried on by putting up a modest amount of capital—10 percent or so—and can produce quick and spectacular profits, and staggering losses as well.

THE PRICE OF PESSIMISM

Professor Falk, as we saw, finds the planet and mankind in grave danger of irreversible catastrophe if the present political structure is not drastically changed during the next few decades. U Thant has given the world and its people only ten years in which to solve the problems of the population explosion, pollution, the arms race, and the aspirations of the developing countries, but he holds out no hope for any drastic change in the world's political structure.

Scientists have said that the accumulation of DDT, dieldrin, and other long-lived killer chemicals in our environment may soon poison all our food or upset our reproductive processes, just as it has already deranged the genetic processes of bald eagles and brought certain species of osprey to extinction. Experts have warned us that carbons in the air from automobile exhausts and factory wastes and the destruction of green forests have left much less oxygen in the air we breathe than there was in the 18th century, and will soon smother us all to death. There is always the risk of a nuclear detonation or a nerve gas spill or a twitchy finger on a missile trigger setting off an irreversible chain reaction, or a monstrous earthquake, or fatally polluting the atmosphere. This planet could always collide with another. There is always something or other.

And there always has been. The air has always been full of warnings that the world was coming to an end, although they were easier to ignore when worldwide communications were not so instantaneous. But so far the human forces that have threatened to finish our planet have been switched off by other human forces, often barely in the nick of time. There is a statistical possibility that the world will end tomorrow instead of at the end of your life expectancy thirty, forty, fifty, or so years from now.

It is necessary to make certain optimistic assumptions. It is necessary to assume that the runaway locomotive's brakes will hold, and that it will skid to a shuddering stop in the nick of time, with its cowcatcher no more than a perilous inch from Pauline's ear.

History has shown that guarded optimism is the right mental approach to investing. While the optimists have plugged along making fortunes over the years, the pessimists have been losing what they had carefully husbanded against a sudden catastrophe to a creeping inflation. Broadly speaking, the most successful investors are the ones who are lucky enough to strike it rich with a few long-shot winners, and to take losses in many more issues than they win with, by cutting their losses short and letting their winnings run.

A GLIMPSE OF A ROSY FUTURE IN A MURKY CRYSTAL BALL

In the years directly ahead, the rate, form, and manner of the deescalation of the Vietnam war will have a psychological impact on the United States economy entirely out of proportion to its actual economic impact. There is no historical precedent for the United States' position in Vietnam, so projections of the results of our future policy there must be political speculation alone. Assuming that the United States and her allies continue withdrawing troops, by the end of 1970 most United States troops will be out of Vietnam. Even if noncommunist governments fall there and in Laos as well, the troops will not go back. Air and naval support units in Okinawa, Thailand, Taiwan, and other countries on the Asian perimeter that maintain a United States presence may well be increased by almost the same amount that the forces in Vietnam are reduced.

While peace in Vietnam in 1971 or 1972 with or without Falstaffian honor may permit a moderate reduction in defense spending, and will give a psychological boost to the economy, peace in Vietnam alone will not dramatically change the portions of the federal budget going into defense spending and the basic economic factors that will control the economic environment in the next five years.

If the Pursides and the Midases settle their long war in an armistice, as it is believed they will, and if the International Monetary

287

Fund evolves into a truly effective international reserve system, the tension and pressure that will be lifted from the world's money system will provide the world with a vastly improved financial outlook. If at the same time the Vietnam war is ending, the psychological impact will be dramatic. The increase in confidence in international liquidity will unfreeze a serious block to present international trade and will give the stock market and all stocks a powerful lift. In these circumstances the Dow Jones Industrial Average might have little difficulty pushing through the magic 1000 level even though the economy as a whole follows the rather unexciting path of the projections in this chapter. Although the idea of expanded international reserves in the form of SDR's may well increase inflationary expectations, such expectations will also provide a powerful psychological lift for stock prices in the stock market.

If, as suggested elsewhere in this book, the International Monetary Fund gradually acquires most of the free world's monetary reserves of gold and establishes a firm, coherent, and visible link between the paper money of the world's national governments and gold, a basis will exist for restoring the forgotten man's confidence in the commodity basis of his money. No basis for such confidence has existed since the Ides of March in money. If, in addition, the fund evolves into an international reserve system with extensive powers to affect rates of inflation and deflation of particular national currencies, there will be a further lessening in grounds for the forgotten man's expectations of inflation. Removing the power to exercise important controls over inflationary expansion of national currencies from powerful national voting blocks and placing it in the hands of the gaggle of governesses at the fund should also lead to a letup in powerful expectations of inflation. And putting the international reserve system directly behind the creation of one new worldwide money based on the dollar will materially reduce the possibilities of further gold and currency panics, and speculative attacks against one or another national currency. Even though the general economy passes through a recession, even though inflation persists, even though the rate of real, noninflationary growth in the 1970's is slower than in the 1960's, the establishment of such an international reserve system would foster the kind of psychological climate for investment that could cause stocks and bonds generally to move up impressively in price during the decade of the 1970's.

18

HOW WE GOT HERE FROM THERE— OR LIFE UNDER THE GOLDEN RULE

*Just as each individual country painfully
acquired a central banking system, so there
ought—ideally—to be a central banking
system for all the countries of the Free World.*
*All sorts of remedies are being suggested.
The main difficulty about many of them is
what I might call the mental hurdles which
they present. It is normal to think of money as
something painfully acquired; a dollar
represents so many drops of sweat or so many
ulcers. There seems to be something immoral
in increasing the credit base by mutual
agreement. It is done often enough in our
internal economies; but the extension to the
international field is hard to swallow. All the
same, I repeat, expanding trade needs
expanding money.*
*The needs of our time demand a new
attitude. An old-fashioned or doctrinaire
approach is not good enough. We must use
the energy and abundance of our free
enterprise system to transform our economic
life. Above all, we must try to jump—even
the older ones among us—the mental hurdles.*

HAROLD MACMILLAN, *Address at Massachusetts
Institute of Technology, April 7, 1961*

ACQUIRING, LOSING, ACQUIRING, LOSING, AND THEN AGAIN ACQUIRING A CENTRAL BANK

Our country's experience in acquiring, then losing, then acquiring, then losing again, and then again acquiring a central bank has been as painful as that of any other. When the United States was young and just beginning to flex her economic muscles, people's clamor for loans and credit was probably even stronger than it has been in

289

recent years. But through gradual development of powers to regulate the private banks, the First Bank of the United States (1791–1811) controlled the overexpansion of credit much more strictly than the Federal Reserve System attempts to do today. These regulatory powers proliferated unplanned, like the banking business of the London guild of goldsmiths, like the classical gold standard, like the Eurodollar system, and like so many other great inventions in economics.

The early private banks, like their distant predecessors, the goldsmiths, issued notes against their deposits, and these notes circulated as currency in the young country. With these notes businessmen paid their federal excise duties to the federal collectors of revenue. The collectors of revenue in turn deposited the notes in the Bank of the United States, which was the chief depository of the government and had offices in the chief seaports and commercial cities.

As fast as it received these notes, the Bank of the United States would demand that the bank that had issued them redeem them in gold and silver (that is, specie). This automatically prevented the bank from issuing more notes, restricted the banks from overextending credit, and held down the rate of expansion of the money supply and the rate of inflation in the country.

In periods of deflation and panic, the Bank of the United States eased the pressure on the private banks and allowed the money supply to grow. The framers of its charter had not clearly envisaged these important central-banking functions that made the bank such a powerful and effective institution. Political opposition to precisely these powers to impose regulatory restraints that made the bank so effective as a central bank finally overwhelmed it. Its Federal charter lapsed, but it continued to operate as an ordinary commercial bank under a New York state charter.

THE BOOM IN LOCAL BANKS, AND THE BUST

The Second Bank of the United States (1816–1836) under Nicholas Biddle recognized and developed similar central-banking functions. But these responsibilities usually had to be exercised as restraints on overexpansion of credit, so the private banks once again resented them and complained of oppression. It was an expansionary period in industry and transportation. Business was growing and developing and exploiting the resources of the new country, so the very conditions that made central-bank credit restraint necessary also made it objectionable. Speculative and impatient businessmen and traditional agrarian opponents of bankers in general and monopolies in particular joined forces against it, and President Andrew Jackson prevented the renewal of its charter. So in 1836 the Second Bank of the United States expired.

President Jackson then had the collectors of revenue deposit the government's tax collections and other funds in banks incorporated under state law. This touched off a boom in the business of setting up new local banks, which turned into a bust with the panic of May 1837. There followed a disastrous deluge of bank failures, bankruptcies, and a business depression, and the surviving banks stopped paying out gold and silver and coin in specie. A year later a group of New York bankers took the lead in resuming specie payments and firmly established New York as the financial center of the country.

A CONTINENT-WIDE CHECKERBOARD OF CURRENCY CHAOS

In letting the Second Bank of the United States expire without providing for any sort of a successor, the federal government abandoned responsibility for the money system of the country. Each individual state established its own separate state banking system with its own separate rules and regulations. Across the whole country the money system was a checkerboard of currency chaos.

In those days bank notes were the principal circulating medium because checkable demand deposits had not grown to the magnitude of today. State bank notes varied in design and size and material, and also in the degree of protection accorded to the note holder and in the limitations on total issue. At one time about 1600 banks issued approximately 10,000 different kinds of notes. Principal financial houses used a publication known as a "Note Detector" to enable them to distinguish counterfeit notes from genuine ones. If the note of a state bank circulated in another state at all, it could only be at discounts ranging up to 10 and 15 percent and more. As a result, the notes of most state banks had only local circulation.

A Private Central-Banking System,
and New York State's Central Bank

Most states' regulatory systems were directed toward controlling the note liabilities of banks, and for the most part left the banks' depositors to fend for themselves, without official protection. Some states followed the federal example and abdicated public responsibility to the banks themselves for issuance of bank notes. Other states took constructive measures to keep bank currencies strong.

State governments were not the sole source of regulatory control over issuance of bank notes; some private bankers themselves established controls over note issue. For example, the Suffolk Bank of Boston arranged to redeem the notes of all New England banks that would maintain balances with it, and it systematically called on other banks for payment of their notes. When notes of the New England banks that maintained deposit balances with the Suffolk Bank came in, the notes were debited or added to the balances of the depositor banks.

When the First Bank of the United States had received a note from a private bank, it had demanded payment in specie, and it thus regulated such banks as their creditor. But when the Suffolk Bank received a note from one of the other New England banks that maintained deposits with it and added the note to the bank's deposit balance, the Suffolk Bank in effect regulated other banks' note issue as their debtor. The latter relationship is a step more advanced than that between the Bank of the United States and private banks. It is typical of the relationship of present-day national banks and the Federal Reserve System, and of modern commercial banks in foreign countries to the national central bank of their country.

New York State law provided for a safety fund administered by the state to redeem the notes of banks that failed with contributions from each state bank proportional to its deposits. A later law provided that a bank that issued notes had to deposit a proportionate reserve of United States government or New York State securities with the state controller.

In order to finance the Union's war effort, President Lincoln sought to establish a strong national currency acceptable throughout all the states. The National Bank Act of 1863, which was patterned on New York State banking law, provided that national banks could issue notes on the security of government bonds pledged in Washington, D.C., with the controller of the currency, and that their notes would be redeemed through governmental reserve deposits. Thus the nationwide banking system of the federal union evolved as a combination of the private central-banking procedures of the Suffolk Bank and New York's central-bank reserve system.

"THE MOST POWERFUL GROUP OF PRIVATE CITIZENS IN AMERICA"

From this in turn evolved the present Federal Reserve System under the Federal Reserve Act of 1913, consisting of twelve federal reserve districts. Each has its own Federal Reserve Bank, whose initial capital is subscribed by the commercial banks that are members of the system. All twelve reserve banks are coordinated by the seven-member board of governors of the Federal Reserve System in Washington. The twelve-man federal reserve open-market committee includes these seven, plus five representatives from the twelve districts. The Federal Reserve Board in Washington, together with the twelve regional federal reserve banks, is now the United States' central bank. The President appoints Federal Reserve governors for fourteen-year terms, but the board considers that its allegiance is primarily to Congress and not to the executive branch. An "accord" signed in 1951 between the Treasury and the Federal Reserve System recognized its independence.

The board members have rightly been called "the most powerful group of private citizens in America." * The Federal Reserve System, like other national central banks, operates to control the supply of money and credit in the national economy. Through regulation and manipulation of monetary policy, the central bank seeks to foster real growth and a reasonably stable price level in the country, to curb inflationary tendencies, and to prevent recessions and depressions. If business is getting worse and jobs are scarce, the Federal Reserve acts to expand money and credit by increasing the reserves available to banks for lending, by reducing their reserve requirements, or by buying government bonds in the open market in order to place more funds in the hands of the banks, or by making loans to

* Paul A. Samuelson, *Economics,* Seventh Edition, 1967.

to member banks and thereby helping the member banks' reserves to grow.

On the other hand, if inflation occurs and spending threatens to become excessive, and prices rise rapidly and there is full employment with many job vacancies and no one to fill them, then the central bank cuts down on the reserves available to banks for lending. This is done by raising reserve requirements, selling securities in the open market to force deposited funds out of banks and back to the Federal Reserve system, and raising interest rates on the loans it makes to member banks for their reserves—that is, the central bank raises the "discount" rate. It also regulates the rates of interest banks can pay depositors on certain types of deposits. For example, by limiting to $6\frac{1}{4}$ percent (under Regulation Q) the interest commercial banks can pay on certificates of deposit when prevailing money-market interest rates are higher, the central bank causes the commercial banks to lose deposits, deprives them of lendable funds, and curtails the amounts of demand-deposit credit available for private borrowers and municipal governments to use for more expansion.

The Federal Reserve is also responsible for the currency itself. Practically all United States currency in circulation today is in form a "Federal Reserve note" and is so legended.

Until the Ides of March of money in 1968, 25 percent of these Federal Reserve note liabilities had to be backed by Federal Reserve gold certificates, which represented gold on deposit with the United States Treasury. As we have seen, Congress repealed this 25 percent gold-backing limitation during the Ides of March of money in 1968. The argument for doing this was to show foreigners that all our gold was available for international purposes, not for domestic purposes, and thus restore foreign confidence in the huge foreign paper-dollar balances held abroad.

The fallacy of this argument, of course, was that foreign confidence in the gold-backed dollar and domestic confidence in the nongold-backed dollar are not simply two separate and distinct issues, in two separate watertight compartments; they are one and the same. If the dollar is strong and stable domestically, it will be strong and stable for international purposes. If it is not strong and stable domestically, it will not be internationally. Domestic stability is what counts; international stability is illusory and temporary if domestic stability does not exist.

Foreign holders of dollars are not really interested in exchanging the dollars they hold for gold itself. They want their paper dollars to maintain real value and a stable level of purchasing power in terms of goods and services in the United States market.

Maintenance of the value of foreign-dollar holdings is an important responsibility of the Federal Reserve System. But until recently this importance has been overshadowed by concern with purely domestic monetary objectives.

GREAT EXPECTATIONS OF GREAT INFLATION

When Congress took away the 25 percent gold-backing from the domestic dollar currency in March 1968, the effect was to reduce, not enhance, international confidence in the dollar. Notwithstanding the "freeing" of the entire United States gold reserve for international purposes, foreign holders of dollars could easily observe that removing gold-backing from the domestic dollar would excite further domestic expectations of inflation. Indeed, the international bankers' announcement removing the gold-backing from the international dollar on the very same Ides of March dispelled even any temporary illusions about gold-backing that foreign holders of dollars might otherwise have entertained. The subsequent persistent trotting inflation in the domestic economy, and the economy's resistance to the almost desperate monetary and fiscal policies the Federal government and the Federal Reserve have had to take to try to curb it, are persuasive evidence of the persistent strength of inflationary expectations. They also indicate the strong distrust of all paper money, foreign and domestic, in the era ushered in by the Ides of March in money.

THE FEDERAL RESERVE—POWER WITHOUT POLITICS

Presidents have often criticized the Federal Reserve for politically unpopular policies—tight money, for example—and so have members of Congress. But it seems probable that the elective officials who criticize it most publicly should privately support its independence most strongly, since it spares them the onus of taking responsibility for unpopular economic action.

Popular elective processes can no more operate effectively or

295

promptly in economic affairs than a majority vote can create gold or oil reserves in a country's earth, or pass a law that will make all foreigners accept its currency at face value at all times and places.

So far, the consensus has been that it is preferable to maintain the Federal Reserve System independent and insulated from the immediate political demands of elected officials and the people as well, and so far popular antagonisms have not shoved it back into economic and historical limbo with the First and Second Banks of the United States. Their fate remains a grim reminder that national central banks operate effectively at ever-present peril to their own existence.

It is the whole point of the Federal Reserve System that "the most powerful group of private citizens in America" exercise their vast powers over our domestic economy far removed from and independent of the elective political processes that control Congress and the President. The very reason for such independence is to make it possible for the Federal Reserve System to "lean against the wind" of political popularity in the direction of sound, long-term, real growth and monetary stability.

Such general approval of the principle that an agency independent of popular political forces should exercise these vast powers over the economy does not contradict the criticisms of the actual results of the Federal Reserve's exercise of these vast powers, as described in Chapter 13. The Federal Reserve has often seemed to act on factual assumptions that differed from nearly everybody else's, and indeed has seemed to act "by the seat of its pants." Thus it has often "leaned against" a different wind than blew on everybody else's telltale, and seemed like the solo violin virtuoso who was "fine-tuned" to the key of A Major when the rest of the orchestra was playing the G Minor concerto.

Every modern country has a central banking institution that is a counterpart to the Federal Reserve, although most of these also carry on additional functions that the Treasury performs in the United States' system. Examples are the Bank of England, the Bank of France, and the Deutsche Bundesbank of Germany. The purpose of all these central banks is to help the government handle its own transactions, to coordinate and control the commercial banks, and to help regulate money supply and credit conditions within the country. None of them enjoys the same freedom that the Federal

296

Reserve does to take action contrary to the fiscal and monetary policies of the elected government of the country at the same far remove from the bruising political tides within the country.

THE ECONOMIC ORGANIZATION OF THE FREE WORLD IS SOMEWHERE BETWEEN THE SECOND BANK OF THE U.S. AND THE NATIONAL BANK ACT OF 1863

Contrast the vast powers the Federal Reserve exercises with so much independence over the entire economic life of the United States, occasionally acting in the economic sphere entirely at cross purposes with the popular policies of the elective government, with the comparatively modest powers the International Monetary Fund presently exercises in the international economic sphere.

As outlined in Chapters 4, 5, and 6, the International Monetary Fund today sees its role as one of maintaining fixed exchange rates between national currencies and of allocating drawing rights on the fund among the various countries to permit them to overcome short-term, temporary shortages of foreign currencies with which to carry on international trade. Creation of the special drawing rights discussed in Chapter 14 provides a modest increase (partly nonrepayable) in the amounts available to each country to smooth out short-term imbalances in its international trade accounts.

On a time scale comparable to United States banking history, the countries of the free world are somewhere between where the states of the Union were after the demise of the Second Bank of the United States and before the adoption of the National Bank Act of 1863.

Drawing rights on the fund possessed by small, economically weak countries—like balances that small, remote New England banks kept with the Suffolk Bank of Boston—give some assurance to others that the small countries' currency obligations are not worthless, and make them acceptable in foreign trade. But these activities of the fund fall far short of furthering "the enjoyment by all people of access on equal terms to the markets and to the raw materials which are needed for their economic prosperity" envisioned by the Atlantic Charter.

Whether world business is getting better or worse, the fund has no discretionary powers to expand or contract money and credit within the world system as a whole, by increasing or reducing the reserves available to national central banks for domestic lending, or by

controlling the amount of money national central banks make avail
able in each country, or by buying or selling securities to central
banks to place more funds in their hands, or take excessive funds
away from them, or by controlling interest rates in the free world's
economy.

More than a quarter of a century after Bretton Woods, it is time
that all forgotten men who have to pay 9 percent for a mortgage
when they buy a new house because nobody and no country can do
anything effective about the escalation of worldwide interest rates
got impatient for more action. Establishment of an effective international reserve system is too important and urgent a matter to be
left to world economic officials.

Ease of modern travel and communications, increasing use of the
dollar in transactions among all countries, interpenetration of all
national economies by multinational corporations and international
banks and banking relationships, and international monetary and
political organizations all weave all countries of the free world tightly
together, and leave them with far less scope for independence in
their money and banking policies than the separate states of the
United States had during the 19th century between the demise of
the Second Bank of the United States and the National Bank Act
of 1863. It has been estimated that 70 percent of international trade
is carried on in terms of dollars. Why, then, should the mental
hurdles Mr. Macmillan finds in the way of establishing an international reserve system be so much harder for everyone to jump?

THE REAL HURDLES IN THE WAY OF AN
INTERNATIONAL RESERVE SYSTEM HAVE VANISHED,
AND THE MENTAL HURDLES ARE ILLUSIONS

At Bretton Woods in 1944, John Maynard Keynes offered a plan
for an International Clearing Union. This would have moved the
free world far in the direction of an international organization that
would accomplish some of the things the Federal Reserve System
has been trying to accomplish for the United States in its domestic
economy since 1913.

Keynes's plan was rejected primarily because of United States' opposition on two grounds: the United States as the chief surplu

298

country argued that it would simply be making "handouts" through such a union, and that the removal of gold-backing for currencies through the union's "overdraft" features would lead to strong worldwide expectations of inflation and consequently to inflation itself.

By the standards the United States imposed upon herself, the United States is no longer a surplus country; America is the greatest debtor nation in the history of the world. She has removed the gold-backing from her dollars both domestically and internationally, and the powerful persistence of the inflationary expectations of both domestic and foreign holders of dollars confirms that practically everybody is aware of what has happened—except possibly a few members of Congress and the Treasury officials who have been assigned to romance them.

The real hurdles that stood in the way of Keynes's plan no longer exist, except as mental hurdles. Now indeed, we should seek the creation of an international reserve system for the very same reasons we opposed Keynes's international clearing union: to save the dollar from international instability, and to provide a sufficient measure of credible control over the issuance of nongold-backed paper dollars to quiet the leaping expectations of inflation that removal of the gold-backing has excited.

The real hurdles disappeared from the track long ago. The mental hurdles are illusions. It is time we stopped trying to jump over what is not there and realized that the straight track toward an international reserve system is clear and inviting, particularly for deficit key-currency countries such as the United States and Britain.

An international reserve system does not look nearly so inviting to surplus countries such as West Germany, Italy, and Switzerland. But there is no gainsaying the gross strength and power of the United States' domestic economy, the ability of the independent Federal Reserve System to persist in strict measures to maintain this strength, and the relatively smaller size and fragility of the domestic economies of the other countries of the free world, including West Germany.

It is therefore clearly the present duty of the United States, with the cooperation and invaluable contribution in brainpower of British economic thinkers such as Macmillan, to lead the free world down the clear track that will show the International Monetary Fund how to become a true International Reserve System.

Earlier chapters of this book spotlighted the foundations of the world money system as it now exists under Aquarius and found it full of cracks and fissures. Freshets of hot money, inflationary expectations, and national budgetary red ink, in quickening confluences, seemed to be eating away the pilings and joists and threatening the whole structure with total collapse.

After the gold-exchange standard collapsed in 1931, distrust spread to all paper moneys and fortified the Pursides' faith in gold metal as the only reliable reserve. All through the 1930's the "invisible hand" of the free market proved incapable of providing sufficient exchange assets, and each independent country adopted "beggar-thy-neighbor" economic policies, set up trade barriers, and prolonged the low level of economic activity that the Depression had created.

During World War II the Atlantic Charter transmuted national economic objectives into international economic goals. At Bretton Woods, Lord Keynes' plan for an International Clearing Union with overdraft facilities for national central banks was rejected in favor of Harry Dexter White's International Stabilization Fund, which merely provided national central banks with temporary foreign funds with which to counteract massive short-term international speculative movements threatening to depress particular currencies. Since World War II the International Monetary Fund has modestly regulated these "drawing rights" and has maintained the narrowly fixed exchange rates provided for in the articles of agreement of the fund except where "fundamental disequilibrium" of a particular currency appeared, in which case a significant devaluation has been permitted. The World Bank, the International Development Agency, and the International Finance Corporation have helped less-developed countries and countries with little or no domestic foreign exchange obtain foreign exchange to raise their living standards.

Panicky holders of paper dollars turning them in by the hundreds of millions for gold metal at the London gold pool during the Ides of March in money in 1968 forced the United States to repudiate her basic pledge to redeem paper dollars for gold. Since then we have seen sudden panic selling of French francs and British pound sterling, panic buying of German marks, sudden traumatic jumps in the prices of gold and silver to feverish levels, insistent demands by foreign central bankers that the United States impose controls on Eurodollar deposits, and retorts by United States economic officials that the problem was solely one for the European central bankers where the foreign dollar deposits were held. In addition, there have been complaints that American multinational corporations were establishing American economic hegemony abroad, while at the same time American restrictions on foreign investments cut down the expansion of multinational corporations abroad. We have heard European economic officials complain with ever more urgency that the system can work only when the United States supplies liquidity by running international deficits, and that every dollar of deficit that the United States runs injures confidence in the system. We have seen the whole system caught in the cross fire of the long gold war between the Pursides and the Midases.

CONSEQUENCES OF A COLLAPSE OF THE FREE WORLD'S SYSTEM

A collapse of the system would probably result in the United States' complete repudiation of any obligation to buy or sell gold to or from foreign central banks or anyone else, restrictions on all international payments through foreign-exchange controls, import restrictions of all sorts, prohibitions against capital transfers, and blocking of deposits of foreign nationals. Collapse would mean the end of convertibility of most currencies, including the dollar and the pound, and the elimination of these currencies from official reserves of central banks, staggering losses to central banks that did not match depreciation of the key currencies with equal devaluations of their own currencies, reduction in worldwide production and employment, and ever more import restrictions and export reductions. In short, collapse would bring a return to the stagnation and depression that the world suffered through during all of the 1930's after Britain abandoned the gold standard in 1931. The only final solution for the worldwide depression of the 1930's turned out to be worldwide war.

Considering all that has happened, it is a wonder that we still have a system at all, but we do. Conceivably the present system could continue more or less indefinitely in its present form, but this depends on some rather shaky assumptions: That confidence in the dollar and in the pound sterling will be fully restored; that nothing at all will be done about an increase in the price of gold; that all other coun tries will be willing to accept paper dollars indefinitely instead of refusing them as at Orly and Heathrow in 1968; and that the growth of foreign-exchange reserves of the free world through new gold pro duction, selling of gold from hoards, and the willing acceptance of ever-growing balances of paper dollars by other countries will see the system through without organic change. Rather like Venice, the sys tem is still with us but the foundations are a far from reassuring sight.

The first difficulty with trying to make any plan for salvaging, im proving, reforming, or replacing the present system is that the most distinguished economists and monetary officials are in total disagree ment about what really ails it. Sir Roy Harrod and all United States Treasury officials, for example, contend that growth in world mone tary reserves have been far too slow; Per Jacobsson and most French and German officials deny that either the size of the reserves them selves or the rate of increase is inadequate.

Karl Blessing, president of the Deutsche Bundesbank and governor of the International Monetary Fund for Germany, said at a fund meeting in 1965:

> I can see no urgent need for additional international liquid ity. The fact that some deficit countries are short of reserves is no justification for a global increase of liquidity. We cannot bring the tide to a higher level because a few ships have run aground.

Such a salty metaphor can hardly have been lost on a seaborne nation like Britain.

Notwithstanding the high standing of all the United States and British economists and government officials who have made assertions to the contrary, there seems to be no evidence for the claim that the need for reserves rises proportionately with world foreign trade, or vice versa.

Pierre-Paul Schweitzer, managing director of the International Monetary Fund, shot this one down when he stated at the 1965 annual meeting:

> International liquidity is needed for settlement of deficits and surpluses among monetary authorities, not to finance trade; trade is financed by banking and commercial credit. The need

for international reserves is affected by the arrangements that exist among monetary authorities, and it does not bear a clear and simple relationship to the growth of trade.

THE PRESENT SYSTEM PROVIDES INADEQUATE DISCIPLINE, OR ELSE IT IS TOO HARSH

Some experts find that the present system is out of kilter because it gives countries running balance-of-payment deficits too much time in which to cure them; equally brilliant experts, usually in the United States and Britain, find that it gives them too little time to get over their troubles. The first group cites, for example, the willingness of foreign countries to accept ever-increasing amounts of paper dollars abroad as parts of their monetary reserves. This postponed their demanding gold from the United States, postponed substantial gold outflows from the United States, and thus postponed for eight or ten years the warning to the United States that these outflows would have given.

They argue that the present system enabled the United States to continue reckless fiscal and credit policies that brought her to the bankrupt position she now occupies by the standards she has imposed upon herself. For countries like the United States whose currency is used as a reserve, the system provides inadequate discipline; but for countries whose currencies are not reserve currencies, it provides too harsh a discipline. Thus, they say, as between sovereign and equal free-world nations, the system operates inequitably, in the United States' favor.

The second group responds that the fault of the present system is that it does not give countries like the United States and Britain sufficient time to cure the present deficits in their international payments.

There is general agreement that the system must be changed, but changed to what?

303

19

THE FUTURE OF MONEY

CORDIALS, CATHOLICONS, ELIXIRS, EPITHEMS, AND
OTHER ECONOMIC ANODYNES

Forty or more serious proposals for reforming the international monetary system have been offered publicly by the leading economists and monetary officials of the world. Because of the many different diagnoses of what is wrong with the present system and of what should be accomplished in a proper system, many of these plans tend to cancel each other out. Essentially they fall into five classifications, but many of the plans combine features of two or more of the five separate classifications mentioned below. These are:

1. Extension of the existing gold-exchange standard (a) with a continuing increase in dollar and sterling reserves and (b) with the adoption of additional key currencies such as the deutsche mark and the Swiss franc.

2. Additional mutual assistance among national central banks (a) with safeguards against overly expansive national credit and fiscal policies and (b) with extension of domestic credit and expenditures.

3. Centralization of monetary reserves and creation of reserves based on John Maynard Keynes's original idea at Bretton Woods for an International Clearing Union with overdraft facilities. Thus (a) there would be overdraft facilities available to deficit countries, (b) a world central bank would be given autonomous authority to create world money reserves, and (c) the world central bank would also have authority to finance aid to underdeveloped and less developed countries.

4. There would be an increase in the price of gold (a) with the present gold-exchange standard continued or (b) with the present gold-exchange standard abolished.

5. The present narrowly fixed exchange rates would be made more freely flexible (a) in order to make internal monetary policies in each country more independent of each other and more responsive to the condition of the national currency on world markets and (b) because internal monetary policies are too independent of their effects on the

world money system, and maintaining fixed rates imposes too many hardships on individual countries.

TRANSMUTING THE INTERNATIONAL MONETARY FUND INTO AN INTERNATIONAL RESERVE SYSTEM

To the preceding five types of proposals that have been made by others, a sixth might be added.

6. An International Reserve System would be established through modifying and expanding the existing activities of the International Monetary Fund and changing its name to the International Reserve System to reflect more accurately the evolution in its duties and responsibilities. Through evolutionary changes and amendments to the present articles of agreement of the fund, the International Reserve System would be responsible for the integrity and availability of one international currency, based on the international dollar presently known as the Eurodollar, but which under the evolving system might come to be known as the Reserve Dollar, or Fundollar, or Worldollar, or just plain dollar. Responsibility for the presently outstanding foreign-held dollar claims against the United States' gold reserve would be assumed by the International Reserve System as guarantor, in consideration for transfer to it of a substantial part of the present United States gold reserves. Responsibility for foreign-held pound sterling balances would also be assumed by the system as guarantor, as would the obligations as guarantor that the United States and other countries have already undertaken to foreign holders of sterling balances, and Britain would transfer a substantial part of her national gold and foreign currency reserves to the system's reserves.

The system would adjust the monetary price of gold upward to increase the value of the national reserves deposited with it, and the value of the gold newly mined each year as well, and would thereafter control the price of gold. The system would relieve the United States of her political commitment to buy and sell gold at $35 an ounce because none would be available to change hands at that price for any purpose. Because gold would have been stabilized under the control of the system and placed squarely behind the international dollar, or Reserve Dollar, the name of the international dollar currency backed by gold at the new price through usage and custom might even become the Gold Dollar or, eventually, the "golder."

305

But before going more deeply into the details of this book's type (6) proposals, one should contrast briefly a few of the proposals of types (1) through (5) that leading economists and economic officials have presented as blueprints for a new and better world money system. Out of the turgid slag heap of mostly unverifiable assumptions about the world money system, this polite form of adversary procedure may serve to extract a little truth and understanding in somewhat the same way it serves to do in courts of law and equity.

MULTIPLE RESERVE CURRENCY UNITS
À LA BERNSTEIN

Some leading economists would build on the existing system by adding several additional "key currencies" to the dollar and pound sterling as the key reserve currencies. Instead of the present "gold-exchange" standard or "key-currency" exchange standard, as the present system is called, such plans would create a multiple-currency reserve system.

Edward M. Bernstein, a former assistant to the Secretary of the Treasury and Director of Research and Statistics of the International Monetary Fund, proposes the creation of "reserve units," each of which would be equal to one gold dollar and would consist of the eleven leading currencies in agreed proportions. For example, a reserve unit might consist of fifty cents in United States currency and lesser amounts of marks, sterling, francs, lire, Canadian dollars, yen, guilders, and so forth. The participating countries would be free to hold their reserves in any form—gold, foreign exchange, or reserve units—but their holdings of gold would have to be matched by a minimum amount of reserve units.

All countries would agree to convert official holdings of their currencies to this ratio of gold and reserve units. The actual proportion of gold to reserve units would be subject to agreement and would change over time in the direction of a greater proportion of reserve units to gold. The International Monetary Fund would serve as the trustee for holding national currencies and issuing or creating reserve units. The value of the reserve units would be guaranteed in terms of gold. Thus the fund's holdings of the eleven individual reserve currencies would have to be the subject of a new guarantee in terms of gold value similar to the guarantee that now applies to the fund's other holdings of currencies. Each country would pay the trustee 2 percent per annum on its currencies held by the trustee, and the trustee would pay each country 2 percent per annum on its average holdings of the reserve units. Participating countries that held reserve currencies, dollars, and sterling could continue to do so. If any of these countries would prefer to reduce dollar holdings, for example, and obtain composite IMF reserve units with a gold guarantee, the immediate effect would be that the United States would lose gold and gain reserves in the form of reserve units.

The American dollar would continue to be widely used in international trade and payments, but its present function as almost the sole reserve currency would be severely restricted. Since European countries have shown a clear preference for holding gold over foreign currency (dollar) holdings, the initial agreed proportion of gold to the reserve units would probably be quite large. Initially, the conversion of official balances of a currency might be 90 percent in gold and 10 percent in reserve units.

Broadly speaking, the Bernstein plan substitutes an international reserve unit for an equivalent amount of convertible currency. The reserve unit is heavily dependent upon gold. To create this new unit, much of the United States gold reserve would have to be withdrawn because a large portion of foreign-held dollar reserves could be converted into this new currency.

The plan would help countries such as West Germany that now have currency surpluses held in dollars to secure the maintenance of value of these reserves. It would not increase total international monetary reserves nor help solve the deficit in the United States balance of payments. The plan does not increase the overall amount of international resources available to help finance more world trade. It does not create any new purchasing power to help the underdeveloped countries pay for the necessities of life. It does not help developed countries such as Britain, which has long-term, persistent deficits in international payments, settle their international debts, or increase confidence on the part of foreign holders of such countries' currencies.

XENOPHON ZOLOTAS AND THE GOLDEN GUARANTEE

The governor of the International Monetary Fund for Greece, Xenophon Zolotas, has proposed a plan somewhat similar to Mr.

Bernstein's. His plan's key provision is that every country whose currency is used in the foreign reserves of other central banks and treasuries (dollars and sterling primarily) must provide a gold guarantee. This would not necessarily be an obligation to redeem the currency in gold, but a gold clause that would protect all foreign monetary authorities against losses in their holdings resulting from devaluation of the dollar or sterling, for example. Central banks could then deposit their reserves of gold and convertible currencies (other than their own) with the International Monetary Fund, relying on the protection of the constant gold-value guarantee.

Such deposits would earn a modest, periodically adjustable rate of interest and would be freely usable by the owner countries just as they use drawings within the "gold tranche" at the fund at present. These provisions would make it more attractive for central banks to hold large portions of their reserves in the form of foreign claims and deposits with the International Monetary Fund rather than in the gold itself.

"WHERE BALANCE-OF-PAYMENTS ADJUSTMENT IS CONCERNED, THERE IS NO SANTA CLAUS—NO ESCAPE IN THE GUISE OF LIQUIDITY"

By contrast, the proposals of Robert B. Roosa, Undersecretary of the Treasury for Monetary Affairs during the 1961–64 period (the period that provided for multiple currency reserves), reject the idea of any "gold guarantee." In Roosa's view, guarantees of compensation for losses in the event of devaluation are unnecessary, cumbersome, harmful, and worthless.

Roosa believes that confidence in the dollar as a reserve currency must be beyond suspicion, and that it need not and cannot be bolstered by gold guarantees. In May 1962, when he was Undersecretary of the Treasury, the United States began to hold various foreign currencies as part of her own foreign reserves. For example, the Federal Reserve Bank of New York paid $50 million to the dollar account of the Bank of England in New York against a corresponding payment by the Bank of England of nearly eighteen million pounds to the sterling account of the New York bank in London. A similar arrangement was made with the Banque de France. These reciprocal arrangements were designed to provide "forward cover" to the currency of both parties. It was also announced as United States policy that during any temporary or persistent surplus in her overall balance of payments, the United States would not reduce her liabilities to foreign monetary authorities—which would lower the total of international reserves—but would acquire foreign currencies instead.

These currencies would be added to the United States' gold and other reserves so that her total reserves would increase. Thus it would be possible, in principle, to make world reserves increase, both as the result of a United States deficit and as the result of a United States surplus.

Payments from the United States in the case of a deficit could increase the dollar holdings of the recipient countries, while payments to the United States in the case of a surplus would increase the foreign currency holdings of the United States. During 1962, arrangements for bilateral "swing credits" or "swaps" through mutual holdings of currencies were concluded by the United States with France, England, the Netherlands, Belgium, Canada, Switzerland, and West Germany.

The Roosa plan envisages a more or less continuous holding by the United States of moderate amounts of the convertible exchange of various leading countries as a means to permit the holding of a smaller gold reserve. The net effect would be to "multilateralize" part of the job performed now by the two key currencies, the dollar and the pound sterling, within a framework that would place great stress on further cooperation among the monetary authorities. Eventually, the leading financial countries whose currencies are used in international trade would contribute their own currencies to a "fund-unit" account upon which they would receive a corresponding "checking-unit deposit." A country would qualify if its currency were used as a reserve asset or for International Monetary Fund drawings. The checking-account deposit could be used by a country "to lend, invest or make grants at its discretion through payments to other monetary authorities or international financial institutions." The currencies deposited in the accounts would remain in the account. These reserves would only be used to reduce the total of fund units or to dissolve the arrangements. Each country would agree to maintain the external convertibility of its own currency through the purchase and sale of gold at a fixed price related to $35 an ounce.

The plan thus assumes that every member country would be willing to hold fund units in its reserves because they would be "as good as gold." A central bank that held fund units could convert the units into gold, so if European countries, for example, decided to hold more reserve units than dollars, or reserve units in place of dollars, the United States would have to acquire these reserve units by running balance-of-payments surpluses, or paying out more of her gold stock in exchange for reserve units. Thus claims on the United States gold stock would arise from two sources: foreign dollar holdings and foreign reserve fund units holdings.

TRIFFIN'S VISION OF A WORLD CENTRAL BANK

Professor Robert Triffin of Yale has raised serious questions about the adequacy of international liquidity. He assumes that current levels of gold production are inadequate for the growing requirements of liquidity, and that national reserve currencies, particularly the dollar and the pound, should not be used as international reserves. Triffin stresses that the United States is not able to solve her balance-of-payments problem without depriving the rest of the world of a large portion of its future liquidity.

He points out that large conversions of foreign-held dollar balances into gold might leave the United States in "overall equilibrium," with our gold losses being offset by parallel reductions in our indebtedness abroad, yet still lead to a major dollar crisis and a loss of confidence by foreign holders. Such a crisis would force the United States to choose between deflation, devaluation and a complete embargo on gold, drastic cuts in foreign aid and military defense programs, and tariff increases and other trade and exchange restrictions. The restoration of overall equilibrium in the United States balance of payments would also dry up the major source by far of current liquidity and monetary reserve increases for the rest of the world.

Many of the problems Triffin perspicuously saw as specks on the horizon are now economic thunderclouds looming directly over our heads, threatening to loose a deluge upon us.

RUSHING BACK AND FORTH FROM ONE
RESERVE CURRENCY TO ANOTHER

These various proposals for multiple currency reserve standards, or entirely new currency or reserve units, represent a curious reversal in the history of thought on international monetary economics. According to Gresham's Law, if three international currencies supplied from sources independent of one another are convertible into each other at fixed rates, the scarcest of the three will go into private hoards. Every student of monetary economics remembers the bimetallism debate. When both gold and silver were international money, convertible into each other at a fixed rate, there was periodic trouble depending on the relative scarcity or abundance of one or the other. People were always rushing from one money into the other, just as during 1967 and 1968 people rushed from the pound to the dollar, from the dollar to gold, from the dollar to the deutschemark, from the franc to the deutschemark and Swiss franc, back to the dollar and into gold.

The world now has three principal international moneys—gold, dollars, and pounds sterling—and there are periodic rushes from one to the other, or sometimes, indeed, out of all three. This is to be expected since dollars, pounds, and gold are all produced in quantities determined completely without regard to the ratios in which, at fixed rates of exchange, the world may wish to hold them.

Many of the experts whose plans have been reviewed here (without attempting to do justice to their complex details, or the powerful arguments for and against them) hope to find safety in larger numbers of reserve currencies, with six or eight or even fifteen or twenty international moneys, and fixed exchange rates between them. Some advocate entirely new world currencies, with arbitrarily coined names, reminiscent of Lord Keynes's "bancor." Years of monetary history, particularly the years of the classic gold standard, have shown that currency crises can be eliminated most effectively by having only one international money.

A COMEBACK FOR GOLD IN THE CENTRAL ROLE?

Gold has played the part of the one international money in the past, and many a Pursides in all countries today following Jacques Rueff and Roy Harrod and even Arthur Burns would like to see it play the central role again. But its usual unavailability in sufficient quantities, its unequal distribution as a resource among countries, the fact that gold holdings earn no interest and prevailing interest rates are high, the myths and legends that surround it, the passion women and politicians have for it—in short, all the quirkiness that surrounds it—disqualifies it for a comeback in the central role.

This is not to say that gold does not have an important transitional role to play in the evolution of one international money under the control of an international reserve system, whatever may be the role of gold in the monetary system in the very long run.

Just as a successful new world-money system would not insist on a return to the rigors of the classic gold standard, neither would it petulantly insist on blotting out any monetary role of gold. It would weld the age-old strength of the Pursides' mystic faith in gold onto the structure of the new system, not force it into the ranks of the antagonists of the new system.

Many of the experts' plans are drawn on a sheet of blank paper, in generalized form, and seek to create an entirely new system, or a new currency, or to reform the present system, by means of a grand design, as was done at Bretton Woods. Without the pressures of global war, most other great economic inventions have "jest growed" from evolving quietly out of existing situations and practices into something else that came to be recognized after the fact as a new and remarkable invention.

No symmetrical, generalized blueprint or master plan can deal effectively with, nor successfully ignore, such special problems as the $41 billion of foreign paper-dollar holdings the United States has pledged herself to redeem for gold metal, when she only has $11 billion of gold metal; the more than $10 billion of outstanding foreign claims against British sterling balances of little more that $2 billion; the apparent inability of the United States and Britain to balance their international accounts to prevent the further buildup of foreign paper-dollar and paper-sterling claims against their domestic reserves; and the unwillingness of the surplus countries, particularly those of the European Common Market, to continue to accept and hold United States dollars and pounds sterling in their reserves.

It is not easy to handle the persistent demands of the Pursides of the world for gold metal instead of paper dollars or paper sterling or other paper currencies, regardless of governmental fiat and reassurances from governmental officials, or the $30 billion or so of Eurodollar deposits abroad on which United States banks are willing to pay as much as 11 or 12 or 13 percent interest, or the worldwide preference of practical men for using American dollars in international

312

commercial transactions to the point where approximately 70 percent of free-world trade is carried on in dollars.

A Single International Currency Already Exists— U.S. Dollars in the Form of Eurodollars

There is no need to try to invent a brand new currency with a freakish name and then try to make all bankers and businessmen use it as their single worldwide reserve unit or currency. As a practical matter, a single worldwide currency already exists. It is, of course, the United States dollar in its various different forms. As a purely domestic currency within the United States, its creation through bank loans, deposits, and currency is regulated by the activities of the Federal Reserve System. During most of 1969 the Federal Reserve System, through impressive application of the "money-supply" control policies discussed in Chapter 13, brought the growth of the domestic money supply almost to a standstill.

Early in 1969 there was about $45 billion of United States currency in circulation and, in addition, the member banks of the Federal Reserve System held reserves to meet Federal Reserve requirements of about $28 billion. On the basis of these reserves, the member banks make loans, expand credit, and create deposits in favor of customers. The total of about $73 billion was the United States' monetary base as reflected in the Federal Reserve System's bank reserve equations. In relation to this monetary base, foreign-held dollar obligations and Eurodollar deposits are of significant magnitudes.

Out of a total of about $41 billion of foreign-held dollar claims, as much as $30 billion are in the form of Eurodollars, foreign-held deposits in the form of dollars. In 1969 United States banks borrowed an estimated $10 billion or more of Eurodollars from their own foreign branches at interest rates that for a time ran as high as 13 percent.

Conflicting National Interests in the Regulation of Eurodollar deposits

European central bankers suddenly stopped complaining about being forced to hold unwanted dollars and started complaining that the United States was stripping Europe of much-needed dollars and driving up interest rates within European countries. They demanded that the United States impose restrictions on bringing foreign-held

313

dollars back to the United States. United States bankers retorted that regulation of Eurodollar deposits was primarily a question for the central bank in each country where the Eurodollar deposits were held. (Although traditionally claims of London or other foreign branches against their New York head offices are not subject to regulation by the country where the branch is located, this is becoming a thing of the past.) Yet there is no gainsaying that the transaction has important international consequences. It provides more loanable funds in the United States, and it deprives the country where the branch is located of loanable funds, although the Federal Reserve in the United States may be trying to restrict the availability of loanable funds, and the central bank in the branch's country may be trying to increase it and hold down local interest rates as well.

INTERNATIONAL RESERVE SYSTEM REGULATION OF EURODOLLAR AND OTHER INTERNATIONAL CURRENCY DEPOSITS

Thus it is obvious that the creation and use of Eurodollar deposits has international consequences whose regulation does not properly fall under the control of one separate national government or another. They should be regulated by an international reserve system, much as interstate commerce among the states of the United States, and the nationwide currency that circulates among them, is regulated by federal agencies such as the Federal Reserve System.

The Eurodollar is the single most important international currency of the free world. It is in the interests of all free-world countries holding vast amounts of Eurodollars that they be under the regulation of an international reserve system for the good of all.

Foreign-held dollar claims against the United States gold supply total something over $41 billion; Eurodollar balances may be as much as $30 billion, and of this $30 billion at least $10 billion are claims by United States branches against their domestic head offices. This vast fund of international liquidity in the form of foreign-held dollars can be constructively used for financing and expanding international trade and commerce, or, on the other hand, can continue to be a dangerous and destructive demand note on the United States gold reserve that could more than wipe it out at current gold prices. It thus constitutes a serious threat to the safety of the whole structure.

It seems clear that Eurodollar deposits, and indeed all other forms of international currency deposits—that is, deposits denominated in

314

the currency of one country made in the banks of another country, such as Eurosterling deposits and Eurofranc deposits—have such important international consequences that neither the country whose currency is used, nor the other country in whose local bank it is deposited, can effectively regulate the transaction. Obviously, because of the vast size of the Eurodollar market in comparison to the size of the Eurosterling and other foreign-currency markets, the chief object of regulation by the international central bank would be the Eurodollar market. Since all international currency deposits would be under the control of the same international reserve system, there would be no profit in flight from one currency to another to escape from the regulatory system.

The international reserve system would establish percentage reserve requirements imposed through foreign countries' central banks and the Federal Reserve System, upon the amount of Eurodollar deposits and other international foreign-currency deposits. It could raise and lower these national central banks' reserve requirements from time to time, and permit the international deposit reserve requirements to be lower or higher from one country to another, and as between one currency and another.

The International Reserve System would carry out these functions through each nation's central bank, in somewhat the way the Federal Reserve Board carries out reserve requirement regulation and control through each of its twelve separate Federal Reserve District Banks. On occasion it would make different reserve requirements applicable from one district to another. There would be a constant exchange of information between each national central bank (acting somewhat like a Federal Reserve District Bank) and the headquarters of the International Reserve System.

At the outset, at least, no more than twelve or fifteen national central banks—those of the most economically developed free-world members of the present International Monetary Fund—would participate directly in the system, and the central banks of lesser members of the fund would correspond through one of the twelve or so principal central bank members.

ADJUSTING NATIONAL CENTRAL BANKS' RESERVE
REQUIREMENTS FOR INTERNATIONAL DEPOSITS

By adjusting reserve requirements for international deposits upward or downward, the International Reserve System would pursue objectives designed to promote the overall economic interests of all members of the system. By raising national reserve requirements for Eurodollar holdings "across the board," it could limit the amounts foreign countries could add to such holdings, and the amounts United States banks' head offices could withdraw from their foreign branches (assuming central banks where the branches were located extended control to their local dollar deposits).

This would also put more pressure on the United States Federal Reserve to maintain pressure on the domestic economy sufficient to preserve the international value of the dollar. By raising national central banks' reserve requirements for Eurosterling or other foreign currency holdings to a higher level than rates for Eurodollar reserves, the system would slowly force international transactions out of other international deposits of national currencies and into the one international currency based on the dollar regulated by the system. By raising one national central bank's reserve requirements for international holdings and lowering another's, the system could reverse flows of international deposits away from "surplus" countries and toward "deficit" countries.

By agreeing to fulfill the new role that is being forced on it by the international controversy over regulation of Eurodollar deposits and, by extension, of all other international currency deposits, the International Monetary Fund will be taking the first steps in its evolution toward becoming an International Reserve System. At the same time, it will remove an element of uncertainty and risk from these proliferating types of international currencies, and will lend a force for stability and security to the system as a whole. It will be acting not as a mysterious foreign "engine of inflation" to create new opportunities for deficit countries to increase their deficits, but (through national central banks) to place reserve requirements on the extent to which deficit countries can increase or export their deficits.

Each Country's Net Position with the Fund Will Be Determined in International Dollars

As a second step in its evolution into an international reserve system, the fund would denominate each country's present net position with the fund in terms of Eurodollars or international dollars or Worldollars. The fund would purchase national currencies and pay for them by creating deposit liabilities of the fund in their favor; or, in other words, make loans to their central banks denominated in Worldollars. The fund would be obliged to buy the currency of any member country by establishing a fund deposit in its favor denominated in Worldollars. The fund would also buy all gold offered to it by member countries at a price to be fixed by the system by creating in favor of the member a Worldollar deposit of the equivalent amount with the system. Each member country would commit itself to accepting Worldollar deposits in settlement of obligations of other member countries to it.

Worldollar deposits would be international legal tender and fully transferable, but once created, they would not be convertible back into gold through the system, except in the discretion of the system. Gold could be used as a means of international settlement bilaterally between one country and another, more or less as the equivalent of Worldollar deposits, and member countries could continue to hold gold as part of their domestic monetary reserves if they chose to do so.

If another member presented foreign-held dollars to the United States and demanded gold, the United States would not be required to redeem the dollars in gold at $35 an ounce. Instead, the United States could deposit the equivalent amount of gold with the fund at the higher Worldollar price fixed for gold, and the fund would credit the other member's account with an equivalent sum of Worldollars. No one country would be required by another to redeem its currency in gold at a fixed price, but it could do so if it so desired.

The International Reserve System and the Worldollar in Full-Scale Operation

National currencies could also be used optionally as means of international settlement to the extent that both parties were satisfied to accept them, and would serve as stores of value. The fund would be required to purchase a national currency for Worldollars at a fixed price whenever the currency was offered by a member, but there would be fixed limits on the amount of any one national currency other than Worldollars that the fund was required to hold. If the member's currency exceeded the fixed limits, the fund could require it to repurchase the excess part of its currency by spending Worldollars or some other member's acceptable currency.

317

In addition to these controls to ensure the integrity of the Worldollar, the fund would have the power to lend Worldollars directly against a member's currency and grant it overdraft facilities and temporary standby credits, more or less as extensions of powers and practices already exercised under the General Arrangements to Borrow and the various countries' multilateral "swaps" and credit arrangements. The fund could sell liquid investments in one or another member's domestic money markets if it appeared necessary to "sop up" excessive money and credit there, and thus carry on an internationally discriminating "open-market policy."

SPECIAL DRAWING RIGHTS WOULD BE ACTIVATED SOLELY IN DENOMINATIONS OF WORLDOLLARS

Special drawing rights that have already been authorized would be activated on the scale presently contemplated (see Chapter 14), but would be added to each member's Worldollar deposit with the fund and would not be available in the member's own currency. Coupling the activation of special drawing rights in a limited amount each year with the assumption of reserve regulation by the international reserve system would serve to dispel the widespread expectations that such "overdrafts" would lead directly to worldwide inflation of paper currency. Apart from such special drawing rights as have already been authorized, there would be no further creation of "overdraft" reserves, at least until a few years' experience operating under the system had demonstrated clearly the need for additional reserve creation of this kind.

There would be no special provisions to assist underdeveloped countries as such, no more than the United States Federal Reserve System includes among its functions extra aid to underdeveloped urban and rural areas. The World Bank and other satellite organizations will continue to expand their efforts in this direction dramatically, as we saw in Chapter 7. An effort to engraft such functions onto the International Reserve System itself would only weaken it, and possibly confuse and frustrate the efforts to aid underdeveloped countries and foster birth-control efforts that agencies with more experience in doing these things have already undertaken.

The key to this proposal for an international reserve system is the substitution of balances of Worldollars in the system for balances of national currencies. This would mean that all member countries would initially have to hold a certain proportion of their monetary reserves in Worldollar deposits with the system, the way member banks of the Federal Reserve System keep reserves on deposit with Federal Reserve banks. The system would provide for moderate interest payments on some or all of such reserves. Such Worldollar balances would be attractive also because they would escape the risks involved in holding separate national currencies, such as devaluations, day-to-day fluctuations, defaults in payment, and blocking and other national restrictions on currency transfers.

They would be more attractive than gold because they would be more easily transferable, would earn interest, and would avoid the speculative downside risk that is inherent in any large holding of gold. Over time, the system could adjust the percentages of its reserves that each member central bank was required to hold in Worldollars or could, optionally, hold in Worldollars.

Using "Old Gold" as the Worldollar Monetary Base, and "New Gold" for Additions to World Liquidity

Consider, for example, the serious downside risk inherent in the United States' still large holding of gold metal as a monetary reserve, and the even greater risks such holdings involve for France and Germany. At present, at least, there is a $35 "floor", but the free market price has actually fallen below the floor at times. If all demand for gold as a monetary reserve were removed, the supply would far exceed the demand, and market forces might well drive the price well below $35 an ounce.

Therefore it is in the interest of these countries to shift the risks of large holdings of monetary gold reserves to the international reserve system at a higher price, in accordance with the suggestions in Chapter 16.

An increase in the price of gold has two separate effects, which should be distinguished both in theory and in policy. First, would be an upvaluing, a doubling for example, of the existing gold stock both in monetary reserves and in gold presently held outside the system. The second effect would be an increase in the value of annual additions to gold stocks. The revaluation in the existing gold stocks might be compared to a "capital gain," and would broaden the monetary base at one moment, but would not necessarily increase the available supply of money.

319

On the other hand, purchases of newly mined gold at an increased price would gradually increase the supply of money automatically, and would make it possible for deficit countries to turn their foreign-trade accounts to surplus without forcing other countries into deficits.

In 1934 in order to "sterilize" gold profits resulting from devaluation of the dollar, the Federal Reserve banks and all private holders of gold were required to sell their gold stocks to the Treasury at the old price, and the Treasury paid for the gold with gold certificates, which took the place of the gold itself among the assets of the Federal Reserve banks. A part of the revalued gold that was not needed to cover the gold certificates was later used by the United States Treasury to pay its subscription to the International Monetary Fund.

THE INTERNATIONAL RESERVE SYSTEM ASSUMES ALL U.S. LIABILITIES TO FOREIGN HOLDERS OF DOLLARS

If the United States were able to surrender substantially all of her remaining monetary gold reserves to the system at a higher gold price to provide it with Worldollar reserves, in exchange for the system's assumption of all liabilities to foreigners to exchange paper dollars for gold, the United States would in all likelihood be making a good bargain. And it would be a good bargain for the other countries as well. The liquidity of foreign central banks that held dollar claims against the obviously inadequate United States gold reserve would be strengthened by the substitution of a Worldollar claim against the whole system, covered by more impressively valued gold reserves. The United States' own reserve position would be unchanged, with its Worldollar reserve deposit in the system substituted for its reserve of monetary gold. Interest payments on foreign-held debt would be assigned to the system and eliminated, so the United States' current account position would be improved.

WITH ONE WORLDOLLAR CURRENCY THE NEED FOR ENFORCING FIXED EXCHANGE RATES DISAPPEARS

The establishment of the Worldollar as the one universally acceptable worldwide currency through the International Reserve System would gradually eliminate the need for the present elaborate system of using national monetary reserves to "peg" the value of each national currency against all others at fixed rates. Gold and foreign exchange reserves are really needed only if exchange rates are not permitted to move to the level that would conform to the market at the moment. There is always a price at which the quantity of supply and demand are equal although it may be subject to fluctuations from day to day.

The Worldollar would be the single currency in which all significant free-world transactions were expressed, and other free-world currencies would be familiarly expressed as fractions or percentages of it. The question of "fixed" or "freely floating exchange rates" would gradually become academic.

It is hardly necessary to describe the advantages this would produce: freedom from devaluations and fears and risks of devaluations, simplification of world trade and travel, and the possibility of greater improvements in economic standards of all countries.

A Sigh for the Loss of One Illusory Sovereignty for Another

Sovereignty is still a nation's most cherished possession. Freedom from effective regulation by national sovereigns is a multinational corporation's most cherished possession. Freedom from control by national sovereigns is the quality of gold most cherished by speculators. Sovereign nations purport to have sovereignty in international economic matters, but this is a pretense that has worn thin.

In many ways the United States and her people have less sovereignty in economic matters than any other country, because of the wide use of her dollar in worldwide trade, her multinational corporations and banks, and the huge foreign-held dollar claims against her gold and products. The United States is tied to the free-world system the way Gulliver was tied down by the Lilliputians. Even sovereignty over her domestic economy has been turned over to the independent Federal Reserve System in Washington, which would of course work closely with any International Reserve System.

Any country that felt its political sovereignty would not permit it to participate in the establishment of the Worldollar under the International Reserve System would be politely advised that it was under no obligation to participate in any way. Nor would it continue to be allowed to use drawing rights in the fund beyond existing rights, nor would it participate in any future additions of special drawing rights to its reserves in the form of Worldollars. If the "sovereignty" opposition can be overcome as a matter of United States domestic politics, no other country's opposition on sovereignty grounds need trouble us further. The last of the mental hurdles we have to jump on the way to an International Reserve System and one worldwide money is the easiest of all to clear.

20

ONE NEW WORLD OF MONEY

It is now sixteen or seventeen years since I saw the Queen of France, then the Dauphiness, at Versailles; and surely never lighted on this orb, which she hardly seemed to touch, a more delightful vision. . . . Little did I dream that I should have lived to see such disasters fallen upon her in a nation of gallant men. . . . I thought ten thousand swords must have leaped from their scabbards to avenge even a look that threatened her with insult. But the age of chivalry is gone; that of sophisters, economists, and calculators has succeeded.

EDMUND BURKE
REFLECTIONS ON THE REVOLUTION
IN FRANCE (1790)

A manufacturer of sweatshirts emblazoned "Money Isn't Everything" has gone out of business.

The Wall Street Journal,
JANUARY 3, 1969

Economic growth is psychologically unsatisfying. Grandmother, living in the year 1900 and being told of the economic growth that was in store for society in the century ahead, would have expected perhaps to be able to hire a second maid, or even a table waitress and a cook. Instead, progress brought her a vacuum cleaner and a washing machine.

And today's housewife, reading that the world's present total population of 3.5 billion will rise to 4 billion by 1975 and will double to 8 billion shortly after the turn of the second millennium A.D., wonders why she cannot find even one cleaning woman she can afford.

More troubling than these gritty little domestic problems are the cosmic signs Professor Falk sees that indicate mankind is following the dodo into extinction; and U Thant's prediction that we have only about ten years left in which to solve the problems of defusing the population explosion, stopping world pollution, curbing the arms race, and raising world living standards.

According to Professor Falk, the only hope for reversing our present trend toward "irreversible catastrophe" is a drastic change in the political structure that now prevails.

Yet U Thant does not suggest that the United Nations, which once seemed to be the most promising political structure the world had created, can do anything about the trend in its present form, and he holds out no hope that drastic change will bring anything better. He calls upon the nations to "subordinate their ancient quarrels" and launch "a global partnership" to save the world.

One thing that seems true of all countries' political institutions today, even the oldest and strongest such as our own country's and Britain's, is that they are less and less able to govern their people effectively in the face of rising economic expectations, rising populations, rising levels of literacy, and, on the part of political leaders, an assiduous effort to cultivate the lowest common political denominator. The Chief Executive of the United States was elected for four years by just over 43 percent of the electorate in a checkerboard of mostly nonurban states, at the same time the legislative districts produced a Congress controlled by the opposite party.

The worst are full of passionate intensity, and the best lack all conviction. When Harvard's President Pusey called in Cambridge cops to stop Harvard students from assaulting deans and rifling private files in the university's administration building, the political freedoms supposedly ordained by natural law for each individual, including university deans, and graven on our Bill of Rights, were exposed as precious, rare, not widely understood, and fragile. The tides that threaten to engulf political freedoms are not articulated by the best, nor the worst, but seem to rise directly from incidents of general economic discontent (such as substandard Cambridge private housing near the university) or social discontent bred by economic dissatisfactions.

Europe's population is growing at a rate of less than 1 percent a year while Latin America's rate is more than 3 percent. Costa Rica, which now has 1.7 million people, will have 75 million in a hundred years if its present rate of population growth continues.

Despite the emptiness of the satisfactions it brings a housewife, notwithstanding the rising expectations it brings to once passive populations whose numbers grow so much faster in poverty than in relative affluence, one new world of money must make worldwide economic growth its first order of business, its grand objective, and its quest. This is not a matter of choice; it is a matter of necessity. Poverty in a poor country with an expanding population multiplies to the limit of subsistence and beyond. In rich countries such as ours and Britain, when real economic growth slows down and governmental welfare payments remain at the same or a higher level, the additional purchasing power bids up all goods, services, and prices. The resulting inflation without real growth impoverishes all.

In Latin an *aera*, from which our word "era" is derived, referred to the items of an account, counters, or brass, or, indeed, money. One might say that the era of religion, having persisted from the beginnings of civilization, ended with the French Revolution, which ushered in what Edmund Burke described as the age of "sophisters, economists, and calculators." Burke was ahead of his time. The age that arrived when no swords leaped from gallant men's scabbards to avenge the Dauphiness was the age of political nations which, in turn, expired without knowing it during World War II, when Bretton Woods ushered in at least the possibility of one new world of money.

The present is truly the age of "sophisters, economists, and calculators," and the world is still waiting impatiently to welcome them on center stage as the kings and emperors and dictators and generals and other gorgeously caparisoned performers pick up the corpses and shuffle off into the wings of the past historic era.

But the economists and calculators need a hard kick from the

324

prompter to stop playing general understudy as they have for twenty-five years and step confidently out into the spotlight. We can wait no longer. We should begin to press them forcefully toward establishing one money for the world under the control of one international reserve system for the world.

What has been the cost of the failure of one new world of money to realize that it has been born and is already twenty-five years old? The cost is incalculable.

Because the preponderance of Britain's imports over exports and other foreign earnings placed that country's foreign balance of payments in deficit, thereby lessening foreign confidence in the pound sterling, Britain's Labour government made a deliberate attempt several years ago through conscious economic policy to force the country into an economic leveling off and, indeed, a recession.

When the United States' balance of payments turned into a deficit a few years later, the President, the Federal Reserve, and Congress for the first time in economic history made a deliberate attempt to force the country into a recession by imposing the income tax surcharge, by proposing repeal of the investment credit, and by making money "tighter" than it had ever been before in the history of the United States. They appeared to be successful in the attempt. Real economic growth was slowed almost to a standstill in both countries.

Yet in one new world of money the true quest is economic growth. Even the most productive countries have no production time to lose if they are to keep their own poor and the exploding populations of the poor countries of the world from engulfing the living standards that they have managed to reach so far through effective expansion of production and capital.

Obviously, unlimited expansion of production to relieve the misery of populations increasing without limit on a small, finite planet cannot go on forever. But that is another book. We have no choice but to continue to expand production for at least a while longer.

In classical economic theory, within one economic system, it was more or less assumed that supply would create its own demand, because all sellers are buyers, at least potentially, and because production involves a payout of funds almost equal to the cost of the product put on the market. The balance, interest, and depreciation, plus the producer's profit, becomes demand just as the workers' wage does. In

325

the real world the population explosion, the pollution of the earth, the depletion of resources, the arms race, the space race, and the pyramiding of money credit all create demands for production far beyond anything envisaged by a closed economic system.

Yet Britain and the United States, two of the world's most productive countries, purposefully forced themselves into recessions and slowdowns of production for what appeared to be sound domestic economic reasons. From the point of view of the world as a whole and its peoples, such policies appear to be folly. Ironically enough, Britain, leading the way as usual, recently discovered that over a period of many years the figures she used in measuring her exports had been substantially understated. Instead of having a trade deficit, as economic planners had believed, Britain had actually had a trade surplus for many periods. The whole well-reasoned and courageously applied deflationary policy that had caused so much suffering was largely founded on false figures.

All of the foregoing is a large oversimplification of many abstruse economic matters, many issues, and many complex economic factors of cause and effect, for which apology is herewith tendered. It is intended to drive home an important point.

National political states today are almost helpless to deal effectively with the most serious problems that confront all the people of the world, who have to live in the states willy-nilly. The problems are not neatly compartmented within national boundaries. Neither can they be framed in political terms. From whatever direction one approaches them, the answer comes back that more money is needed, and not just printing press or inflationary money, but more money resulting from real economic growth.

What the world needs to support more people every day and their rising expectations is a true and expanding capitalism. But it cannot give that name to its quest because Karl Marx used it for his book that taught half the world's people to hate the idea of it, and the name.

An international reserve system, gradually acquiring all world monetary gold reserves standing behind one world currency initially based on the international dollar is the most hopeful basis for one new world of money.

Le dieu defini est le dieu fini. For the quest itself, the idea of one new world of money is enough. No narrow definition should be allowed to smother any popular mystic force that will drive true converts onward toward their grail.

For the religious and the antireligious, the next revisers of the American Standard Version of the New Testament could help out by finding a new apocryphal remark for Timothy to the effect that "The love of money is the root of all goods." To give the movement proletarian appeal in the Marxist countries, and egalitarian appeal in the free egalitarian countries, there is "Workers of the world unite— you have nothing to lose but your change," because for it you will be paid world dollars, at Orly and everywhere else.

For sophisters, economists, and calculators who aver that an idea does not exist unless it can be put into a word, the word for one new world of money is monetism: A philosophy, or secular religion, that envisages the creation of one international world of money.

In white clapboard frame houses on elm-shaded streets of small Midwestern towns where etchings of Abraham Lincoln gaze down from the parlor wall and talk of money is still a grave breach of good manners, talk of monetism instead will allay suspicions of overweening greed or materialistic thinking. And the Great Emancipator himself will be pleased that his National Bank Act of 1863 and one nationwide currency showed the way to the International Reserve System and one worldwide money.

THE MONETARY ATLAS SHIFTS THE WORLD OF MONEY
TO THE INTERNATIONAL RESERVE SYSTEM, AND ALL
HIS GOLDEN APPLES AS WELL

One day when mighty Hercules, the great-grandson of Perseus and a direct descendant of Danae and the shower of gold, was lurching about in the void looking for his eleventh labor he came to Atlas the Titan, whose name has not become a household word for high intelligence any more than Hercules' has. Hercules' eleventh labor was to fetch the golden apples from the Hesperides, who were Atlas' daughters, and carry them to King Eurystheus of Mycenae.

Hercules offered to take the burden of the globe on his own shoulders while Atlas collected the golden apples from his daughters. Atlas accepted at once, shifted the globe to Hercules' back, and went off to look for his girls. But when Atlas returned with the golden apples he refused to give them to Hercules; he was not about to take back all that dead weight on his own two shoulders.

327

Atlas laughs at Hercules, and says he will take the golden apples to King Eurystheus himself. As Atlas starts toward Mycenae, Hercules groans, seemingly resigning himself to the everlasting burden of the whole world on his back.

But then he very casually says, "By the way, Atlas, would you mind just taking the globe back for a moment, so I can put a pad up here on my shoulders." He may have added, "Something is really digging into me, like a mountain range in Antarctica, perhaps."

Atlas shrugs, and agrees to take the globe back, provided it is only for a moment. Hercules shifts back the load, picks up the golden apples, and trundles off to Mycenae with the inedible fruit. Atlas roars out at him in helpless rage.

Among the stories of Hercules' dozen labors and innumerable other adventures that classical poets have handed down to us, the story of how Hercules talked Atlas into taking back the weight of the whole world on his own shoulders is the one example there is of Hercules doing something that was intelligent, or at least rather smart.

Having taken over the burden of carrying the world of money on her back from the former economic Atlas of the world, Great Britain, the United States would display intelligence at least equal to that of Hercules, if she could manage to shift the crushing burden of supporting the free world's money system to the International Monetary Fund, as the pivot of the evolving new international reserve system.

Going Hercules one better, the United States should also turn over to the system all her golden apples as well, along with all her obligations to redeem foreign-held paper dollars for gold. This would form the principal reserve basis for one new worldwide money based on the dollar in its various worldwide forms. She could then trundle off to Mycenae unencumbered by golden apples of doubtful value, and unworried by foreign-held dollar obligations of unimpeachable validity.